Maryland Board of Health

Sixth Biennial Report of the State Board of Health of Maryland

January 1886

Maryland Board of Health

Sixth Biennial Report of the State Board of Health of Maryland
January 1886

ISBN/EAN: 9783337269180

Printed in Europe, USA, Canada, Australia, Japan

Cover: Foto ©ninafisch / pixelio.de

More available books at **www.hansebooks.com**

BIENNIAL REPORT

OF THE

State Board of Health

OF MARYLAND,

JANUARY, 1886

"*People who are living in the midst of general unsanitary conditions are in a worse plight than people living in the crater of an extinct volcano; for not only may any one of the severest epidemic diseases break out among them at any time, but they are continually sacrificing unnecessary victims to the demon filth.*"—Prof. CORFIELD.

ANNAPOLIS:
GEORGE T. MELVIN, State Printer.

1886.

MEMBERS
—OF—
THE STATE BOARD OF HEALTH
OF MARYLAND.

RICHARD McSHERRY, M. D.,* *President*, Baltimore.
HON. CHAS. B. ROBERTS, Westminster.
JAS. A. STEUART, M. D., Baltimore.
J. CRAWFORD NEILSON, C. E., Harford County.
ST. GEO. W. TEACKLE, M. D., Baltimore.
J. M. H. BATEMAN, M. D., Easton, Talbot County.
C. W. CHANCELLOR, M. D., *Secretary*, Baltimore.

*Deceased.

REPORT
OF THE
Secretary of the State Board of Health of Maryland,
1886.

"In nothing do men more closely approach to the gods than in giving health to men."—CICERO.

To his Excellency Henry Lloyd, Governor, and the Honorable the General Assembly of Maryland:

In accordance with the provision of the Act of Assembly of 1880, chap. 438, sec. 6, which requires that the Secretary of the State Board of Health "shall, at each regular session of the Legislature, submit a full report of his investigations, with such suggestions and recommendations as he may deem proper," I herewith present the following

REPORT.

Though no provision exists in this State for the collection and registration of vital statistics, the Secretary has by correspondence and other means gathered sufficient data to enable him to say that an unusually satisfactory condition of the public health now prevails in the State, and has prevailed for the past two years.

The efforts made by the board through printed reports and circulars, public lectures and private correspondence, and by other means to disseminate sanitary information among the people have combined to reduce both sickness and the death rate in the State considerably below the average of preceding years. It is a source of congratulation that no disease has generally prevailed, and no widespread epidemic has visited any section of the State during the two years ending December 31, 1885.

DEATH OF DRS. WARD AND McSHERRY.

Since the publication of the last biennial report death has deprived the Board of two valuable members, Dr.

J. Robert Ward and Prof. Richard McSherry, both of whom occupied the position of President at the time of their death, making four Presidents of the Board who have died since its organization, viz: Prof. Nathan R. Smith, Prof. F. Lloyd Howard, Dr. J. Robert Ward and Prof. Richard McSherry.

Dr. Ward had been a member of the Board from the time of its organization, and had, by a modesty and ingenuousness of conduct, secured the affectionate attachment of his colleagues, as well as their highest respect.

Dr. McSherry succeeded Dr. Ward as a member of the Board, by appointment of Gov. McLane, and was immediately thereafter elected President. He had long attained eminence both as a physician and sanitarian ; and another eminence, that of a happy blending with the discharge of his protracted and arduous professional duties, the graces of a Christian gentleman.

WORK OF THE BOARD.

It is gratifying to note the increased interest which has been awakened throughout the State in sanitary matters. Until lately the people entertained a very inadequate conception of the laws of health, now there is an obvious tendency to a deeper and more enthusiastic interest in everything that pertains to the protection of the public health, and the sphere of sanitary inspection and regulation is likely to be much greater in the future than it has been in the past, not only because the occasions for interference will be more numerous, but because a greater understanding of sanitary needs will make the necessity more obvious.

The Board has been greatly embarrassed by the action of the last Legislature in reducing the appropriation for necessary expenses from $1,200 annually to $200 for the fiscal year ending the 30th September, 1885, and making no appropriation for the present fiscal year, thereby placing the Board in the anomalous position of a body charged with important and responsible duties and yet deprived of the means of efficiently executing them. Surely, while yellow fever still flickers "like the baleful fires of the tomb" along our Southern coasts, and cholera has already aroused from its natural *habitat* in the East and is sweeping westward; while that trinity of woe, malaria, diptheria, and typhoid fever still holds high carnival in our midst, it is no time to withdraw the watchmen who guard the public safety, or call in our picket line, and hope to meet the destroyer with the *brutum fulmen* of State economy or the guerrilla warfare of unorganized local efforts.

Of the twenty-nine State Boards of Health now existing in the country, the Maryland Board was the fourth organized; and, in proportion to the means and powers vouchsafed, it has accomplished equally valuable results with other boards having plenary powers and almost an unlimited amount of money. It is quite unreasonable to expect that the Maryland Board should accomplish the same results with $200, or even $1,200, annually, that other boards attain with appropriations varying from $5,000 to $50,000 annually. But much has been done by this Board, even with the limited means at command, and under a more liberal State policy and a somewhat improved organization, much more will be done to serve the interests of the public health.

The special work accomplished by the Board since its organization was fully set forth in the biennial report of 1884, which may be restated in the following summary:

1. The inspection of State institutions.
2. The inspection of county almshouses and prisons.
3. The inspection of charitable institutions receiving State aid.
4. A special census of the insane population of the State in 1877, by personal visitations of the Secretary of the Board to the various institutions where they are confined.
5. A census of the idiotic and imbecile paupers in the State.
6. A census of the blind and deaf-mutes in public institutions in the State.
7. The suppression of nuisances, by the exercise of *advisory powers*, in various localities.
8. The organization of local boards of health in most of the counties of the State, under the provisions of section 4, act of 1880, chapter 438.
9. The delivering of public lectures on hygiene, in many of the principal cities and towns of the State, by the secretary.
10. The investigation into the causes of the epidemic of diphtheria in Frederick city in January, 1882.
11. The investigation and "stamping out" of small-pox in Charles county, by rigid isolation of cases and systematic vaccination.
12. The examination of various localities in the State, at the request of local authorities, physicians, and prominent citizens, with reference to the existence of prevailing diseases and the best method of arresting the same.

13. The organization of sanitary conventions, to be held annually or semi-annually, in different sections of the State.

14. The collection of a library of reports, documents, and scientific works upon the subjects within the peculiar sphere of the Board.

15. The preparation of six extended reports on general and special sanitary subjects, for publication by the State, containing a very considerable fund of information and suggestion, statistical and otherwise.

16. The preparation, printing, and distribution of forty or fifty thousand circulars on the following subjects, namely:

1. How to resuscitate persons supposed to be drowned.
2. Drainage, with suggestions as to the most fruitful source of typhoid fever.
3. Sanitary rules for the prevention of scarlet fever.
4. Prevention of diphtheria.
5. Sanitary precautions to prevent the spread of small-pox.
6. Special instructions for disinfection.
7. Rules for the management of infants.
8. Rules for the management of children over two years of age.

Since the last report the aid of the Board has been invoked by a number of communities and individuals in suppressing nuisances and in investigating the cause or causes of existing disease; but in several instances, from want of the necessary means, no adequate assistance could be rendered. In every case, however, where the nuisance complained of was of such magnitude as to endanger the health of a community, the secretary has promptly visited the locality, and in most cases secured an abatement without resort to other than *advisory* measures. But in several instances the authority and the recommendations of the Board have been disregarded by the offending parties, and as no means had been placed at the disposal of the Board which would enable it to enforce an observance of the sanitary laws of the State applicable to existing grievances, it was forced to abandon further efforts to protect the communities or individuals making complaint.

This was notably the case in connection with several of the fifty or sixty nuisances complained of by persons living in the "Belt," especially on the line of Gwynn's Falls, into which stream fetid matters are suffered to flow from slaughter-houses, hog-pens, stables, and from certain factories, giving rise to offensive and unwhole_ some smells, which are calculated not only to affect seriously the public health, but also to impair the value of property in the immediate vicinity.

INSPECTION OF NORTHEAST, CECIL COUNTY.

In June, 1884, upon a request from the town authorities the Secretary visited officially the town of North East, in Cecil County, for the purpose of aiding in the suppression of certain nuisances which were deemed prejudicial to the health of the community. The nuisances complained of consisted in a filthy slaughtering establishment, and several filthy cesspools in the heart of the town, which the authorities had not been able to suppress. In company with the President and Secretary of the Board of Town Commissioners the Secretary of the State Board made a very thorough inspection of these nuisances, and being satisfied that they were obnoxious both to the comfort and health of the citizens, the advisory powers of the State Board were exercised with the most satisfactory results.

In each case the nuisances, which, if they had been suffered to continue, would probably have given rise to some serious disease, were promptly abated, and without any recourse to law. It may not be out of place to observe here, that, with rare exceptions, the Board has found a very hearty and ready response to its advice in all matters pertaining to the sanitation of premises, offending parties, as a general thing, yielding a ready and willing acquiescence to the advice and authority of the Board. In most instances where insanitary conditions exist as a result of private negligence, they are maintained either through ignorance of the evil effects likely to arise from such conditions, or from a want of knowledge as to the proper method of dealing with the same, rather than from a disposition to injure or inconvenience others. A little timely advice and counsel from one who is familiar with such matters, will usually accomplish all that may be desired; and herein consists one of the most important and valuable functions incident to the work of the State Board of Health.

INSPECTION OF UNION BRIDGE, CARROLL CO.

About the middle of August, 1884, a petition signed by a large number of the most prominent citizens of Union Bridge, Carroll County, was received by the State Board of Health, asking that some action be taken by the Board to suppress an intolerable nuisance which existed in that town and threatened the health and lives of the community. The nuisance consisted in a filthy slaughter-house and several disgustingly filthy pig-pens upon the premises of one Reek. The Secretary of the Board immediately visited the town and found that the complaint was well founded, but deemed it best, before resorting to other measures, to make a personal appeal to Reek, and counsel with him as to the best mode to abate and overcome the evils complained of. This was done with the result shown in the following letter from the mayor of the town:

LETTER FROM MAYOR RINEHART.

MAYOR'S OFFICE, UNION BRIDGE, Sept. 27, 1885.

DR. C. W. CHANCELLOR,

Secretary State Board of Health:

DEAR SIR.—Your favor of the 25th instant was received yesterday, and at a meeting of the Council last evening, I called attention to the subject-matter contained therein. There seems to be no further cause for complaint against the slaughter-houses &c., which you visited and found in a state of nuisance. Mr. Reek is, and has been for the past two weeks sending all the refuse of his butcher's shop to the country every day or two, and he has disposed of his hogs.

Thanking you in the name of the citizens of Union Bridge for your kind and prompt attention and interference,

I remain, yours truly,

(Signed) DAVID RINEHART, *Mayor.*

INSPECTION OF ELKTON, CECIL COUNTY.

On the 2d day of September, 1884, the Secretary of the Board received the following communication from W. J. Jones, Esq., President of the Town Commissioners of Elkton, Cecil County, Maryland.

MAYOR JONES'S LETTER.

DR. C. W. CHANCELLOR,

Secretary State Board of Health:

DEAR SIR.—There is now prevailing in this town what our physicians say is epidemic typhoid fever. One case has proved fatal and others are likely to prove so. There are many conjectures as to the cause, and it seems to be a case calling for the action of your Board, as provided in the Act of 1880, chapter 438, section 3. We desire that one or more of the Board of Health shall visit us at once, so that we may have their advice.

Please telegraph me when to expect a visit. We deem prompt action necessary.

Yours truly,

(Signed) W. J. JONES,
Pres't Town Commissioners of Elkton.

In response to this urgent appeal the Secretary telegraphed Mayor Jones to expect him immediately, and he reached Elkton the evening of the same day the letter was received. A thorough investigation was made into the cause and progress of the existing fever, and as will appear in the report given of the proceedings of the Second Sanitary Convention held at Blue Mountain House, September 17th and 18th, 1884, which accompanies this report, the Elkton fever was found to have originated and spread from the use of a contaminated milk supply. This fact being made known to the citizens the use of the milk from the dairy to which the source of contamination was traced was absolutely and entirely abandoned, and immediately thereafter the progress of the disease was arrested. In consequence of the limited funds of the Board only an imperfect analysis of the water used in rinsing the milk vessels, and which was undoubtedly the source of all the trouble, could be made; whereas a thorough analysis should have been made in order to determine the quantity of the obnoxious matter in the water, and also in the milk after it had been contaminated by germs of disease contained in the poisoned water, which was drank by the cows and which was used to rinse the udders of the animals and the milk vessels, and perchance to dilute the milk.

It is gratifying to note that the intelligent and philanthropic owner of the farm, (but not the operator of the dairy,) whence this poisoned milk supply was drawn, fully appreciated the importance and necessity of adopting the sanitary measures advised, and has put the premises in such condition as to preclude the probability of a recurrence of the evil.

SANITARY CONDITION OF SMITHSBURG, WASHINGTON COUNTY, MD.

In the latter part of the fall of 1884, the following letter addressed to Prof. McSherry, then President of the Board, was referred to the Secretary for such action as he might deem proper in the premises;

LETTER FROM MAYOR D. A. PIKE AND OTHERS.

PROF. RICHARD MCSHERRY,
 President State Board of Health:

DEAR SIR—As Mayor and Councilmen of the town of Smithsburg, Washington county, Maryland, we respectfully ask your attention to the fact that there is within the limits of our town a slaughter-house belonging to a certain Seigler, which we deem a nuisance, and believe the emanations therefrom are prejudicial to the health of the inhabitants. We earnestly invoke your aid in this matter, which we deem of great moment.

With deep interest in the welfare and progress of the State Board of Health and its grand objects, we remain, very respectfully,

D. A. PIKE, <i>Mayor.</i>
C. A. BALDWIN, M. D.,
J. H. ROHRER,
JAMES MATTEN,
Councilmen.

As the funds of the Board were exhausted by previous investigations, the Secretary was debarred from visiting the town and making a personal investigation into the grievances set forth in the foregoing letter, but the following official notice was sent to Mayor Pike to be served on the offending party:

"OFFICE STATE BOARD OF HEALTH,
Baltimore, Sept. 30, 1884.

"MR. SEIGLER, *Butcher:*

"Information having been received at this office that the present condition of your premises, located at Smithsburg, Washington county, Mayland, is detrimental to the public health, you are hereby notified to abate the nuisance complained of, without delay, otherwise you will be proceeded against according to the law made and provided in such cases.

Respectfully,

"C. W. CHANCELLOR, M. D.,
"<i>Secretary State Board of Health.</i>"

Mayor Pike was requested to communicate with the Secretary of the Board and inform him whether this official notice was respected and complied with by the party offending, but as no response was returned, it is fair to presume that the nuisance was promptly abated.

A NUISANCE AFFECTING THE CITY OF BALTO.

Another case of nuisance was brought to the atten--

tion of the Board by Health Commissioner Stewart, existing at the slaughtering establishment of Charles Meister, on Pennsylvania avenue extended, beyond the city limits. This nuisance was caused by rendering the refuse of the slaughter house, and manufacturing within the area of the establishment, the *debris* into a fertilizer, which was represented to be very offensive to the inhabitants of this thickly populated locality, and often the disagreeble odor was wafted directly into the city.

Accompanied by Sanitary Inspector Brown, of the City Health Department, the Secretary visited the establishment and found that the escape of offensive gases into the surrounding atmosphere, with the liquids flowing from the establishment, created an intolerable nuisance. Such establishments should not be permitted to exist in densely populated neighborhoods, for however perfect the condensation may be some of the gases will escape, and these gases are not only offensive, but are poisonous if inhaled in a concentrated form. It was represented that the offensive odor from this establishment was at times perceptible at the distance of more than half a mile from the premises, and at the distance of a few hundred yards it was scarcely tolerable.

Under these circumstance it was deemed proper to take action, and the following official communication was accordingly sent to the proprietor:

CHARLES MEISTER, ESQ.:

DEAR SIR—I have visited your establishment and find that the odor emanating therefrom is very disagreable and manifestly injurious to the public health. I trust you will, without delay, take the necessary steps to correct the evil. My own belief is that this can only be effected by ceasing altogether the process used by you in manufacturing fertilizers out of the *debris* of your slaughtering establishment, within the limits of a thickly populated neighborhood. As at present conducted, the business is a nuisance that calls for immediate abatement, and it is to be hoped that in the interest of the health and comfort of your neighbors, and others at a distance who are affected thereby, you will not postpone action in the matter. Please be kind enough to let me hear from you, at your earliest convenience, what course you propose to take, and oblige,

Yours respectfully,
C. W. CHANCELLOR, M. D.,
Secretary State Board of Health

No response having been made to this letter, the usual official notice was served upon Meister, and the nuisance was, very soon thereafter, so far modified that no further complaint has been made against the establishment.

A COMPLAINT FROM PRINCE GEORGE'S COUNTY.

On the 15th of September, 1884, the following letter was received:

FORESTVILLE, PRINCE GEORGE'S COUNTY,
September 12, 1884.

DR. C. W. CHANCELLOR, *Secretary State Board of Health:*

DEAR SIR—Mr. George Blaine, of this place, who is deeply interested in the Prince George's County Almshouse, asked me if I would write and ask you, if it is in the line of your duty, to visit the said almshouse prior to the next session of the Circuit Court, October 6th, prox.? If you will drop him a card at the above postoffice he will meet you in Washington.

Yours respectfully,
WM. BRASHAW.

In reply to this letter, Mr. Blaine was informed that the Secretary had no authority to inspect almshouses or any public institution, without an order to do so from the Governor of the State, but if authority were obtained from his Excellency, Governor McLane, the inspection would be cheerfully made. In reply the following letter was received from Mr. Blaine:

DR. C. W. CHANCELLOR, *Secretary State Board of Health:*

DEAR SIR—I have written Gov. McLane asking him to request you to visit the almshouse of Prince George's county during the present session of the grand jury, October 6th, and during the week. The nearest point from which to reach the almshouse is Upper Marlboro. I will be found at the courthouse during the sessions of the grand jury.

Thanking you for your promptness in replying to Mr. Brawshaw's letter, I am yours, respectfully,

GEORGE BLAINE,

No order was received from His Excellency, and consequently no inspection of the house was made.

At the regular quarterly meeting of the Board in October a resolution was passed setting forth the necessity of having annual inspections made of all public hospitals, asylums, prisons and other institutions, as provided for in the act of 1880, chap. 438, sec. 6.

A PROPOSITION TO PROTECT DREDGERS.

At the same meeting a resolution was adopted by the Board calling the attention of His Excellency to the shameful sanitary condition under which the oystermen of the State pursue their avocation, and offering the services of the Board in an effort to ameliorate the hardships and sufferings of this class of the community; but in the absence of authority and pecuniary means His Excellency did not approve the suggestions of the Board,

NUISANCES AT OAKLAND, GARRETT COUNTY.

The following letter was received from Vice-President Spencer, of the Baltimore and Ohio Railroad Company, on June 25, 1885:

BALTIMORE AND OHIO RAILROAD COMPANY,
OFFICE OF THE VICE-PRESIDENT,
Baltimore, June 24th, 1885.

DR. C. W. CHANCELLOR, *Secretary State Board of Health:*

DEAR SIR:—I beg to enclose herewith copy of a complaint this day made by our superintendent of hotels (Mr. Walker) to Dr. J. L. McComas, President of the Board of Health of Oakland, regarding a nuisance which exists there and which is a matter of grave importance to us and the public in connection with the hotel owned and operated by this company at that place.

I am advised that there has been some communication with you on this subject already, but I believe no formal complaint has been lodged until now.

As the time is short, and the necessity for prompt action urgent, I beg to ask that you take such official action as may secure a speedy remedy of the evil complained of.

I enclose herewith transportation to Oakland and return, and this letter, in connection with your own transportation, will be sufficient for you to take with you any or all members of the Board of Health if you so desire.

Your early attention will greatly oblige,
Yours respectfully,
S. SPENCER, *V. P.*

In response to the above communication the following letter was sent:

OFFICE STATE BOARD OF HEALTH,
June 26th, 1885.
S. SPENCER, ESQ., *Vice-President B. & O. R. R. Co.*

DEAR SIR.—Your favor of the 24th inst. is received. I wrote to Mr. Walker, Superintendent Hotels two month ago that I would visit Oakland if the necessary expenses of the trip were provided for, the Board having no funds at command. Subsequently, in a personal interview, I told Dr. McComas the same thing, but until now I have heard nothing in regard to the matter, and concluded my services were not required.

The last Legislature made no provision beyond a meagre appropriation of $200 to carry out the objects for which the Board was organized, and this amount has already been expended. I am, however, entirely willing to aid as far as I can in suppressing the nuisance complained of, and for this purpose will send Dr. McComas a formal notice (a copy of which I herewith enclose for your information) to be served on the party or parties offending. Should they fail to respect this notice, the only alternative is for your attorney to apply to the Circuit Court (in the name of the Board) for an injunction to restrain the party or parties from maintaining the nuisance, or bring the matter to the attention of the grand jury, should that body be in session.

Attorney-General Gwinn, in May, 1881, advised the Board, in a written opinion, that it had no power over such cases, except to send the notice above referred to, after which its functions under the law ceased and the parties affected would have to prosecute the matter at their own expense. This opinion you will find published in the Biennial Report of the Board for the two years ending December 31, 1881, a copy of which was sent to President Garrett. If you should decide to prosecute the parties offending as above suggested, it will give me pleasure to render you any aid I can.

At this time I am suffering from the effects of a recent attack of illness, and am physically unable to travel, but even if I were able to go to Oakland as you suggest, I could accomplish no more by my presence than serve the notice, in person, which I now send to Dr. McComas, with the request that he will serve it in the name of the Board. But if my presence should be required hereafter to testify before the courts in the case as to the nature and evil effects of the nuisance, I will be pleased to obey a summons from you. Inasmuch, however, as my presence will not probably be needed for some time, (or until the initiative is taken in the matter) I return the pass you kindly sent. Similar notices, sent in like cases to other parties creating and maintaining nuisances have been, almost without exception, respected, and I trust and believe that this action will be quite sufficient to insure you the relief sought.

Very truly yours,
C. W. CHANCELLOR, M. D.,
Secretary State Board Health.

OTHER APPLICATIONS FOR RELIEF FROM NUISANCES.

Many other applications have been made to the Board of a similar import, from every section of the State, during the present year, but the means placed at its disposal have been entirely inadequate, especially as we have no power to command the services of any States Attorney or of any police agencies. The Secretary has, however, endeavored to performed the functions of his office as best he could without money, and in urgent cases has, at his own expense, visited a number of localities where nuisances were alleged to exist, and has in almost every instance succeeded in suppressing the evils complained of by advisory measures.

LOCAL BOARDS OF HEALTH.

As stated in the last biennial report, the efforts of local boards of health, wherever they exist, have been of too unorganized a character to accomplish anything of real value, and, as at present formed, would, in the face of threatened or actual epidemic disease, be quite useless. In view of this fact it is all important that some efficient code of public health laws be enacted, so that each county, town or city in the State, may have its local health board to act in co-operation with the State Board of Health.

SANITARY LEGISLATION OF 1884. GOV. McLANE'S LABOR BILLS.

The Legislature of 1884 passed several laws ostensibly in the interest of sanitary reform which have proved utterly inoperative and valueless:

First—With reference to the act, entitled "An Act to protect the health of those employed in factories, manufacturing establishments and work shops in the State of Maryland," (chap. 265 Laws of Maryland, 1884,) it is found that no provision was made for rendering effective the objects as specified in the several sections of the act, viz: "That all factories, manufacturing establishments or work shops in the State shall be kept in a cleanly condition, and free from effluvia arising from any drain, privy or other nuisance; and no factory, manufacturing establishment or work shop shall be so overcrowded while work is being carried on therein as to be injurious to the health of the persons employed therein; and every such factory, manufacturing establishment or work shop shall be well and sufficiently lighted and ventilated in such manner as to render harmless, as far as practicable, all the gases, vapors, dust or other impurities generated in the course of the manufacturing process or handicraft carried on therein. which may be injurious to health, &c."

There is not a more important law, so far as the protection of human life is concerned, upon the statute books of Maryland, yet it is rendered nugatory and utterly inoperative, by reason of the failure of the Legislature to provide for any inspection or sanitary supervision of these places. The matter properly belongs to the State Board of Health, whose duty it is to "make sanitary investigations and inquiries respecting the causes of disease, and especially epidemics, *the causes of mortality and the influence of locality, employments, habits and other circumstances and conditions upon the health of the people.*" With this view of the case, the State Board of Health, at its quarterly meeting in October, 1884, passed the following resolution:

"*Resolved*, That the aid of this Board be tendered his Excellency, Governor McLane, in rendering the provisions of the Act of 1884, chapter 265, section 1, relating to the health of these employed in factories, manufacturing establishments and workshops in the State, and that the Secretary of the State Board of Health be requested to co-operate with His Excellency and make such inspections and investigations as the latter may direct, to the end that the law may not be a dead letter upon the statue books of the State."

This resolution was duly presented to Governor McLane, but inasmuch as the Legislature had not provided for any inspection of, or report upon the condition of these establishments, he was not willing to accept the offer of the Board, preferring to leave the whole matter to the chance visitations of grand juries.

THE EFFECTS OF UNHEALTHY OCCUPATIONS.

Previous to the Act of the General Assembly of 1884, chapter 265, the evil effects of the unsanitary condition of "factories, manufacturing establishments and workshops" was so notorious that his Excellency, Governor McLane, deemed it necessary to bring the matter to the attention of the Legislature.* It was thought, at the time, that the Act which he suggested and which was passed by the Legislature would be a great boon to the laboring classes, but it soon became evident that this Act was not fitted to accomplish the object for which it was ostensibly intended in the sanitary regulation of our industries. The facts eliminated prove this, and also that further legislation on the subject is urgently demanded. Our great operative industrial classes are entitled to be cared for and protected, as to their health, in the pursuit of their avocations. They are the backbone and sinews of the State's strength. It is estimated that fully 3,000 of this class are annually lost to the State through disease and death. For a moment consider the effects of this loss from a merely economical point of view. Taking, then, the figures to be 3,000, and reckoning the average wages of each at $10 a week, there is thus a yearly loss in wages to the industrial wage class of upwards of $1,500,000. So much for the money aspect of the question. But what of the needless waste of life and its attendant sickness, of the consequent impoverishment, pauperism and demoralization, and the increasing legacy of hereditary disease? Could Adam Smith, the great political economist, reappear he would, looking back and gathering up the lessons of the past, place a prefatory note to his "Wealth of Nations," somewhat in these terms: There are two primary and fundamental considerations upon which the stability and permanency of governments, national, state and municipal, rest. The first regards the health of the people, the other their education. Any system of government without full provision made for these will be incomplete; and, in regard to the former, the best guarantee of security will be wanting. Therefore, above all things, let no State in its administrative capacity be without its health department, composed of wise and energetic men, whose supreme duty it shall be to vigilantly administer the laws, the aim of which shall be to protect the health of every citizen, and especially to surround that of the dependent industrial population with every possible safeguard. A State, such as ours, of 1,000,000 of people, with a large manufacturing industry, a busy and flourishing commerce,

---
*See Governor McLane's "Labor Bills," Laws of Maryland, 1884.

cannot afford to waste the lives of its citizens. Are not labor and capital the two pillars upon which a free commonwealth rest? Disease paralyzes labor and wastes capital. It ought, therefore, to be the primary object of an enlightened State to prevent disease, preserve health and prolong life, and to maintain the whole people in the highest efficiency, alike for the labors of peace and, if needs be, the struggles of war.

THE ACT OF 1884, CHAPTER 357.

Under the Act of 1884, chapter 357, the Governor of the State was empowered to appoint "a board of commissioners to inquire into the practicability of making a complete survey of the swampy, badly drained and water-soaked lands of the State, and their effect upon the public health, and to suggest measures for abating the same, with an estimate of the cost, &c., &c."

The importance of such a measure can only be estimated by reference to the experiences of England, Holland, Belgium, France and other European countries in draining their marsh lands and thereby rendering them not only healthy localities, but lands valuable for agricultural purposes. In view of this well established fact, the board, soon after the passage of the act by the Legislature, adopted the following resolution:

"*Resolved*, That the Secretary of the State Board of Health be, and he is hereby directed to communicate with his Excellency, Governor McLane, and direct his attention to the importance, from a sanitary standpoint, of giving prompt consideration to the provisions of the Act of 1884, chapter 357, relating to the appointment of a board of commissioners to inquire into the practicability of making a survey of the swampy, badly-drained and water-soaked lands of the State and their disastrous effects upon the public health."

The Secretary, in obedience to the above instructions from the Board, had a long personal interview with his Excellency on the subject, and it was finally decided that the failure of the Legislature to provide any means for carrying out the provisions of the act would preclude the possibility of any practical execution of the same.

THE PRACTICABILITY AND ADVANTAGES TO BE DERIVED FROM DRAINING THE MARSH LANDS OF THE STATE.

There is no *physical* difficulty in the way of draining the marsh lands of Maryland. Engineers can furnish plans and execute the work if the financial means are provided. But when we come to consider the actual performance of the work there will be a host of conflicting interests, and even many whose lands and health would be benefited will persist in declaring their satisfaction with the present state of things, miserable as it is, and their disbelief in the practicability of any scheme of improvement, or the ultimate profit to be derived therefrom.

There are not less than 500,000 acres of marsh lands in Maryland which could be reclaimed. Now, if for more accurate and closer calculation, we should deduct one-fifth, we shall then have 400,000 acres remaining, which, when drained and prepared for cultivation, will readily produce 40 bushels of corn or one and a half tons of hay per acre, and will command from $30 to $50 per acre, or in round numbers will average $40 per acre. Upon this basis, which is believed to be reasonably accurate, we may formulate, as the practical result of good drainage and cultivation, the following :

ESTIMATE.

400,000 acres of unreclaimed land, at $1 per acre....................................	$400,000
Expenses of draining and improving 400,000 acres, at $10 per acre.....................	4,000,000
Total cost.......................	$4,400,000

CREDIT.

Reclaimed lands, 400,000 acres, at $40 per acre...............................	$16,000,000
Deduct cost of drainage, &c...............	4,400,000
Net profit.......................	$11,600,000

In their present condition these marsh lands are worth nothing, and yield nothing but an unlimited supply of malarial fevers. When drained and cultivated in a proper manner they will produce 40 bushels of corn or 1½ tons of hay per acre. Four hundred thousand acres then will give 16,000,000 bushel of corn, which at 50 cents per bushel will be $8,000,000 gross product. It will require about 10,000,000 bushel of corn in addition to the wheat and other crops to supply man and beast in the counties where these marsh lands exist, which, when deducted from the gross product, will still leave 6,000,000 bushels at 50 cents per bushel—equal to $3,000,000 saved annually to the farmers of this section.

If the above estimate is within just and correct limits, there cannot or should not be any reason in the minds of practical, thinking men, in or out of the Legislature, to cause them to look upon this important work with fear and trembling, or want of faith in the possibility of executing the same.

The experience of England and Holland has proved in the most conclusive manner that by drainage and the introduction of agricultural improvements the greatest changes may be effected in the health of a district, and that it is quite possible to have luxuriant crops produced on the same soil where formerly noxious vapors abounded and impregnated the inhabitants with disease and death.

Before the marshy districts in England and Scotland were drained, strangers hardly ever ventured to visit them, from the certainty of being subjected to an attack of ague; but since the improvements which have been effected by drainage they have become as healthy as any other parts of the kingdom.

HYGIENE IN THE PUBLIC SCHOOLS.

As a body charged with the general care of the sanitary interests of the people of the State, the Board have had under consideration the advantages which would arise from adding to the curriculum of the public schools lessons in hygiene, and at a meeting in January, 1885, passed the following resolution:

Resolved, That the Secretary be requested to communicate by a circular letter, with the various school authorities throughout the State, and request that they take into consideration the importance and feasibility of embracing in the regular course of studies of the respective schools under their charge, lessons in hygiene, with the view of educating the rising generation in the art of preserving life with the enjoyment of more perfect health."

DIFFICULTIES AS TO PUBLIC HEALTH.

The Board have experienced the difficulties of enlightening the general public upon the all important subject of preserving a high degree of public health, and it would seem that to successfully educate the people in this branch of knowledge, we must begin in the schools. It is true that there are already a burthensome multitude of studies embraced in the school curricula, but the demand of the age is for the practical and useful as distinguished from the theoretical and ornamental. Could any one doubt that a knowledge of the laws of health would be of more practical use to nine-tenths of our pupils in every day life, than a knowledge of music, or the study of history with its myth and mystery, its truth and fable, its error and exaggeration.

SCHOOL BUILDINGS AND VENTILATION.

It is generally conceded that many of the school buildings in the State are to a greater or less degree defective in facilities for proper ventilation, while some are so dangerously situated as to drainage that they should not be used for school purposes until so grave a defect is remedied.

As to ventilation, there is yet much room for improvement in this vital matter, both in dwelling houses and school buildings. Especially does the school room call for the successful application of the inventor's art in this direction. It is probably true, that our schools, in the newer buildings, are as well equipped as those of any other State, but as long as there is room for improvement, and particularly, as long as any just complaints whatever are made, there should be attention and effort at reform.

The importance of pure air as a vital condition of health cannot be overestimated; and the imperative duty of providing it for our young and growing children, when they are confined to tasks of brain work, is always and especially pertinent to urge. One of the greatest defects in the proper ventilation of schools, whether the building is provided with modern appliances or not, is the neglect of the teachers in each room to give proper attention to the matter. No self-operating system of ventilation has yet been found adequate to all occasions. No two schools are alike in their needs of temperature regulation; the external atmospheric conditions constantly change, and must be studied for adaptation.

It is the duty of janitors of school buildings to see that every room is kept heated to a proper temperature, but the changing of the air by the ventilating apparatus, or other means, as occasion demands, is the duty of the teacher, and experience and good judgment must be their guides.

The judicious attention and action of a teacher will often avai to counteract, very materially, the lack or defects of a system of ventilation, while the best system in the world is practically worthless if not intelligently operated. Too much stress cannot be laid on these facts. They are the direct cause of most of the trouble in the ventilation of schools everywhere. The fault is not so much due to ignorance as to lack of carefulness on the part of authorities and teachers. Particular pains should be taken to instruct new teachers, and regularly to remind them of the general principles of proper ventilation, and as to the proper manner of operating whatever means are afforded. There are no teachers who could not readily comprehend such instructions, or, if there are, they have no business to be intrusted with the care of children.

INFECTIOUS DISEASES IN SCHOOLS.

It is often through the medium of schools that the diseases which are communicable from one person to another, such as small-pox, scarlet fever, diptheria, measles, &c., are spread throughout the community, and consequently a heavy responsibility rests on trustees and teachers, both in the interests of school children and the public, to guard against the approach of these diseases. The law vests or should vest the teachers with power to exclude all children affected with or exposed to any contagious disease until a medical certificate is shown that all danger of infection had passed. It should also vest the trustees with plenary powers to make such regulations on the subject as they may see fit.

The teacher should not only keep his school-room well ventilated and clean—that is necessary in the interest, of health, whether disease is in the neighborhood or not—but he should *watch* for the indications of the approach of communicable diseases. When such indications appear in the locality, he should find out if any of his scholars have been exposed to them by living in or visiting houses where the disease may exist; he should find out, whenever his scholars are absent through sickness, whether the disease is one of this class or not; he should promptly exclude any pupil with eruptions of the head, face or hands until satisfied that there is nothing of the nature of ringworm, favus, itch or any such contagious disease. And herein consists one of the great advantages of local health organizations, which could assist the teacher in his work as a sanitary officer.

RULES TO BE OBSERVED BY TEACHERS AND TRUSTEES OF SCHOOLS.

The following rules should be adopted by Boards of Trustees:

1. Small-pox—All pupils will be excluded from the schools until they produce a physician's certificate of

effectual vaccination. All pupils residing or visiting in any house where small-pox exists, or within twenty yards of such house, will be excluded until twenty days after the recovery of the patient.

2. Scarlet fever—All pupils coming from any house where scarlet fever exists will be excluded until twenty days after the recovery of the patient, except children who have previously had the disease, who will be excluded until ten days after the recovery of the patient.

3. Diphtheria—All pupils coming from any house where diphtheria exists will be excluded until ten days after the recovery of the patient.

4. Measles—All pupils coming from any house where measles exists will be excluded until the recovery of the patient, and the patient will be excluded until ten days after recovery.

5. Other diseases—All pupils afflicted with mumps, whooping-cough, chicken-pox, or any eruptive disease of the scalp will be excluded until complete recovery.

6. The evidence in regard to time of recovery from any of the above-mentioned diseases will be a physician's certificate.

7. In excluding pupils from any house in which smallpox, scarlet fever, diphtheria, or measles exists, two or more dwellings must be considered as one house, if there is any direct communication between them, or any opening from one into the other, or if it is possible to enter or leave the two residences by means of the same hall, stairway or door, or if the rear yards are used in common.

8. Whenever it comes to the knowledge of a teacher that a pupil has visited a house where smallpox, scarlet fever, or diphtheria exists, or has attended the funeral of any person dying of either of these diseases, such pupil shall be at once excluded from the school and the case investigated by the teacher, who shall then decide whether or not the pupil shall be excluded for the full period required by these rules. In cities the case may be referred to the inspector for investigation and decision.

9. Whenever the teacher has reason to believe that any pupil has been afflicted with or exposed to any disease not specially referred to in the above rules, which may render such pupil a source of infection or contagion, he will exclude the pupil until he has received satisfactory evidence that all danger has passed away.

THE REDUCTION OF MORTALITY IN CHILDHOOD.

Statistics show that nearly half the deaths that occur are of children under five years of age, the majority of these scarcely seeing the light, and none of them surviving a year. How very shocking, since, if we except the inherited and the acute diseases, children are, as a rule, exempt from those influences that help to swell the death-rate at maturer ages.

That nearly half the children born should thus perish is the more to be deplored when we discover that the vast majority of deaths originate from causes that might reasonably be deemed avoidable—*i. e.*, atmospheric or other impurity, mismanagement as to food, &c.—which exert their influences in infancy with much greater fatality than in adult life, and for obvious reasons, since the susceptibility is inversely to age; hence it is that in populous towns the mortality among children is higher than in rural and healthier communities, in which, as a rule, those born healthy are seldom ill, if correctly managed.

In reference to the inherited and acute ailments of childhood, deficiency of stamina—vital power—being among the former, and certain of the eruptive diseases, as well as the more serious inflammatory complaints among the latter, it must not be inferred that these are unamenable to measures of prevention, since it is surprising how greatly we are enabled to rectify the *tendency* to debility and the inception of disease even *anterior* to birth, when too often the mischief is unwittingly done by the mother, who produces in her offspring future diseases of body or some degree of physical deterioration. Few mistakes, for example, are more common among women than that of regarding the very natural process of child-bearing as something seriously debilitating or otherwise abnormal, to be counteracted by change in habits and mode of life, as the indulgence of various fancies and cravings, the consumption of more and richer food, stimulants, &c. These are errors directly conducing to harm, by heating the blood, producing a full habit of body, and probably fostering, as a curse for after years, those very evils it is intended to avoid.

Again, a scrofulous, consumptive or otherwise delicate tendency in the child may arise from the occurrence of conception when one or other, or both parents are laboring under or recovering from weakness or disease. As certainly, also, may epilepsy and idiocy be often traced to the intemperance of one parent or both, and under favoring circumstances pulmonary diseases may also be transmitted.

By popularising information that ought to be possessed by everyone, whether mother or nurse, who has or is likely to have the care of children, we may hope to be, in some degree, instrumental in remedying much prevailing ignorance in such matters. During infancy and childhood, in many cases, much may be done towards securing a healthy future; and it becomes a plain duty not to withhold such knowledge, and thereby risk disease and misery—through neglect and mismanagement—that we might possibly avert at a period so critical.

Essential benefit may be conferred upon the poor, and through them upon the whole community, by such reforms as may be silently effected by sanitary and similar associations, having for their golden aim the mitigation of human wretchedness; and what more promising field for those whose merciful mission it is to "go about doing good," than that of inculcating the simple, obvious laws of cleanliness, ventilation, &c., the infringement of which is so often followed by misery, disease and death?

Prevention is a mighty power for good, and at no stage of life can more effective measures be adopted than in childhood, when, other things being equal, the foundation of a vigorous and happy future may be laid. By correct training, and the right management of infants and children, a life of health and consequent happiness may be secured to many who otherwise would drag out a miserable existence, ending only in untimely death.

The prevailing neglect, in our educational system, of the laws that regulate the varied functions of life seems as anomalous as it is deplorable, since it not unfrequently happens that the very cattle in our fields, and the plants in our gardens are better understood and cared for by those whose duty it it to tend them, than are many children by those on whom devolve *their* care and culture.

THE COLLECTION AND REGISTRATION OF VITAL STATISTICS.

The subject of an efficient registration of deaths, births and marriages has been urged in the last three reports of the State Board of Health, and a bill, prepared with great care, was introduced in the last Legislature, but it was never fairly brought before any committee and died without consideration. Outside the city of Baltimore no vital statistics are collected, and yet a correct system for the collection and classification of the records of births, marriages and deaths is the very groundwork of all public hygiene. We are as yet very far from paying to this matter the serious attention which its importance demands. European nations are so careful in this respect that they keep a record of their citizens even when they are absent from their homes, and request the vital statisticians of all foreign countries to certify to the death of their citizens occurring abroad.

While every community is bound by the mere principles of self-interest and economy to establish such a system of registration as shall enable it to know its own life-history, and the influences which are moulding it for better or for worse, it is, nevertheless, true that Maryland has, as yet, made no adequate provision for this purpose. Without this means of knowledge, respecting the peculiar sources of danger to life, it is not probable that the State will ever have effective sanitary work. Complete statistics of disease and death, where obtained, supply the knowledge of relative dangers to life from each recognized cause of death, and such statistics also lead to a knowledge of many causes of death not previously known, and which cannot otherwise be ascertained. It becomes, therefore, a matter of necessity that we should study these records if we would promote the health and safety of the people.

By such records the health of a town or county is shown at a glance. The efficiency of preventive measures, such as vaccination, is tested, and the progress and mortality of disease traced. By statistics we ascertain the proportion of deaths to the whole population, and without the existence of such statistics our knowledge of the number of deaths, births and marriages in a community must be vague, uncertain and often erroneous.

The most important statistics required for health purposes are:

I. The annual mortality.
II. The annual rate of increase of population.
III. The causes of death.
IV. The amount of sickness to population.
V. The births to population.
VI. The relative number of live and still-born children.

VII. The number of vaccinations to population.
VIII. The mean ages at death.
IX. The number of marriages to population.

Hygienists must not be satisfied with merely the annual rate of mortality, but the deaths should be grouped and classified with (1) male and female; (2) under and over five years; (3) grouped according to the age at death, &c.

Although a large number of facts are required for any certainty of deduction, we are not precluded from reasoning upon a small number. There are many facts which, from their nature, cannot be collected, but there is always a balance of probability in favor of the average even of a smaller number of facts approaching closely to the true average.

THE POLLUTION OF WATER COURSES.

The subject of the pollution of streams, ponds, wells, springs and other sources of water supply used for domestic purposes is a question of great importance to the public health. It is a matter which may yet seriously vex our people, and, therefore, a subject which should be considered and settled before it becomes practically beyond control on account of increasing population, large expenditures of money for public improvements, manufactories, &c. Indeed, the pollution of our rivers has already begun, and the evil will increase from year to year with the increase of population, unless all contaminating influences are excluded by timely precaution on the part of the public authorities.

The Rivers' Pollution Commission of England and the Committee of the State Board of Health of Massachusetts to "investigate the question of the use of running streams as common sewers, in its relation to public health," show that such efforts to preserve the purity of streams are no novelty in this age. There is really no necessity for such pollution, since all excretal matters may be otherwise provided for, and it would seem, upon the ground of simple justice and equity, that each manufactory or trade should be required to clean its own waste or sewage; not of course convert it into perfectly pure water, which is unnecessary, but to deprive it of its power to become a nuisance to others when discharged into public waters or elsewhere.

It can safely be asserted that Baltimore has at this time one of the best and healthiest water supplies in the world, and which has undoubtedly, exercised a potential influence on the health and comfort of the community. But the Gunpower River, the principal source of this supply, has many tributaries, and the purity of the whole water supply of the city might, in a short time, be destroyed, should filth and decomposing matters be permitted to flow into any one of these tributaries. And what is true of Baltimore is also true of other places in the State, especially Frederick city and Cumberland, both of which have excellent water supplies if guarded against the disastrous effects of pollution.

Recent investigations have established beyond question the fact that diseases, often of the most fatal character, are conveyed into the system through the medium of polluted drinking water. An example is furnished in the recent terrible scourge of typhoid fever from infected water in the Town of Plymouth, Pennsylvania. With a population of 8,000 souls, 1,200 were stricken down with fever, and there were nearly 150 deaths in a few weeks, all directly traceable to water pollution, occasioned by the excreta of one typhoid fever case, cast upon the snow, and subsequently, by the melting of the snow, was carried into the stream which supplied the inhabitants of Plymouth with drinking water. If the fecal discharges from one fever patient, carelessly cast upon the surface of the earth can thus infect the wells or reservoirs of a city to such an extent, or if the sewage of a town three miles distant, with a few tan vats, can give rise to such a fatal epidemic, what may we not expect when the filth of privies, slaughter-houses and manufacturing establishments is suffered to flow into streams which are tributary to the water supplies of our cities and towns.

As an instance in point, take the waters of George's creek that flow into the Potomac river, not many miles above Cumberland, which city draws its water supply from the Potomac. George's creek carries with it the sewage of Lonaconing, Barton and other villages in the mining districts of Alleghany county, which employ several thousand hands, whose excretal sewage, to a large extent, passes into the creek. In addition to this the refuse waters and *debris* from a number of manufacturing establishments, tanneries and slaughter-houses flow into the stream and pass down to mingle with the drinking water of Cumberland, and thus the inhabitants of the latter city are at the mercy of the villagers on the line of the Potomac and its tributaries above the city.

The exact influence or even presence of the sewage

and trade pollution which may have passed into a stream cannot, when in minute quantities, be discovered by the chemist, and yet they may be sufficient to render the water, not merely repulsive or suspicious, but more or less dangerous for domestic use.

The opinion of the English Rivers Pollution Commission is very decided on this point. "No process," says the commission, in its report of 1868, "has yet been devised of cleansing water once contaminated with sewage so as to make it safe for drinking." And again: "Among the numerous processes for the cleansing of polluted water with which we have been acquainted there is not one which is sufficient to warrant the use, for drinking, of water which has once been contaminated with sewage or other noxious matters."

To devise a system by which rivers and other watercourses may be protected against pollution, so far as possible, is indeed a difficult undertaking and must be a work of time; but, beginning with what can be done, the difficulties will gradually solve themselves. When a beginning is made, however imperfectly, the necessities of the case will create the ambition to remedy what is amiss or incomplete and some satisfactory solution of this difficult problem will, in all probability, follow. The first step is to direct the State Board of Health to devise a system and present the same to the Legislature for such action as that body may see fit to take, with the view to the preservation of the health and lives of the inhabitants of the State.

POLLUTION OF THE WATERS OF CHESAPEAKE BAY.

Using rivers and estuaries as receptacles for sewage and offal was first tolerated on the assurance that it would be unrecognizable to the senses, and, consequently, wholly inoffensive through the enormous dilution resulting from admixture with the volume of water receiving it, and minute calculations were produced to prove the degree of the resulting dilution. Experience, however, has shown that this argument is a fallacy, inasmuch as the mixing in question does not take place. The most offensive solid substances float persistently on the surface, and are, when the water is a running stream, soon deposited on its banks. In tidal waters the evil is quite as great. The sewage not only poisons the water and renders it obnoxious to smell, but in the case of bays or estuaries the solid matter settles to the bottom in the form of a noxious mud, structive to animal life. In this way the finest bays and harbors in the world have become stinking pools.

The most conspicuous example of the pollution of a large volume of water by sewage matter is furnished by the bay of Naples, in Italy, which receives only the refuse water and street washings from the city of Naples, with a population of 400,000, but even this amount of sewage, free from human excrement, has so contaminated the waters of the bay that its surrounding shores, teeming with lovely villas and villages, once the abode of thousands of happy people, are now in a measure desolate and deserted, their owners and occupants, in many instances, having fled in disgust from the sickening stench arising from the surface of the water, and which, probably, furnished an important factor in the origin and progress of the terrible epidemic of cholera that has recently visited Naples and the vicinity of the bay.

This experience, taken in connection with the proposed construction of a system of sewerage for Baltimore city which would have its outfall, indirectly if not directly, into the Chesapeake bay, is a matter for serious consideration by the Legislature.

It is estimated that the whole volume of sewage of Baltimore city and its environs, including human excrement, the worst and most dangerous source of pollution, will aggregate nearly one million tons annually, and if this should be permitted to flow into the bay the result may easily be anticipated. As to the amount of disease and discomfort which, sooner or later, it would occasion in the counties adjacent to the bay, we must naturally speak with some caution. It is chiefly among dense populations, or where the poison is very concentrated, that we should naturally expect the worst results from this source; but that filth infections, either of air or water, will seriously depress the vital powers, and that it is one of the chain of causes producing epidemics are matters of common observation.

As to the effect that the emptying of such an enormous volume of human excrement into the bay would have upon the fish and oyster supply—this is also a matter for serious contemplation. It is well-known that fish do not now exist, or only to a very limited extent, in the waters of the "Basin" at Baltimore, whereas they were found in considerale quantities before it was contaminated by sewage matter; and it is believed that the deposit of any considerable quantity of excreted sewage, in the form of filthy mud, upon the oyster beds of the bay would greatly lessen, if not absolutely destroy, this valuable source of food supply and revenue to the State.* The oyster is of much more delicate organization, and consequently more easily affected by extraneous circumstances than either fish or crabs. Again, it is altogether doubtful whether either fish or shell-fish existing, in filth-polluted water, were at all possible, if such a thing could be used for human food without great detriment to health.

THE EFFECT OF MILL-DAMS AND STAGNANT POOLS ON THE PUBLIC HEALTH.

The causes of a great number of diseases are imperceptible to our senses, and it is one of the duties of the State Board of Health to get at these hidden causes and root them out. Malaria is one of the most powerful hidden causes of diseases, but it is also one of the most preventable. A fertile source of this disease is the obstruction of the natural flow of water, caused by the erection of mill-dams, artificial ponds, locks, &c. The destruction of one form of organic matter is always accompanied by the production of another form, which is regarded as the product of the decomposing process. It is generally acknowledged among the medical profession that scarlet fever, diphtheria, and even consumption, have originated from one form or another of malaria. Mill ponds, fish ponds, and other stagnant pools of water, sometimes act as generators and dischargers of this deadly poison, although their presence may never have been looked upon as in any way insalubrious. The amount of decomposing animal and vegetable matter which forms in still water during warm weather is sometimes enormous, and to this cause may be attributed the insanitary effects of all stagnant pools of water.

At times when rivers and streams are high, the unhealthy effect of mill-dams and other obstructions is not felt, because the overflow of water purifies the streams by carrying with it all miasmatic troubles. Dr. Arnott relates a case where a mill-dam was erected, and within a year or so afterward the neighborhood was infested with ague and malarial troubles, but when the mill was burnt down some years after and the dam destroyed, all signs of the presence of malaria disappeared. The occurrence of floods sometimes has its beneficial as well as calamitous side, by washing away

*In 1883, twenty million bushels of oysters were gathered in the waters of Maryland (Chesapeake bay), worth, on an average, thirty cents per bushel, or a total value of six million dollars.

mill-dams and other obstructions, and by destroying all decomposing matters collected in the river and vicinity. Where mill-dams or other obstructions cause sickness they should be removed, and not to do so is a criminal offence morally, if not legally.

It is the duty of the State Board of Health specially to urge this matter upon the attention of the Legislature. The census of the United States for 1880, will show that about one-half of the total number of deaths in the country are caused by diseases due for the most part to miasms consequent upon soil saturation and stagnant water; and that fully three-quarters of the victims to this baleful influence might be saved by proper drainage and disinfection. Many a community has been ravaged by malarial diseases which would have remained unscathed, or, at worst, would have escaped with slight visitation, had proper sanitary authority been exercised to put the community in a state of defence against this dreaded foe.

SUGGESTIONS ON RURAL HYGIENE.

A dry, well-drained site for a dwelling-house is generally conceded to be requisite for a healthy home. The relation of damp, sodden foundations, and wet, undrained surroundings to such diseases as rheumatism, diarrhœa and consumption is recognized by nearly all intelligent persons.

The soil about the house may be contaminated by soakage from leaky cess-pools, privy vaults, pig-pens, stables, and from decaying heaps of garbage and filth. The contamination of the ground air (which is the air that fills the spaces between the particles of the soil to several feet below the surface) is more deleterious to health than the vile odors that may render the air disagreeable. A house standing upon a gravelly foundation rests upon two-thirds earth and small stones and one-third air. Now, as in this climate, the houses are warmed a great part of the time, they act upon the same principle as a chimney, and suck up or draw in this ground air, which is colder than the air of the house. Now, if the air, contaminated from contact with a soil polluted by kitchen or chamber slops, soakage from privy-vaults, cess-pools, pig-pens, stables, or any decaying mass or accumulation of filth in outhouses or surroundings, is drawn into the house, as must of necessity happen if any such sources of pollution exist near by, the air of the house is to this extent contaminated and devitalized, and becomes the predisposing cause of such diseases as diptheria, cholera infantum, croup, catarrh, lung fever, consumption, and a host of minor ills that depress vital energy, lessen the working power, and shorten life. The products of decay from vegetable putrefaction in the cellar are, by the same law of natural philosophy, drawn up to devitalize the air of the occupied rooms.

If cess-pools are used they should be cemented watertight, ventilated thoroughly, and frequently emptied. The soil saturation resulting from ordinary careless methods sooner or later become factors in the production of disease.

It is hardly possible to fix the limit of perfect safety for the distance that should exist between privy-vault, cess-pool, &c., and the well for drinking water. It is safe, however, to say that at the ordinary distance which obtains at most country houses both valt and cess-pool should be cemented water-tight.

The principles of drainage are practically recognized by every farmer almost, who knows, from experience, that a drain draws from a larger area after it has been made awhile, and that channels of communication are formed in the soil along which the water finds its way to the drain. Still it is seldom that they apply this to their wells, and we find privies, cess-pools, and pig-pens situated within a few feet of wells.

A common error in this connection is to conclude that if the water from the well is clear, bright, and sparkling, and offends neither taste, sight, or smell, it must be pure. The reverse, however, is true; for water that is decidedly contaminated by the products of organic decay may be pleasant to both sight, taste, and smell, and yet dangerous to health or life.

The driven well, if driven deep enough, avoids contamination from surface water. The water from deep wells, when not contaminated by surface water, is of the best possible quality. Surface water, which is always liable to carry filth, may be excluded by laying the upper three-fourths of the wall of the well in cement.

Infiltration of the soil from a privy vault may be prevented by cementing the vault so as to make it watertight. The earth-closet system is to be unqualifiedly commended, and any one with the slightest ingenuity can construct one that will answer all requirements, with an ordinary packing box and a large-sized coal hod, furnished with the requisite materials. If dry earth is not readily obtainable, ashes will serve equally as well. The advantages and comfort of this system, especially in the winter months, for women and children, more than outweigh any slight trouble that may be involved.

Excessive shading of house and grounds is not uncommon, and while shade trees add much to the attractiveness of a country place, dense shading of the house and grounds induces dampness, and produces ill health by the exclusion of sunlight. The soil is often kept damp and unwholesome, and a constant decay of leaves and other vegetable substances near dwellings is occasioned by dense shrubbery. Fresh air and sunlight should have the fullest access to all the immediate surroundings of the house. Human beings require sunlight as well as plants, and this should not be excluded from a country residence by too many shade trees with dense foliage. In the back yards and gardens rank vegetation and a filthy, saturated soil are to be avoided, as they often give rise to sickness. The prompt removal of all filth before decay commences is a sanitary maxim which should never be neglected.

THE DANGER OF KEEPING PIGS AND OTHER ANIMALS NEAR HUMAN HABITATIONS.

It is not necessary to say much in demonstration of the nuisance arising from the keeping of hogs and other animals in a town or village. The reports of health officers in all parts of the country abound in illustrations of it, yet it is a matter of fact that animals, especially pigs, are habitually kept in the midst of populous towns and villages in a most uncleanly and unwholesome manner. Health officers would cut the knot of the difficulty by altogether forbidding the keeping of pigs within the precincts of any city, town or village, if they had the power. But it is not solely amid aggregations of population that such nuisances are occasioned. A single animal badly kept in or near a solitary house may be a source of injury to the inhabitants of that house.

The offensive odor from ill-kept and ill-managed pigstyes will travel with the wind considerable distances, and they should not be permitted within a defined limit of inhabited dwellings either in town or country. The nuisance has its source in the usually filthy condition of the styes themselves, in the accumulation of matter often in a fermenting condition, and in the storage and subsequent preparation of the food. The swill tub in most towns and villages is an institution, and throughout the year, during hot as well as cold whether, the process of filling it goes on.

Uncleanliness is properly reckoned as the deadliest of our present removable causes of disease. "It has," says Mr. Simon, "been among the oldest and most universal of medicial experiences that populations living among filth, and within direct reach of polluting influences, succumb to various diseases which, under proper conditions, are comparatively or absolutely unknown; and the broad knowledge that filth makes disease is represented in the oldest records which exist of legislation meant for the masses of mankind."

The universal experience of medical men affirms the fact that diseases are exceptionally frequent among residents in proximity to stables, cow-sheds, and pig-styes especially, where effluvium is concentrated within a confined space by peculiarities of locality, &c.

SLAUGHTER-HOUSE NUISANCES.

This question has been discussed in several of the Biennial Reports of the State Board of Health, wherein an effort has been made to open the eyes of the public and the Legislature to the dangerous and disgusting results arising from the present practice of slaughtering animals in the heart of a large city, or in the midst of a dense population. It cannot be denied that this practice has become a serious evil in Baltimore, Frederick city and Cumberland, but it is to be feared that the custom is too rooted to be easily eradicated—nothing short of a pestilence will arouse the public to a sense of the dangers which surround them in this respect.

Slaughtering is usually conducted within a building specially arranged for the purpose; but frequently this is not the case, and animals are slaughtered for food in an open yard, in some stable, or inappropriate outhouse, or in an open shop forming part of the butcher's dwelling-house. These slaughter-houses are usually to be found in neighborhoods occupied by poor people, often in narrow, close, ill-ventilated streets or courts. *They would not be tolerated in better neighborhoods.*— My observation of private slaughter-houses has given me a very unfavorable general impression of them. No doubt many, especially in the larger cities, are well paved and kept clean; but generally any filthy place appears to be regarded as good enough for "pounding" and slaughtering animals intended for human food. Usually in the smaller slaughter-houses the yards are trodden in dung and litter many inches thick, while the floors are encrusted and the walls begrimed with blood and filth.

The nuisances arising in connection with slaughtering are usually confined to the immediate neighborhood. They may depend: 1. On the uncleanly manner in which the animals are kept prior to slaughter, and (especially if sheep) to the peculiar odor arising from animals themselves when they are kept in an open yard close to the windows of inhabited houses. 2. On the uncleanly condition of the slaughter-house (a condition which is aggravated when it is not properly paved and drained), or on an uncleanly mode of conducting the several processes of slaughtering. Where there are no proper means of drainage (which is the usual condition in Baltimore), blood and filth may flow out upon the surface of the ground outside the slaughter-house, and there stagnating and becoming decomposed, they may give rise to offensive effluvia. 3. On the retention and accumulation upon the premises of hides, skins, blood, fat, offal, dung and garbage, which after a time, varying with the state of the weather, undergo decomposition and become offensive. 4. On the uncleanly condition of blood-tubs or other receptacles, either kept in the slaughter-house or in the yard. 5. On blood and other decomposable animal liquid matters flowing into drains or sewers with which untrapped pipes of other premises communicate directly or indirectly. The utmost care is necessary to prevent any slaughter-house in a populous neighborhood becoming a nuisance, under the most favorable circumstances of location and drainage, but where the drainage is bad, which in an unsewered city like Baltimore, is invariably the case, slaughter-houses must in every instance be deemed necessarily a nuisance calculated to bring, sooner or later, evil consequences.

These nuisances may, by their operation on the senses, produce similar functional disturbances to those which evil odors from other sources are apt to occasion, and in so far as they are filth nuisances, they are unquestionably injurious to the health of persons exposed to their influence. Dr. Alfred Carpenter has stated his belief that blood and garbage from slaughter-houses, when undergoing decomposition, may cause the development of scarlet fever in persons exposed to their effluvia. He lays considerable stress on the influence of decomposing vertebrate blood in giving origin to this disease. Dr. Spear, the health officer of South Shields, England, declares that in two instances, during the two years he held office, he had traced back the infection of local outbreaks of this disease to butchers' premises, being unable to trace it back any further. The experience of Dr. Steuart, many years Health Commissioner of Baltimore, tends also to corroborate this view of the injurious effects of slaughtering establishments.

It is scarcely necessary for me to say that I have myself arrived at a very decided opinion on the subject, and have consequently (but hitherto fruitlessly) urged the State authorities to pass the necessary legislation to insure the success and universal use of public abbattoirs, and thus to place the health authorities in a position to deal with unwholesome slaughtering places in the towns and cities of the State, more efficiently than they can now deal with them. It is the common opinion of most of the medical practitioners of the day, that the course of zymotic diseases and the type assumed by them have been unfavorably influenced by exposure to slaughter-house effluvia. There appears moreover, to be a general impression among medical men, that women living in houses where they are exposed to this effluvia, make bad recoveries after child-birth. Dr. Bradley, of Jarrow, England, says that he is strongly impressed with this fact, as the result of a long and extensive obstetric practice, that it is now a rule with him to advise women approaching their confinement to quit such places.

And there is also another less direct way in which the effluvia from a badly kept and badly managed slaughter-house may conduce to the injury of the public health; namely, through the influence which the septic effluvia from them may exert upon the recently killed meat. It is a common practice to hang up the dressed carcass to cool and "set" within the slaughter-house. When the slaughter-house is too warm or charged with septic effluvia, the meat is liable to imbibe septic matters from the slaughter-house atmosphere. Septic effluvia must be abundantly present in the air when the slaughter-house is badly kept and badly arranged or managed; such effluvia, for instance, may originate from a badly kept yard communicating freely with the slaughter-house, from blood or filth encrusted upon the walls or lying in the fissures of the flooring, from skins or fat too long retained, or from a drain having its inlet within the slaughter-house itself. And such absorption of septic ferments are apt to conduce to early decomposition of the meat, especially in the warmer season of the year, or when the meat is the product of animals which, although diseased, are not so diseased as to render the meat, *in the opinion of the butchers*, unfit for human consumption. It is well known to medical men that some meat apparently good and wholesome, meat not obviously tainted, may produce, when cooked and eaten, very serious disturbance in the system of the consumer, symptoms distinguishable with difficulty from choleric symptoms or symptoms of irritant poisoning.

INSPECTION OF ANIMALS.

The necessity of a rigid inspection of all animals intended for human food, both before they are slaughtered and afterwards, has heretofore been urged by the State Board of Health as a means of guarding the public against the mischiefs which arise from the use or consumption of unwholesome meat, but thus far no legislative action has been taken in the matter. I have myself experienced an instance in which a piece of beef, apparently sound when viewed at the butcher's shambles, presented, after being cooked and served at the table, unmistakable evidences of a septic condition; there was some alteration in the meat, possibly in the fat, having affinity with putrefaction, but not itself the ordinary putrefaction which betrays itself by odor. This condition could not have been detected in the raw meat, except by an expert, hence the necessity of proper inspection laws, and a close scrutiny of every animal, both before and after being slaughtered, and this can only be accomplished under the abattoir system, which consists of improved buildings for slaughtering purposes, having thorough drainage and every facility for cleanliness, cooling chambers for storage and for thoroughly removing animal heat; also, an improved process for the utilization of all offal. The advantages of this system are numerous and important. It concentrates all the business of slaughtering at one point; it permits of the handling of the refuse offal without removal through the streets by wagons, carts, &c., before the material begins to decompose or become offensive. The animals for slaughter are not required to be driven from one section of the city to another, at the risk of life and property from vicious animals; it affords ample facilities for strict inspection of stock by municipal authorities before and after slaughter. It is not only diseased animals that are unfit for human food, but those that have been over-driven and worried, and are killed when too hot; pregnant animals, &c. All of these can be under the inspection of authority, provided all animals are slaughtered at one place. When public abattoirs are under the control of authority they *must* be kept in a wholesome condition, and in the matter of slaughtering animals for food, as well as the inspection of both live stock and carcasses, the abattoir system is unquestionably superior to any other; it concentrates the business, it obviates the necessity of driving stock through closely populated parts of the city, and it will remove a great source of nuisance, viz., the effluvia from slaughter-houses scattered in every section of the city.

ANOTHER FRUITFUL SOURCE OF DANGER.

Recent investigations have conclusively established the fact that brass, nickle-plated or other metal faucets impart certain poisonous properties to beer and other malt liquors, which, when drawn through them and taken into the stomach, often produce painful and sometimes fatal disorders. This evil has become so great, in a sanitary point of view, that some State and city boards of health have felt called upon to take cognizance of the matter, and forbid the use of such faucets by venders of beer, soda-water and other beverages.

Section 208, of the Sanitary Code of the Board of Health of New York, provides, that "in the sale or keeping of any beverage or drink, no person shall keep or use any tap, faucet, tank, fountain or vessel, or any pipe or conduit in connection therewith, which shall be composed of or made with brass, lead, copper or other metal or metallic substances that are or will be affected by liquids, so that dangerous, unwholesome or deleterious compounds are formed therein or thereby, or such that beer, soda water, syrups or other liquids, or any beverage drink or flavoring material drawn therefrom, shall be unwholesome, dangerous or detrimental to health." Adopted July 22, 1884.

The Brooklyn Health Department, under date of September 2, 1885, has issued the following:

*To Druggists, Confectioners, and all Dealers in
Soda Water, Lager Beer, and other Beverages:*

You are hereby notified of the following official action taken in reference to the sale of soda water, lager beer, and other beverages:

By virtue of the power conferred upon me by law, I do hereby declare the following practices dangerous and detrimental to the public health, and do prohibit the same in the city of Brooklyn:

The selling, delivering, or draughting of soda water, mineral water, syrups, flavoring extracts, lager beer, or other beverages, through pipes, faucets, or taps composed in whole or in part of copper, lead, zinc, or other poisonous material, unless such pipes, faucets, or taps are so lined, coated, or protected as that the soda water, mineral water, syrup, flavoring extracts, lager beer, or other beverage cannot come in contact with the copper, lead, zinc, or other poisonous material composing the same.

(Signed) J. H. RAYMOND, M. D.,
Commissioner of Health.

This action was taken on the report of Chemist Bartley, of the Brooklyn Health Department, who investigated the subject of beer drawn through metal faucets, and submitted the result of his inquiries to Health Commissioner Raymond, in which he says: "The practice of drawing beer through brass or copper faucets is injurious to the consumer, because deposits of metal are often found in the beverage."

The *Scientific American* of September 6, 1885, calls attention to the dangers which lurk in metallic faucets, when used for drawing beer, in the following strong language:

"Dr. Cyrus Edson, of the New York City Board of Health, a careful and experienced man, said that so far he had devoted himself to the mode of drawing beer in the saloons and beer halls, for in this there was even more danger to the public health than was likely to be found in the adulteration of the beer. He showed the writer a long copper spigot or tap, similar to those in general use, and which he had taken out of a beer saloon. He had it cut through lengthwise, in order to exhibit the corrosion that had taken place from the constant presence of beer. Its interior was a mass of corrosion, green and spongy. Beer, he said, which passes through such a spigot must always be more or less injuriously affected, that which remains the longest being, of course, the most contaminated. The first person who calls for beer in the morning where such a spigot is used would get beer which has stood all night in these poisonous surroundings; in other words, he would get beer that is absolutely poisonous."

I would strongly urge the necessity of some action in this State, in order to protect our citizens against the poisonous effects of beer and soda water when drawn through metal faucets, which is the case in a majority of instances where these beverages are sold. This can be done only by legislative enactment, the State Board of Health having no power in the premises beyond merely advising the public as to the evil results, and such advice cannot well be brought to the attention of children and the laboring class, who are the greatest sufferers by this traffic.

In this connection, it is gratifying to state that an enterprising Baltimore firm, Messrs. Friedenwald Bros., manufacturers of Patented Specialties, have devised and placed on the market a most ingeneous apparatus for drawing beer, ale, &c., from casks, which, if the vendors of these beverages could be induced or required to use instead of the poison generating brass or copper spigot, it would be a great boon to the public health. This apparatus consists of a self-ventilating, wood-lined faucet, possessing strength, durability and simplicity, and so constructed that the fluid to be drawn does not come in contact in any way with metal, thereby preserving it pure and sweet, regardless of the time it may remain in the faucet.

The Messrs. Friedenwald have also produced another important hygienic arrangement, the non-corrodible stopper. It is well-known that many beverages, such as ale, porter, &c., are injuriously affected by contact with the ordinary rubber stopper, and are sometimes thereby rendered inadmissable as beverages. The rubber of the new stopper is so coated with a compound of perafine, applied to its inner face, as to render it perfectly devoid of taste or smell however long it may be exposed to contact with the corroding liquid. It may also be used to advantage in bottling ascidulated mineral waters, especially the carbonice waters, as no absorption or escape of the gases can take place, and no corroding effect will be manifested.

DISINFECTION AND DISINFECTANTS.

"It is to cleanliness, ventilation and drainage, and the use of perfectly pure drinking water," says Mr. Simon, "that populations ought mainly to look for safety against nuisance and infection. Artificial disinfectants* cannot properly supply the place of those essentials; for, except in a small and peculiar class of cases, they are of temporary or imperfect usefulness. That no

---
*The word "disinfectants" is used to cover. not only those true disinfectants which permanently destroy infective matter, but also those agents which merely arrest the process, or absorb the offensive products of organic decomposition.

house refuse—not only excremental matter, but also no other kind of dirt or refuse, should remain on or about inhabited premises, is a first rule against infection. That the air within the house should never in any part of the house be stagnant, but should always be in course of renewal from without, by uninterrupted and abundant supplies of fresh air, is a condition of equal importance. And that all water meant to be used for drinking or cooking should be drawn from sources which cannot have been polluted by any kind of refuse matter, is a third most important rule for the avoidance of infection."

If dwelling places have within them any odor of drainage particular examination should be made, (1,) whether the filth which house-drains are meant to carry away is retained in or near the premises in ill made drains, or sewers, or cesspools, or perhaps is leaking from house-drains within the house; (2,) whether, inside the house, the inlets of drains and sinks are properly rapped; and, (3,) whether the drains and sewers are sufficiently ventilated outside the house. All water-closets within houses should have free openings for ventilation from and into the outer air. Of a cesspool, the only true disinfection is to abolish it. In country places, where proper drainage is not provided, the nuisance of open privies may be best avoided by the use of the so-called earth closet.

If a sewer is much complained of as stinking into the public way, generally the presumption is, that, from original ill-construction or some other cause, it does not properly fulfill its object, but has filth accumulated and stagnant in it; and such a sewer, besides occasioning nuisance in the public way, may be the source of some serious danger to the inhabitants of houses which drain into it. It is most important that all sewers should be well ventilated at points where their effluvia will be least injurious, and ordinary drain pipes may be used to conduct the effluvia to a distance.

For artificial disinfection on a large scale, *the agents which commonly prove useful,* are—quick lime, chloride of lime, carbolic acid, sulphate of iron, perchloride of iron and chloride of manganese. The following are also efficient disinfectants, but, being dearer, are less suited for large operations: Sulphate of zinc, chloride of zinc, chloride of soda and permanganate of potash. In certain cases chlorine gas, or nitrous acid gas, or sulphurous acid gas may advantageously be used, and in certain other cases, powdered charcoal or fresh dry earth.*

Quick lime, recently burnt, may be used, either in the form of dry powder, or, stirred up with about ten times its bulk of water, as milk of lime. *Chloride of lime* is best used with water, and thoroughly mixed with it, in the proportion of a pound to the gallon; or of the solution as commonly sold, about two pints may be mixed with a gallon of water. *Carbolic acid*, in the fluid form in which it is commonly sold, should be dissolved in about eight times its volume of water, with which it must be mixed by strong shaking in a closed vessel. *Sulphate of iron* should be dissolved in ten times its weight in water; a solution which is best effected by employing hot water and stirring. *Sulphate of zinc* should be dissolved in about ten times its weight of warm water. Of *perchloride of iron* and *chloride of manganese*, the common concentrated solution may be used, diluted with ten or twelve times their bulk in water. Of *chloride of zinc*, the common concentrated solution may be diluted with eight to ten times its bulk in water. Of *chloride of soda*, the common solution may be used like that of chloride of lime. Of *permanganate of potash*, an ounce may be dissolved in a gallon of water.

All disinfectants must be used in *quantities proportionate* to the amount of matter or surface to be disinfected. When the matters requiring to be disinfected have an offensive smell, the disinfectant should be used till this smell has entirely ceased, and as often as the smell recurs the disinfectant must again be used.

TO DISINFECT CERTAIN PLACES AND SUBSTANCES.

During the emptying of privies and cess-pools, and whenever temporary disinfection is required chloride of lime, or Reed & Carnrick's solution of hypochlorite of soda, or the sulphate of iron (common copperas), or perchloride of iron, chloride of manganese, or chloride of zinc, will be found available. A dilute solution of one of these agents should be poured into the privy or cesspool, from a quart to a gallon at a time, till the desired

---

*The bi-chloride of mercury or corrosive sublimate properly used is one of the best if not the very best germicide, but on account of its poisonous character its use is not recommended in families. Reed and Carnricks Standard Solution of Sodium Hypochlorite, prepared in accordance with the recommendations of the *American Public Health Association*, is recommended as a safe and efficient preparation for disinfecting and sanitary purposes. Directions for using accompany each bottle.

effect is obtained. Especially where cholera or typhoid fever is present, privies and cess-pools ought to be very frequently flooded in this manner.

Heaps of manure or other filth, if it be for the time impracticable or inexpedient to remove them, should be covered to the depth of two or three inches with a layer of freshly burnt vegetable charcoal in powder. Freshly burnt lime may be used in the same way, but is less effective than charcoal. If neither charcoal or lime be at hand, the filth should be covered with a layer, some inches thick, of clean dry earth. For a privy which has only solid contents, the same sort of treatment is applicable. Earth near dwellings, if it has become offensive or foul by the soakage of decaying animal or vegetable matter, should be treated on the same plan.

If *running sewage*, about to be used in agriculture, requires to be disinfected, the chloride of manganese or perchloride of iron may be best used; but if the sewage is to pass into a river or into any pond or canal, where it might again become offensive, chloride of lime is to be preferred; and in this case a pound of good chloride of lime will generally suffice to disinfect 1,000 gallons of the sewage. For foul ditches and other stagnant drainage, chloride of lime is also the proper disinfectant.

Where it is desirable to disinfect, before throwing away the *evacuations from the bowels of persons suffering from cholera or typhoid fever*, some disinfectants (which here may be chloride of lime or, preferably, the solution of hypochlorite of soda,) should be put into the bed-pan, or other vessel, before it is used by the patient, and more may be added immediately after. Thorough mixture with the evacuation should be ensured. Care should also be taken that portions of the discharges do not remain about the patient's body, or in his dress.

Linen and wearing apparel requiring to be disinfected may be set to soak in water containing, per gallon, about an ounce either of common clear solution of chloride of lime, or that of hypochlorite of soda. Or the articles in question may be plunged into boiling water and afterwards when at wash, be actually boiled in the washing water.

Woolens, bedding and clothing, which cannot be washed, may be disinfected by exposure for two or more hours, in chambers constructed for that purpose, to a temperature of 210° to 250° Fahr. When this cannot be done, the natural disinfectant process of prolonged exposure to air, sun and rain ought to be had recourse to.

For the disinfection of the *interior of houses*, the ceilings and walls should be washed with warm quicklime water. The wood-work should be cleansed with soap and water, and frequently washed with water containing in each gallon about two ounces of the clear solution of either chloride of lime or chloride of soda.

A *room no longer occupied* may be disinfected by chlorine gas, or nitrous acid gas, or sulphurous acid gas. And for this purpose the gases may be produced in the room as follows : *Chlorine gas*, by pouring over a quarter of a pound of finely powdered black oxide of manganese, contained in a jar, half a pint of muriatic acid previously mixed with a quarter of a pint of water, or by pouring over a quarter of a pound of chloride of lime, contained in a jar, a quarter of a pint of muriatic or dilute sulphuric acid ; *nitrous acid gas*, by pouring over an ounce of copper shavings or turnings, contained in a deep jar, three ounces of concentrated nitric acid; *sulphurous acid gas*, by burning an ounce or two of flour of sulphur in a plate or saucer. The process of disinfecting a room by any of these gases requires several hours, and while it is going on, all doors, chimneys and windows of the room must be carefully closed. Precautions to this effect must be taken before the chemicals are mixed, as the person who starts the process, having to avoid the gas, must not afterwards loiter in the room. When the process is at an end doors and windows should be fully opened.

STATE REGISTRATION OF PHYSICIANS.

It is very important, in the interest of the people, that there should be some efficient law to regulate the practice of medicine in the State. The facilities of becoming professional men, with the prefix of "M. D.," are so great that many persons are seduced into an attempt to become physicians without the basis of a primary education or any knowledge of the science of medicine and surgery. There are others again who, having received a good primary education, are induced from motives of economy or convenience to *purchase* diplomas from bogus medical schools without having attained any anatomical knowledge or clinical instruction. A knowledge of the science of medicine is not, like divinity and law, to be acquired by reading books in the closet; it can only be attained by dissection of the dead body, and by clinical instruction in connection with the knowledge acquired from books.

The great multiplication of medical schools in every section of the country, together with the proverbial facilities of becoming practitioners, has so lowered the standard of professional excellence, and so manifestly degraded medical character in the United States that it is to be hoped an enlightened public opinion will in this as in other States take decided steps towards putting down such a vicious system. The statement made some years ago in the annual report of the Attorney General of Pennsylvania that Dr. Buchanan had given information to the State authorities setting forth his dealings with some twenty-two medical colleges in this country alone in the sale and exchange of bogus diplomas, demonstrates the necessity of prompt and stringent legislation which will purge our State of incompetent practitioners. In Illinois, where the diplomas have undergone the careful scrutiny of the State Board of Health, seventeen hundred and seventy-six (1776) incompetent practitioners have been required to stop practice or leave the State. It is unnecessary at present to enter into any statements to show the absolute necessity of the Legislature interfering for the protection of the people in this matter. Events are daily transpiring which must soon direct public attention to the subject with intense and fearful anxiety.

Laws have already been enacted by many of the State Legislatures in reference to this matter, and our own Legislature should be earnestly invoked to secure to the people the same protection in this State. It is their cause, not ours; the people must employ medical men, whether they be ignorant or informed, but if they be ignorant, then it is the people who suffer.

In conferring diplomas, feelings of interest, commiseration and kindness should have no weight. It is a painful thing to send a young man back to his studies who presents himself for a diploma. The kind and generous feelings of the professor rise up and plead in his behalf, and these are more imperative in proportion as the associations have been longer or more close. It is often the case that the preceptor is a professor, and it would seem like condemning him to reject his pupil. Besides, when a student has paid so much money for office and lecture fees, it really seems hard to refuse the diploma. But the vision should be carried further, from the one to the many, from the candidate to the community, and it should be recollected that what to him may be kindness, may to his patients be protracted suffering or death. The tendency of those institutions which confer irresponsible power on the few over the many is to insure the sacrifice of the general to particular interests; and the consideration of such practices should not fail to excite a deep interest in the thinking part of the community. It is time that the physicians of the State should exert themselves to change a system which has so long retarded the progress of their science, and which has been productive of so much evil in communities. Surely there is good sense enough, both in the people and in the Legislature, to listen to their representations.

CHARITABLE AND PENAL INSTITUTIONS.

In the absence of any direction from His Excellency, the Governor of the State, I have not deemed myself justified in making any special inspections of the charitable, penal and reformatory institutions of the State since those made under the direction of Governor Carroll in 1879. The recommendations, however, which I have made in reference to these institutions in past years have not, so far as I am aware, been productive of anything more than temporary results, as each community seems to reverence and admire its own peculiar system of "Poor-house and Jail."

Many persons, willing and anxious to exert themselves in bettering the condition of the poor, have despaired of being able to effect any permanent good. They see the number of charitable institutions daily increasing, and the mass of human misery apparently undiminished. From this they argue that interference would be in vain. They despond, therefore, and remain idle. One of the objects of a regular and systematic inspection of such institutions, and that one not the least important, is to furnish a motive for exertion to such as are now passive, and, if possible, to rouse them into activity by pointing out in what way they may render the most extensive and lasting services to mankind. I have no disposition to repeat the horrors which I have seen in some of the county almshouses. They were laid bare to the public ten years ago, but no statutory provision has been made to correct the evils which a very slight exercise of authority might prevent. The improvement of our almshouse system must of course be a work of time, but it would be very greatly facilitated were these abodes of misery more often visited by the better class of citizens in each county. In the absence of legislative enactments, a voluntary association for the relief of pauperism and crime, by regular and methodical inspection of the county almshouses and jails, at least as often as once in three months, might be organized in each county of the State, and might accomplish a world of good.

The presence of children in such places is their saddest feature. What can be more dreary than the future prospects of a pauper child? All such should be provided with homes, if possible, outside the almshouse; but if compelled to remain there, they should be given every facility for obtaining the rudiments of an education, in the hope of lifting them out of their forlorn condition.

PRECAUTIONS AGAINST SMALLPOX AND OTHER EPIDEMIC DISEASES.

1. In every case where smallpox, diptheria, fever, or any other epidemic disease prevails or threatens to prevail it is of more than common importance that, both by private action and by action of authorities, everything practicable should be done to insure freshness of atmosphere and dryness of soil, and entire absence of dirt throughout the district, especially in and about houses; to guard against overcrowding of inhabitants, and to provide that impure water be not drank. It is of course particularly necessary that whatever proceedings are required to procure the abatement of nuisances should be pressed forward with all practicable dispatch.

2. Proper precautions are equally requisite for all classes of society. But it is chiefly with regard to the poorer population, therefore chiefly in the courts and alleys of towns, and the laborers' cottages of country districts, that local authorities are called upon to exercise vigilance, and to proffer information and advice. Common lodging-houses and houses which are sub-let in several small holdings always require particular attention.

3. Wherever there is accumulation, stink or soakage of house refuse, or of other decaying animal or vegetable matter, the nuisance should as promptly as possible be abated, and precaution should be taken not to let it recur. Especially, examination should be made as to the efficient working of sewers and drains, and any nuisance therefrom, or from any foul ditches or ponds, should be got rid of without delay. The ventilation of sewers, the ventilation and trapping of house drains, and the disconnexion of cistern overflows and sink pipes from drains should be carefully seen to. The scavening

of the district, the state of receptacles for excrement, and of dust-bins, will require particular and sustained attention. In slaughter-houses, and wherever animals are kept, strict cleanliness should be enforced.

4. In order to guard against the harm which sometimes arises from disturbing heaps of offensive matter, it is often necessary to combine the use of chemical disinfectants with such means as are taken for the removal of filth; and in cases where removal is for the time impossible or expedient the filth should always be disinfected. Disinfection is likewise desirable for unpaved earth close to dwellings, if it be sodden with slops and filth. Generally, where any epidemic disease is in the house, the privy requires to be disinfected.

5. Sources of water supply should be well examined. Those which are in any way tainted by animal or vegetable refuse, above all those into which there is any leakage or filtration from sewers, drains, cess-pools or foul ditches ought no longer to be drank from. Especially where the disease is cholera, diarrhœa or enteric fever it is essential that no foul water be drank.

If unfortunately the only water which for a time can be got should be open to suspicion of dangerous organic impurity, it ought at least to be boiled before it is used for drinking, and then not to be drank later than twenty-four hours after it has been boiled. Filtering of the ordinary kind cannot by itself be trusted to purify water, but it is a good addition to either of the above processes. It cannot be too distinctly understood that dangerous qualities of water are not obviated by the addition of wine or spirits.

When there appears any probable relation between the distribution of disease and of milk supplies, the cleanliness of dairies and the purity of the water used in them, should be carefully investigated.

6. The washing and lime-whiting of uncleanly premises, especially of such as are densely occupied, should be pressed with all practicable despatch.

7. Overcrowding should be prevented. Especially where disease has begun, the sick-room should, as far as possible, be free from persons who are not of use or comfort to the patient.

8. Ample ventilation should be enforced. It should be seen that windows are sufficiently opened. Especially, where any kind of infective fever has begun, it is essential, both for patients and for persons who are about them, that the sick-room and the sick-house be constantly well traversed by streams of fresh air.

9. The cleanliest domestic habits should be enjoined. Refuse matters which have to be cast away should never be allowed to remain within doors; and things which have to be disinfected or cleansed, should always be disinfected or cleansed without delay.

10. Special precautions of cleanliness and disinfection are neccessary with regard to infective matters discharged from the bodies of the sick. Among discharges which it is proper to treat as infective are those which come, in cases of small-pox, from the affected skin; in cases of cholera and enteric fever, from the intestinal canal; in cases of diphtheria, from the nose and throat;. likewise, in cases of any eruptive or other epidemic fever, the general exhalations of the sick. The caution which is necessary with regard to such matters must,. of course, extend to whatever is imbued with them; so that bedding, clothing, towels and other articles, which have been in use by the sick, may not become sources of mischief, either in the house to which they belong, or in houses to which they are conveyed. Moreover, in enteric fever and cholera, the evacuations should be regarded as capable of communicating an infectious quality to any night-soil with which they are mingled in privies, drains or cess-pools; and this danger is best guarded against by thoroughly disinfecting them before they are thrown away; above all, they must never be cast where they can run or soak into sources of drinking water.

11. All reasonable care should be taken not to allow infective disease to spread by the unnecessary association of sick with healthy persons. This care is requisite, not only with regard to the sick house, but likewise with regard to day schools and other establishments wherein members of many different households are accustomed to meet.

12. Where dangerous conditions of residence cannot be promptly remedied, it will be best that the inmates, while unattacked by disease, remove to some other safer lodging. If disease begins in houses where the sick person cannot be rightly circumstanced and tended, medical advice should be taken as to the propriety of removing him to an infirmary or hospital. Every sanitary authority should have in readiness a hospital for the reception of such cases.

13. Privation, as predisposing to disease, will require special measures of relief.

14. In certain cases special medical arrangements are necessary. For instance, as cholera in this country

almost always begins somewhat gradually in the comparatively tractable form of what is called "premonitory diarrhœa," it is essential that, where cholera is epidemic, arrangements should be made for affording medical relief without delay to persons attacked, even slightly, with looseness of bowels. So again, where small-pox is the prevailing disease, it is essential that all unvaccinated persons (unless they previously have had small-pox) should very promptly be vaccinated; and that re-vaccination should be performed in cases properly requiring it.

15. It is always to be desired that the people should, as far as possible, know what real precautions they can take against the disease which threatens them, what vigilance is needful with regard to its early symptoms, and what (if any) special arrangements have been made for giving medical assistance within the district. For the purpose of such information printed hand-bills or placards may usefully be employed, and in cases where danger is great, house-to-house visitation by discreet and competent persons may be of the utmost service, both in quieting unreasonable alarm and in leading or assisting the less educated and the destitute parts of the population to do what is needful for safety.

16. The present memorandum relates to occasions of emergency. Therefore the measures suggested in it are all of an extemporaneous kind, and permanent provisions for securing the public health have not been in express terms insisted on. It is to be remembered, however, that in proportion as a district is habitually well cared for by its sanitary authorities, the more formidable emergencies of epidemic disease are not likely to arise in it.

PREVENTION AND RESTRICTION OF CHOLERA.

(A circular issued by the State Board of Health, June, 1885.)

In view of the possibility of cholera making its appearance in this country, the State Board of Health promptly issued the following directions for the prevention and restriction of the disease:

1. In cities or towns the streets should be daily cleansed of all offal, dirt, and impurities whatever, and the gutters frequently washed with running water. In no yard or open lot should any collection of animal or vegetable matters be allowed to remain, nor any cesspool be left unfilled with clean earth.

2. Cellars should be kept dry and clean and the sinks well cleaned out and disinfected with a strong solution

of chloride of lime, or copperas. These substances should also be sprinkled over the floor of cellars. Free ventilation of sitting and bed rooms should be enjoined and practiced, the floors *dry-scrubbed*, and the bedding and bed-clothes aired at least once a day. All kinds of of rooms or halls in which a number of persons congregate together, as in schools, churches, manufactories, &c., should be supplied with a constant renewal of fresh air.

3. Personal cleanliness should be rigidly promoted, by regular ablution or bathing in water of such a temperature as the feelings and experience of the individual teach him to be most agreeable and salutary. Frictions of the skin with a course towel or brush are particularly serviceable. The clothing should be thick enough to protect the body against sudden change of temperature or from sudden cooling after being overheated.

4. Temperance and regularity of life in all respects, which are so serviceable in protecting against most diseases, are required to be observed in a particular degree to ward off an attack of cholera.

5. The exciting causes of the disease are moral excitants, especially fear and anger; intemperance in the use of fermented or spirituous liquors, or in eating and overloading the stomach; acid drinks or large draughts of cold water; the use of crude, indigestible food, whether animal or vegetable, particularly the latter; excessive exertion or fatigue in the heat of the day; exposure to the night air, sitting in currents of air, and particularly sleeping with too light covering. Most of the attacks occur in the night, from 11 or 12 o'clock to 3 or 4 in the morning.

6. Prudence in living during the epidemic period (which usually continues from six weeks to three months); the wearing of flannel, particularly next the body; keeping the feet warm and dry; the avoidance of improper food and drinks; tranquillity of mind and body, are almost certain guarantees against the assaults of the disease, and disarm the pestilence of its malignity.

7. The disease, when abandoned to its course, passes through different stages, in all of which it can be controlled easily, except one, the cold stage or period of collapse, which is in almost every instance preceded by the symptoms of the forming stage, when the disease, if timely treated, may be arrested.

8. The symptoms of this forming stage should be

generally promulgated and persons instructed of the necessity of immediate attention to them. It is ignorance in this respect among the poorer classes of society and their habits of life, leading to indifference and inattention, that plunges so many belonging to this class into the desperate situation so frequently met with when medical aid and human skill are utterly unavailing.

9. The symptoms above referred to are sudden looseness of the bowels, the discharge becoming thin, watery and colorless or whitish, with little odor, vertigo or dizziness, nausea, oppression, pain and cramps of the stomach, with retching and vomiting of a fluid generally resembling dirty river water, attended or soon followed by cramps of the extremities, particularly the legs and thighs.

10. When the foregoing symptoms appear, application for remedial assistance must be made immediately. The delay of an hour may usher in the cold stage or period of exanimated prostration and collapse, from which it is almost impossible to resusticate the expiring energies of the economy. While waiting for medical aid, a mixture composed of equal parts of the tincture of camphor, laudanum and peppermint may be administered in doses of fifteen drops on a lump of sugar or in a little sweetened water every 10 or 20 minutes, according to the urgency of the symptoms.

11. Every preparation should be made by the pubic authorities *in anticipation of the disease*, providing the means of treatment for those who cannot command them, so that aid may be promptly administered to all the moment of attack. These means are a number of small hospitals or houses of reception in various parts of the city or town; stations where nurses physicians and medical students with suitable medicines and apparatus can be procured at all hours, day or night, without delay; the evacuation of certain localities where the occurrence of numerous cases indicates a pestiferous influence; and, lastly, the furnishing to the poor, as far as practicable, wholesome and nourishing food.

By the adoption and observance of the foregoing means of precaution and prevention, in addition to other sanitary measures, the prevalence of cholera may be greatly circumscribed, its mortality diminished, and the public guarded against panic and alarm.

CONCLUSION.

The duties imposed upon the Secretary of the State

Board of Health to submit at each regular session of the Legislature "a full report of his investigations and such suggestions and recommendations as he may deem proper," has induced him to bring prominently to the attention of your Excellency and the General Assembly the importance of prompt and efficient legislation upon the subjects above referred to, and also the necessity for more liberal appropriations to enable the Board to efficiently carry out the objects for which it was created.

Mr. Mill, in his great work on political economy, has said that "The appropriation of money to protect the public health is a duty which the law-maker owes to the people whom he represents, and its performance is a partial discharge of an obligation arising out of the ultimate purposes of goverment everywhere." The obligation to protect the people against injury and death and their property against the depreciation and destruction which result from preventable diseases, rests upon exactly the same basis, and is just as binding as the obligation to protect person and property against the assaults of wicked and lawless men.

There will always be violations of the civil and criminal codes; and so, too, there will always be invasions of diseases in derogation of sanitary law. They hang like armed enemies upon our borders, they spring up like dragons' teeth from our soil.

Respectfully submitted,

C. W. CHANCELLOR, M. D.,
Secretary of the State Board of Health.

PROCEEDINGS AND ADDRESSES

AT THE

SECOND SANITARY COUNCIL OF MARYLAND

UNDER THE AUSPICES OF THE

STATE BOARD OF HEALTH.

HELD AT

BLUE MOUNTAIN HOUSE, WASHINGTON CO., MD.

SEPTEMBER 17TH, 18TH AND 19TH, 1884.

OFFICERS OF THE COUNCIL.

President, Ex-Gov. JOHN LEE CARROLL, HOWARD COUNTY..

VICE-PRESIDENTS.

Dr. JOHN MORRIS, Baltimore.
Hon. THOS. S. HODSON, Somerset County.
C. RIDGELY GOODWIN, Baltimore County.
JOS. K. ROBERTS, Esq., Prince George's County.
Rev. E. K. MILLER, Cecil County.
Rev. ORLANDO HUTTON, Montgomery County.
Col. JAMES G. BARRET, Carroll County.
WM. DUNNETT, Esq., Baltimore.
Dr. JAMES BORDLEY, Queen Anne's County.
Hon. LLOYD LOWNDES, Alleghany County.
Dr. C. W. CHANCELLOR, *Permanent Secretary*, Balto..
ARTHUR STEUART, *Assistant Secretary*, Balto.

COMMITTEE OF ARRANGEMENTS.

Col. JOHN M. HOOD, Baltimore.
Col. L. VICTOR BAUGHMAN, Frederick City..
T. HERBERT SHRIVER, Esq., Union Mills.
JOHN W. DAVIS, Esq., Baltimore.
HARRY WELLES RUSK, Esq., Baltimore.
Hon. J. CLARENCE LANE, Hagerstown.
CHRISTIAN DEVRIES, Esq., Baltimore.
EDWIN WARFIELD, Esq., Ellicott City.
Maj. CHAS. H. LATROBE, Baltimore.
JAS. P. SHANNON, Esq., Blue Mountain..

PROCEEDINGS, DISCUSSIONS AND ADDRESSES.

The second Sanitary Council of Maryland was held in accordance with the following order of the State Board of Health passed June 20th, 1884.

"*Resolved*, That a second State Sanitary Council be held under the auspices of the State Board of Health, about the middle of September ensuing, and that Dr. C. W. Chancellor, Permanent Secretary and Executive Officer of the Board, be and he is hereby authorized and directed to make all necessary arrangements and select a suitable date and place for holding the meeting."

Under the foregoing resolution the following circular was issued and extensively circulated throughout the State:

Second Sanitary Council of Maryland,

UNDER THE AUSPICES OF THE

STATE BOARD OF HEALTH.

The Second Sanitary Council of Maryland will be held at Blue Mountain House, Western Maryland Railroad, Wednesday, Thursday and Friday, September 17th, 18th and 19th, 1884.

The object of these Councils is to awaken an interest in sanitary reform throughout the State, and to prevent as far as possible the introduction and spread of epidemic and pestilential diseases. It is hoped that representative men of every profession or business, as well as the philanthropic women of the State, will attend and endeavor to forward this humane work.

TO THE MEDICAL PROFESSION.

We urge you to evince still further your well-earned character for unselfishness, by attending the proposed Council, and to take an active part in diffusing among the people such information as will tend to secure them from the avoidable causes of disease.

To the Clergy.

It would greatly tend to promote the object of these meetings, if the Clergy would make it a duty to be present and participate in the proceedings of the Council. Their presence and active co-operation would give impetus to the sanitary wave that is gradually flowing over the country, and which will, we trust, improve the moral as well as physical condition of the people.

To Engineers, Architects and Plumbers.

The field of Sanitation offers a wider scope than ever for your talents and influence. You can greatly aid in arousing the people from their sanitary inertness, and in scattering a health breathing influence over those places which, heretofore, have been fever-breeding haunts or hot-beds of disease.

To Editors of Journals.

We especially invoke you to come forward and give to this effort in behalf of the public health your potential influence and support. You have taken upon yourselves the responsibility of publishing journals, not only for the benefit of political parties, but for the good of society generally, and we, therefore, trust you will devote some small portion of your time and attention to one of the most commendable efforts ever made in the interest of the people.

To the Teachers of Public and Private Schools.

No one is more interested or can more effectually help the cause of public hygiene than the teachers of our schools. With you it should be a cherished object to suppress those causes which tend to propagate and spread infectious and contagious diseases, and we would, therefore, urge you to be present and participate in the deliberations of the council.

To Prominent Citizens.

The work of improving and protecting the public health intimately concerns each member of society. It, therefore, behooves all public-spirited citizens to inquire into matters affecting the public health, such as nuisances, unhealthy crowding of dwellings, factories, &c., the appearance of zymotic diseases, such as cholera, typhoid fever, diptheria, &c.; the purity of drinking water, soil saturation, and malarial influences.

Merchants, lawyers, farmers, mechanics,—indeed, all classes of the community are interested in these matters, and will, we hope, unite with us in an effort to suppress the causes of disease, and to lengthen out life with the enjoyment of more perfect health.

TO MOTHERS.

If there is a class of the community to whom the object of the State Sanitary Council is of more vital importance than to any other, that class consists of mothers whose young children so often fall victims to dread diseases. To you mothers, then, we appeal for support in this noble purpose, if only by soliciting your husbands to attend the Council, and aid in securing immunity from those insidious dangers which are ghostly in their form and deadly in their embrace.

To the Ladies of Maryland.

It is in the field of Sanitation where *"woman's rights"* take precedence over those of the other sex; and in that field there is a rich harvest before you. No one is more interested in the preservation of a high degree of health than you. Wherever sickness comes woman is the greatest sufferer; the long night watching, the anxious hours, the weary days of trial and sorrow ever fall to your greatest share;—in times of sickness you are the "ministering angels." To you, particularly, we look for aid in our efforts to promote the general health of the State. Your presence and co-operation will not only cheer the "weary worker," but will also raise us many steps on the ladder by which we hope to attain the highest degree of public health.

To our Law-Makers.

We cannot expect to accomplish as great results as we would desire with the small appropriations made by the last legislature for public health purposes, but we will endeavor to make up in energy what hostile legislation has deprived us of in means, and thereby induce future legislatures to extend their fostering care to the sanitary condition of the people as well as to other material interests. Beaconsfield declared that "the health of the people is the foundation upon which all their happiness and all their power as a State depends, and is, therefore, *the first duty of the Statesman.*" With this view of the obligations resting upon all lawmakers, we earnestly hope that you may be induced to join your influence with our efforts in resisting the approach of "the pestilence that walketh in darkness and the destroyer that wasteth at noon-day."

Addresses and Papers.

A number of interesting addresses and papers have been promised from distinguished sanitarians both at home and abroad; but other contributions are invited, especially upon the following subjects: The Adulterations of Food and Medicines; the Pollution of the Water Courses in Maryland; the Relation of the Diseases of Animals to the Human Race; the Sanitary Problems of the Cities and Towns of Maryland; the Relation of the Press to Sanitary Work; the Relation of Teachers to Sanitary Work; the Physical Dangers of Alcoholic Beverages; the Relation of the Clergy to Sanitary Work; the Duty of State and Municipal Governments in connection with the Public Health; the Disposal of the Dead, &c. Those who cannot attend the meeting may evince their interest by contributing papers, and those who intend to present papers are requested to notify the Secretary as early as possible, giving the title of their papers that they may be listed on the programme which will be issued before the time of meeting.

SESSIONS.

There will be a session the first day at 7:30 p. m., and on the second and third days at 10 a. m., 2:30 p. m. and 8:00 p. m.

Reduced rates will be secured on the lines of Railroad in the State, and at the Hotel, *to all persons attending the Council.*

Admission to all sessions of the Council will be free, and all persons who desire to live long and keep well, or to assist others in doing so, are cordially invited to attend.

For further information address,
C. W. CHANCELLOR, M. D., Secretary,
Baltimore, Md.

SESSIONS OF THE COUNCIL.

FIRST DAY—Evening Session.

The Council met at 8 p. m., September 17th, 1884, and, in the absence of Prof. Richard McSherry, President of the State Board of Health, the meeting was called to order by Dr. James A. Stewart, Health Commissioner of Baltimore city.

The Rev. Campbell Fair, was introduced and invoked the divine blessing upon the work of the Council.

Prof. McSherry, being confined to his home by illness, the address of welcome prepared by him was read by Dr. C. W. Chancellor, Permanent Secretary of the Council.

ADDRESS OF WELCOME.

By Richard McSherry, M. D., President of the State Board of Health.

"Gentlemen and Ladies of the
Sanitary Council of Maryland:

"In the name and on behalf of the Board of Health of the State of Maryland, I at once greet you, and thank you for your presence here. You represent great interests which reach all ramifications of our several existence and welfare. It is within your province to go to the very depths of all of those surroundings which influence the protection of the health, and with it, to a great extent, the happiness of your fellow men, and in the word fellow man, it must be remembered is included every member of the family, from the little stranger in the cradle to the 'Homeward Bound' veterans, who are verging on "the last scene of all that ends this strange eventful history.

" Whatever your individual pursuits—doctors of medicine, of divinity, lawyers or legislators, teachers, editors, engineers, architects, builders, plumbers, farmers, or what not—you are here on a common ground for the common good, in which yourselves, your wives, your children, and your children's children are present or prospective participants. Allow me to make a few passing references to some plain matters of prominent interest. Granted good food, pure air, and pure water in a community, at least one-half of the diseases therein prevalent would disappear at once and forever. You may indicate how these desiderata are to be obtained, if not in perfection, at least in approximation. Good food implies not only the substantial elements which nature furnishes so abundantly in our favored land, but also, as supplementary to nature, art, that is, the food must be well prepared and well served.

"It has been said that God sends us food, but the devil sends cooks. The ladies must come to the rescue, not necessarily to brown their own fingers over pots and kettles and ovens, but to such intelligent superintendence that all the family shall find at the table the daily bread light and sweet and wholesome, and all its accompaniments, baked, boiled, stewed, or roast, no matter how few or how plain the dishes, so well cooked as to please the palate and not distress the stomach. The preservation of this organ in good condition is of prime importance in health and contentment. Pure air, such as we have here at Blue Mountain, is not easily obtained in cities or in malarious districts, or even in country houses with good surroundings, where ventilation is defective. Architects, engineers, and plumbers must co-operate with the doctors in this matter.

"The majority of children dying in Baltimore during the warm months die of foul air principally. The city is ever recking with mephitic odors. How are we to get rid of them? That is a question. Speaking of cities generally, which enlist the attention of all the sanitarians in the civilized world, scientific sewerage can accomplish a great deal, but I think it not yet proved that sewerage is the final and complete remedy for the scourge of cities now referred to. There are gentlemen here, however, of the highest reputation to give opinions upon this subject, based upon much study and actual experience.

"Malaria is subject to correction, and so far as country homes go, or any homes, it holds to reason that proper measures should be in daily use, especially during winter, with artificial warmth, to let fresh air in and foul air out of the house. This seems to be a truism not worth saying, but I have gone into hundreds of houses where such simple precaution is entirely ignored. By pure water we do not mean water chemically pure, but water free from noxious ingredients. Very many diseases are propagated by impure drinking water. Cholera, typhoid fever, intermittent fevers, intestinal worms and numerous other affections befall our race from polluted water. Boiling and filtering are good corrections of water in the house, but, so far as practicable, polluted water should never gain admittance.

"The rivers that supply cities should be watched with the most zealous care to save them from all kinds of filth—animal or vegetable—and in villages or about country homes it should be seen that there are no surface washings or underground channels conveying to the well or spring organic remains or other impurities from adjacent sources—as the barn-yard, the privy, or pig-sty. Here I may make a practical quotation from the address of Dr. A. M. Bell, of the Sanitarium, at our last meeting. In answer to the question, 'At what distance from a well would it be safe to place a privy, vault, or cess-pool?' it should be said, 'The greater the better, but ordinary soils have a lateral drainage area equal to five feet for every one foot of depth; that is to say, a well 20 feet deep is ordinarily the receptacle of any soluble matter in the soil-water for a distance of 100 feet in all directions. Under some circumstances, such as subsoil currents in certain directions, the danger distance is much greater.'

"I have but two other references to make, which may be taken as suggestions. The one is in regard to the ruinous method of education as now pursued. There is too much school-room crowding in every sense. The number of pupils is too great, generally, for the room occupied, but this crowding is certainly not worse than the cramming attempted with a multiplicity of studies. Every physician observes how much injury is done to children by the course pursued, both to the mental and bodily faculties. If the design is to break down teachers and scholars, especially the growing girls, it is being duly accomplished; but if it is to invigorate mind and body, it is unquestionably a failure. The mind and the body are very closely allied, there being between them such correlation of forces that the solid invigoration of the one helps the other, and the impairment of the one damages the other. This is a subject very worthy of the consideration of the convention.

"The final matter to which I will refer is the devising of some means by which a certain social canker may be kept from desolating American homes. The ostrich, it is said, hides his head that he may not see or be seen when pursued by his enemies. But it does not save him. Neither will closing the eyes on the part of the community put any check to the progress of a monstrous evil, which is threatening the very vitals of society. Legislation must be brought to bear, not to make all this world virtuous, but to keep moral lepers from contaminating virtuous families. *Verbum sap.* The board of health is an executive body, and we invite you, as counsellors and experts, to give it your opinions, your advice and information upon the various special and technical subjects bearing upon the great cause in which we are engaged."

The names of the officers of the Council were then read by the Secretary, and on assuming the Chair, Ex-Governor Carroll delivered the following

ADDRESS:

"*Ladies and Gentlemen:*—In accepting the very high honor conferred upon me of presiding over the deliberations of the State sanitary council, I have but one regret, and that is that I am utterly unable to throw any light upon the important questions which will be presented to your consideration. I am here, however, simply in obedience to that spirit and feeling which I trust is growing stronger daily among all classes of our citizens, that however important may be the duties we all owe to the body politic, we can entertain no higher purpose than that of sustaining the proud and charitable efforts of those who are striving to improve the physical condition of the communities in which we live.

"The names of the great leaders of science who have worked out problems by which man is in a measure relieved of suffering, will live in history when the memory of heroes of other fields has passed away, and the whole world looks to-day with interest at the results of that study which seeks to confine pestilence within the narrowest limits, and thus to break the force of the greatest evils which afflict mankind.

"No one can read without the keenest sympathy the progress of the cholera through the fairest portions of Italy, and while we stand in admiration at the sacrificing spirit of her noble King, who in the midst of this carnival of death is there in person to cheer the timid and to give comfort to the afflicted, one cannot but feel that the practical application of the rules of health would have averted this great sorrow and turned into other channels the most fatal epidemic of modern times.

"Who can doubt that Paris to-day would have been in mourning for the loss of thousands of her people had it not been for the discipline of science and the stern efforts of her boards of health, which make the methods of preservation even more important than the questions of cure. Now if this be so, what a solemn warning there is to us in the truth of the assertion, and how surely may we become the victims of disease if we neglect the system by which alone it may be averted. The labors of our State Board of Health, although of comparatively recent origin, have not been without fruit. The energy of its permanent secretary in visiting infected districts and in seeking out the hidden causes of disease has brought confidence and relief to stricken portions of the State, and has often inspired the local authorities with the determination to remove the flagrant causes of suffering.

"Under the influence of his suggestions, and sometimes of his exposures, ill-ventilated jails have been replaced by healthy structures; fetid and pestilential almshouses have been restored to cleanliless and care, and the classification and separation of the unfortunate victims has often been the means of restoring many of them to the enjoyment of blessed health.

"There can be no doubt as to the value of constant inspection and supervision, and this can only be brought about by the public support of an institution fostered earnestly by the State.

"It is to encourage this sentiment that we have met here to-night, and the production of the important papers which will be presented to the world cannot fail to strengthen the cause and to satisfy the public as to any expenditure which is made in its behalf.

"With a full recognition, therefore, of the value of this institution and a strong purpose to sustain its demands, let us now proceed to the important business of the council."

LETTER OF EX-GOVERNOR WHYTE.

The Hon. Wm. Pinkney Whyte was expected to be present and address the body, but was detained by professional engagements. He sent, however, the following letter, which was read by the Secretary:

"*Baltimore, September* 17, 1884.
"Dr. C. W. Chancellor, Secretary, &c., &c.:

"My Dear Doctor—I regret, extremely, that professional obligations prevent my presence with you, at the 'Blue Mountain House,' to-morrow.

"In any case, I could not have attended the Council *as a sanitarian;* for I have no special knowledge to impart upon the subject of sanitary reform.

"I should have joined your convocation, merely as one of those guests, whom you describe in your circular invitation, as *"persons who desire to live long and to keep well."*

"It would be a great satisfaction to me, if I could perform the *role* of a public educator of hygiene—but I cannot.

"It has not been possible for me, amid the absorbing duties of my professional vocation, to penetrate beyond the crust of that knowledge, so essential to such teaching.

"But, as a citizen, thoroughly aroused to the necessity of a wider knowledge among the people in relation to sanitary affairs, I wish to add my earnest approval (whatever that may be worth) of the aims and objects, which the Sanitary Council has in view, and to give it the meed of praise in its public spirited and philanthropic work, to which it is so justly entitled.

"The promotion of health and the reduction of the rate of mortality is one of the most humane efforts, to which man can devote his best energies.

"Health is to the body what a good conscience is to the soul ; without both, life is scarcely endurable. Godliness is the surest help to the one, as cleanliness—which is akin to Godliness—is the best promoter of the other.

"Health to the body is often lost in the neglect of some of the plainest dictates of human reason, by parents at home, and by the teacher at school.

"A knowledge of hygiene and the importance of observing its laws is one of the most necessary elements in the promotion of the health and happiness of the family, and yet it rarely forms any part of the education, either of the school-house or the home.

"It is really here that the foundation must be laid for all successful sanitation.

"As the State is dependent upon the family for the peace and good order of society, so is its health conserved by the orderly and cleanly conduct of the household.

"It is the duty of the State to enforce this knowledge upon the people. They will be slow to receive it, but its benefits will, in time, be recognized and its blessings availed of.

"It took many years to teach the citizen that there was no pauperism in sending his child to the public school, but now he admits, that as the State is to be benefited by the education of the citizen, it is the duty of the State to supply that learning.

"It is a truth universally admitted, and often stated, that the health of a country is not its commerce nor its agriculture; nor its exports nor its imports; neither its military organization, nor its civil constitution; its legislation, nor its judiciary, but its conscience; *i. e.* the moral elevation of its citizens.'

"Suppose a State upon the high road of material prosperity; the arts and sciences flourishing in the largest sense; its wealth expended in splendid buildings and gigantic enterprises; its people expanding mentally, in great intellectual activity, and, yet, its moral sense blunted, its conscience seared, its religious aspirations deadened, how long would that State survive the dissolution of its moral life?

"And so in its physical advancement.

"You may build splendid palaces and lay out noble

cities, and lavish on them all the wealth and beauty which art can fashion, but if the laws of health are ignored and despised, it is a matter of time only, when dissolution and decay shall come.

"But the higher the moral elevation of a people, the more anxious are they to avail of every means to lengthen human life and alleviate human suffering. In the struggle of human passions and the reach for material prosperity the effort at amelioration is slow of progress.

"In almost all large communities, there is much moral corruption, but therein are always to be found the "ten righteous"—the "Sanitary Council" to warn, to exhort, to save—a little body of earnest, thoughtful men, forever plotting for the preservation of the State.

"It is so with the material corruption which festers and destroys wherever men do congregate, and as the body of the public moves with heavy steps, it is in the order of God's providence, that a few skillful, energetic, thinking men should guide it, and devise practical schemes for its well-being.

"The slow and tedious education of a people to make them comprehend any new scheme for their welfare, is necessary before they can appreciate and will adopt it.

"It is a tiresome process and needs all the earnestness and sincerity of the philanthropist. It was through the untiring efforts of John Howard, in many years, that the ague "which haunts the fen and cowers under the mantle of the mist" was driven away from the village of Cardington. The abode of poverty and wretchedness was changed into one of the neatest villages of England by his loving and tireless work.

"In bringing about sanitary reform, nature must be imitated. It always works by gradation. Nature is persistent in her action; like the mills of the gods, it grinds slowly but surely.

"The physical perfection of man does not take place until he is twenty to thirty years old; his moral sense is not completed until between thirty and forty.

"Great results cannot be completed in a brief period.

"Christianity, the greatest blessing to mankind, has not yet accomplished its work, though it has existed for nearly two thousand years.

"I trust, therefore, that this Sanitary Council—the second only this State—will faint not nor be weary, but may re-convene from year to year to mark the progress of sanitary science and of the benefits it has brought to man.

"Pardon this long letter, but it seemed just, that I should fully express my sincere concurrence in your work.
"Truly your friend,
WM. PINKEY WHYTE."

A STUDY OF DIPTHERIA.

After the reading of Governor Whyte's letter, President Carroll introduced Dr. Jackson Piper, of Towsontown, who read an interesting paper on

DIPTHERIA;
Its Sanitary, Preventive and Local Treatment.

(*Dr. Piper's Letter.*)

We are told that in ancient times the heathen worshiped an idol named Moloch. This idol was made of brass and had the face of a calf. It was very large and hollow, so that a fire could be lighted within it. After it was heated very hot, these people used to put their children within its arms, where they were burned to death. While they were being burned, the people beat drums so that their cries could not be heard. This was what they called giving their children to Moloch.

Insanitation is this idol, and skepticism, ridicule and ignorance are its high priests. Their insensate cries would still the voice of Reason and Reform, while our children and ourselves are being sacrificed to the fell Destroyer. Witness the brutal treatment now being displayed in Italy and some portions of France towards the Humanitarians who are striving to stay the ravages of Cholera.. Witness the meanness of our legislators in refusing to enact laws and vote moneys looking towards proper sanitation, and the supreme indifference of our officials in town or country in carrying out the very meagre and imperfect laws already on our statute books.

How to make people *act and think for themselves* is indeed a difficult task. Rules are published and laws enacted, but the former are as idle words and the latter as dead letters from an apathetic public, and from stupid and inefficient officials. Still, an advancement has been made, both by the public and the medical profession. Twenty-five years ago sanitation was scarcely known as a science. Now, the people are gradually awakening to a sense of its extreme importance, and communities are now as keenly alive to local causes as factors of disease, *after the fact*, as sanitarians are to discover and remove the said causes, before. Therefore, it is the bounden duty of the sanitarian by constant iteration and reiteration, to show by incontestable proofs that the public *holds* the *power* to prevent zymotic or contagious diseases, by availing itself of the appliances that sense and science have placed at its disposal. These and like reasons are the writer's apology for presenting to the consideration of this Convention, so thread-bare and oft repeated a subject, as the sanitary treatment of Diptheria.

Without going to the books, he will cite instances in his own practice to show that Diptheria has, first, a spontaneous or sporadic origin in filth;—second, that it is highly contagious, and, third, he will refer you to the powerful arguments adduced by Dr. Chancellor in his very able report of the epidemic in Frederick City in the fall of 1881, to show that under certain conditions of the atmosphere it is terribly infectious.

July 16th, 1880, I attended a child sick with Diptheria, whose prominent symptoms were excessive vomiting and great prostration. This child was brought from the city sick, and there was no case of Diptheria in the neighborhood. The child's sister, who was also its nurse, came for me one morning early, and before I saw her, had entered into play with my children, giving my little girl (about six years old) a button attached to a string which had been, up to that time, about the little nurse's neck, and which dangled on a dress, wet, as I afterwards ascertained, with the vomit from the sick child. My child was discovered with this button in her mouth. Five days after she was taken with Diptheria, and ten days after my son also; and in the course of three weeks, the whole household, three children and three servants, were successively affected, my wife and I alone escaping. We two were the sole nurses on the first two—the servants not allowed to enter the sick rooms, which were on the second and third floors, but were permitted to carry, to and from the doors, utensils, clothes, food, &c. These cases prove direct contagion, which gradually diffused itself throughout the house.

February 27th, 1884, two children of a neighbor were taken with Diphtheria. Several children spent some hours with them before the nature of their attack was ascertained. The stone house in which these children lived had been newly built and was perfect in all its sanitary arrangements. The family moved into it four months after completion, and there had been ample time for its complete drying. There was no Diphtheria in the town at the time, and the children had been kept constantly at home. On investigation it was discovered that the maid had been for several weeks in the habit of emptying the contents of the chambers into the bath-tub, and that the bath-room communicated by double registers in the chimney with the room in which the children slept. Two of the visiting children were, shortly after, taken with Diphtheria. These cases prove the spontaneous origin of the disease through sewer gases, and its after transmissibility by contagion.

May 22d, 1884, a child of Judge David Fowler, of Towson, was taken with Diphtheria; two days after, a daughter of Mr. George Merryman, living five miles distant, and on May 31st, nine days after the first case, my son was seized—the second time after an interval of four years. These three children were in attendance at a private school in the town, which numbered ten pupils at the time the sickness occurred. One of my children complained several time during the spring of the bad taste of the water, and in consequence used it sparingly. Her health being below par, she was kept at home some time before these cases occurred.

The school-room was the second-story front room in a private dwelling. Investigation showed that an open drain from the kitchen had a common covered outlet with an open drain from the pump, which covered drain was choked up, so that the slops and other refuse matter from the kitchen ran into the well, the water of which was milky in appearance and of a foul odor.

The children not only drank of this water, but played over and about the well and drains. These cases show the spontaneous origin of Diphtheria, not only from sewer gases, but possibly from impure water, and all the cases, taken together, admonish us to scrutinize thoroughly our surroundings; to keep away from diphtheritic patients and their attendants; to isolate the sick; to disinfect thoroughly the clothes and excreta, and to instantly remove all children from houses in which the disease has made its appearance. And this brings us to our first consideration: the Sanitary prevention of Diphtheria. This is eminently a most important consideration under the trite axiom that "an ounce of prevention is worth a pound of cure." If it is impossible to remove the healthy, keep them as much as possible in the open air, and let them sleep in rooms the most distant from the sick, with the windows open. A neighbor's house, though it be next door, is better than one's own home on such occasions. A mild case can cause a severe one, so there should be perfect isolation of the sick in the uppermost rooms, and no one but the nurses allowed to enter, and these, once and for all times, to be secluded from the family. The nurses themselves to frequently wash their hands in some disinfecting fluid, and to treat their wearing apparel in the same way, and to wash the hair thoroughly after the cases are over. The poison possesses great vitality, and well persons can be the carriers of the poison. Let the temperature of the children be taken once a day. For years passed I have been in the habit of urging the families I attend to keep self-registering thermometers, and I have reason to believe it has proved a life-saving instrument, giving timely warning of danger, and proving a valuable aid to the information of the attending physician. Unnecessary petting of the patient, kissing or talking over the mouths or diphtheritic wounds must all be forbidden. It would be well to insert a little cotton in the nostrils of the attendants, to be changed often, as it prevents ingress of septic material. Disinfect constantly the chambers, clothing and bed clothes; keep the air of the room cool and fresh. After convalescence, bathe the patient in a warm bath and carbolic soap in another room, and dress in fresh clothes. The room and all its contents, and the whole house, if possible, should be thoroughly fumigated with burning sulphur. After this the floors scoured, using strong carbolic soap; the walls white-washed or re-papered; the wood work and furniture revarnished, and the bedding and all worthless garments burnt. Burials should be strictly private and soon over. The stamping out process is full of trouble and sacrificing expenses, but it is the safest and best, and will save many a valuable life and spare many an aching heart.

Disinfection by carbolic acid is exceedingly doubtful, as it has been shown that the quantities required to destroy the vitality of bacteria is equal to about 17 lbs. in a room $12\frac{1}{2}$ feet square and 12 feet high (capacity 1728 cubic feet), and it would be necessary to scatter this amount over the floor of a room having these dimensions, and to suspend the articles to be disinfected, near the floor for at least six hours, care being taken that all apertures are closed, so that the fumes of the acid may not escape. Another experiment shows that four times the amount of the crude acid (68 lbs.) would not destroy the vitality of the parasites placed upon the floor of the same room for six hours. These and other experiments were made by Dr. Geo. U. Sternberg, U. S. A., at the request of the National Board of Health on May 22d, 1880, and prove that the use of this agent, as a powerful disinfectant, is impracticable, because of the expense of the pure acid and the enormous amount required to produce the desired result. Fortunately, we have disinfectants cheaper, more easily obtained and applied, and more efficacious.

1. Roll or powdered sulphur (brimstone) for fumigating rooms, furs, woolen, carpets, and other and all material.

2. Sulphate of iron (copperas) dissolved in water in the proportion of 1½ lbs. to the gallon for soils, sewers, chambers, &c.

3. Sulphate of zinc (white vitriol) and common salt, dissolved together in water in the proportion of four ounces of the zinc and two ounces of the salt to the gallon and used hot, preferably, for clothing, bed linen, flannel and blankets. As to the manner of applying disinfectants, I would refer to the excellent rules which are published biennially in the reports of Dr. Chancellor, of the State Board of Health, and of circular No. 1 of the National Board of Health, reprinted in Dr. Jacobi's work on Diphtheria. (Edition 1880, page 176.)

I shall now consider the *second* division of this paper: The prophylactic or preventive treatment of Diphtheria by medicines.

Dr. Jacobi says "I shall speak of a remedy which I class among the prophylactic agents, namely, Chlorate of Potass, or Chlorate of Sodium. The reason lies in the fact that the Chlorate is useful in most cases of stomatitis (inflammation of the mouth), and thereby acts as a preventive. The dose of the Chlorate of Potass should not be more than thirty grains in the twenty-four hours for a child two or three years old. A baby of one year or less should not take more than twenty grains a day. The dose for an adult should not be more than a dram and a half (ninety grains), or at most two drams (one hundred and twenty grains). These quantities to be divided and given at short intervals. It is better to give the daily quantity of twenty grains in fifty or sixty doses, than in eight or ten doses; care being taken that no water is given soon after the remedy, for the reason that its local effects would be destroyed by washing it off.

Dr. Brackenridge and Dr. W. Scott have, in the past few years, called attention to the value of Sulpho-Carbolate of Sodium, in doses of five grains to thirty grains, according to age, and given three or four times a day, not only as a preventive in Diphtheria, but also in Scarlet Fever and in Measles. It was given in three families to fifteen persons exposed to Diphtheria, in seven families to twenty-two persons exposed to Scarlet Fever, and in three families to eight persons exposed to the Measles. In every instance the contagion did not extend beyond the individual first attacked.

Dr. P. C. Barker has been using Salicylic Acid for more than ten years, as a preventive in all of the above-named diseases, with very gratifying results. He has never known a second case occur since beginning his experiments. Children have lived and played in the same room, and sometimes have slept in the same bed with the patient, and have entirely escaped. Dr. B. gives the acid in one to five grain doses, according to age, once or twice a day, to be kept up until convalescence has been established and the house has been fumigated. The rationale of these medicines is supposed to be by disinfecting the tissues of the body, and so removing any favorable nidus or starting point for the development of fever germs. They act also locally. At any rate, whatever their action may be, they are innocent remedies in these doses, and are well worthy of the trial. I have prescribed the last two named repeatedly, and the parties escaped sickness, but as other precautions were taken, notably, the instant removal of the well to a distant place, I am not in a position to speak definitely of their results.

The third and last division of my subject, is that of curing the disease by proper, prompt and energetic treatment.

The writer, some four years ago, after losing several patients with Diphtheria, and having, in addition to his own cases, collected all the data of some twenty fatal cases in the practice of several physicians of well-known ability in his neighborhood, became discouraged with the results of the treatment then employed. A letter from the late Dr. Riggin Buckler, received about that time, says: "I have no faith in topical applications, and very little in general treatment. After trying everything, I have fallen back upon the old treatment of Muriated Tincture of Iron, and Chlorate of Potass, and I spray the throat with Lactic Acid." This coincided so nearly with my views, and I was so impressed with the futility of the local treatment used, that I hailed with a gleam of hope the excellent article of Oertel in Ziemssen's Cyclopædia. I determined on the first opportunity to apply this treatment, and, strange to say, the occason came to me in the six cases that occurred in my own family. Up to this time I have treated twenty-two cases after Oertel's local method, and I have not lost a case.

Of the twenty-two cases, two were of the croupous form, one was laryngeal, one septicoemic, and the balance catarrhal, several of the latter being very severe cases. The treatment is in the constant, energetic and *rigorous* application of steam, medicated with Chlorate of Potass or Chloride of Sodium (common salt) applied directly to the diseased surfaces by inhalation. Believing the disease to be local at first, that it depends upon the presence of bacteria and, that the so-called period of incubation is the time that these parasites are at work, the treatment that promises their destruction or removal *before* the constitution is so powerfully affected as to set up blood poisoning, is the treatment beyond all other methods that most concerns the physician and the most important to the sanitarian.

I hold that the medical treatment of all Zymotic diseases is a legitimate subject for Sanitary Science, as much so as sewerage, local causes, or any other like matter, insomuch as every case of contagious disease forms a nucleus for other cases, more potent for harm than the original cause; and its speedy extinction is as much to be desired as the train of causes that set the disease in operation. I am particularly anxious to emphasize the excellent results obtained from steam, for the cases I had lost previously were treated like those of the past four years, except as to the local means used, and none of the fatal cases commenced with symtoms any more severe than those which recovered under the new method. As the application of steam has been so misapplied, I may be pardoned for referring to several authors who have so misapplied it, and in consequence have been the means of bringing it into disrepute.

Dr. Jacobi, who ridicules the germ theory, is as much at sea as to the use of steam. He says, on page 178, "steam, for the purpose of softening the tissues and of provoking the secretion of mucus and suppuration, has been used to a considerable extent in this country and in England. The patient must inhale it directly from a vessel, or in a tent which is more or less closed, or breathe the atmosphere of a room saturated therewith. For the latter purpose, water is kept constantly boiling or lime slaked or red-hot stones put in hot water from time to time." Now this is a stupid misapplication of the method. You are not steaming the disease here, you are steaming the unfortunate patient, already prostrated with a terrible and exhausting disease, to say nothing of his sweltering attendants. Some fifteen years ago I treated a patient, *once*, this way. Of course the patient died. Its poor mother accused me "of cooking her baby alive." I was properly indignant at the time, but at this late date I rather think I did. Dr. Jacobi's own words are the best critique on this way of using steam. He says "the results from this procedure in diphtheria of the larynx have not always been *pleasant*. I have *repeatedly* had the joy of seeing children with croup cyanotic after their removal from an atmosphere of steam, and I can readily see that pure atmospheric air would be more agreeable to a child with stenosis of the larynx, that an atmosphere laden with steam." This means that a child already partly suffocated with a disease that is closing up its wind-pipe would be *further* imperiled by breathing such an atmosphere as he dscribes. I agree with him perfectly here. It is an axiom in logic that when the premises of a proposition are false, the deductions are equally so, so that when he further on remarks— "whoever has noticed the obstinacy with which diphtheric membranes and infiltrations resist *all treatment* for days and *even beyond a week*, will hardly attribute the recovery of mild and favorable cases of diphtheria of the tonsils and of light pharyngeal diphtheria to moist air;"—we will add, that if his cases resist all treatment beyond a week, the sooner he applies Oertel's method the better it will be for his own reputation, and certainly the better it will be for his patients. Aitken, in his Practice of Medicine, volume I, page 523, says: "The temperature of the room in which the patient is confined to bed ought to be kept at 68°, Fhr., and its atmosphere made moist by steam from a kettle with a long spout, kept constantly *boiling on the fire*. If the patient can be kept enveloped in a warm moist atmosphere, so much the better; and this may be done by making a tent with blankets over the bed, and, by aid of a spirit-lamp, a tin kettle of boiling water may be maintained at the boiling point, and the steam thus made to envelop the patient." The absurdity of this sentence is how to keep the temperature of a room at 68° Fahr. with a hot fire, and the room hot enough to keep steam alive, or the use that 68° Fahr. would be to a child in a blanket tent, a hot spirit-lamp beneath, and the sufferer suffocated in steam. Let any one place within these tents a Fahrenheit thermometer and he will be terribly alarmed for the safety of his patient at its amazing height. Oertel's treatment consists in an apparatus that generates steam at some five or more feet from the patient, and this steam is conveyed by a tube or funnel directly to and within the mouth of the patient. A chafing dish with deep sides, or a quart tin-can, around which is wrapped cotton duck, sail cloth or any stiff material some four or five feet long, and gradually tapered towards the top to form the mouth piece, a tripod and a spirit-lamp, with two or three burners, are easily obtained anywhere. A stiff piece of pasteboard around the can and within the canvas will prevent the sides from collapsing from the moisture, and another piece of pasteboard telescoped within the upper portion of the cotton duck makes an admirable mouthpiece, which can be shortened or lengthened as the steam is too feeble or too hot. This piece can be applied close to the mouth, and the vapor is thus prevented from touching the face, which is exceedingly disagreeable to a sensitive child. If still too hot, a burner or two blown out will regulate the heat of the steam, which of course should be as hot and copious in volume as the child can possibly stand. The water is medicated by the addition of table salt or chlorate of potash, ten to fifteen grains to the ounce of water. The steam is to be applied every hour or every half hour, according to the gravity of the case, and each sitting to occupy from fifteen to twenty minutes. The patient is only to be allowed three or four hours sleep for the first and second day. Later on, when the pseudo membranes are being cast off, hourly sittings of fifteen minutes and six or eight hours sleep may be allowed. It is better for the patient to take the steam in a sitting posture, supported by an assistant, as it then can enter the mouth and throat. So long as any secretion of pus is perceived, occasional inhalations every two or three hours, and these to be suspended after the cleansing of the mouth and throat is complete. The mouth can be further washed clean by an atomizer in which is placed twenty drops of concentrated lactic acid to the ounce of hot water; by gargling or mopping the throat in weak solutions of alcohol or carbolic acid or permanganate of potass, two and a half grains to the ounce, or dilute chlorine (containing fifteen to thirty per cent. of chlorine water). These remedies to be used after suppuration and sloughing of the membranes have commenced, and are alternated with the steam so as to secure thorough cleansing of the mouth and its disinfection, as far as this disinfection by such means is possible. In four, or at most five days, my patients were out of danger and the false membrane had disappeared. The shortness of time this treatment requires will admit of its being rigorously applied. Indeed it does not admit of timidity or hesitancy. Every hour lost is fatal.

A catarrhal form may speedily run into a croupous, septic, or gangrenous condition, and any of these dangerous forms must be met instantly and decidedly by this and other measures. Very young children may not submit, and even older ones require kind but firm management. Only one refused me, and that was my own child, and bitterly did I regret it, for her death was the consequence.

In urging the importance of this treatment I do not lose sight of its disagreeableness and irksomeness to the patient, or the perseverance and untiring vigilance it imposes on the attendants. The invasion in my own household on two different occasions familiarized me with a practical knowledge of the method and placed me in a position to speak with some authority on the subject. I was thereby enabled to follow step by step the progress of improvement, and to verify in every particular the results claimed by its author—a speedy recovery, with less loss of strength than attends any other method. I never leave to others the arranging of the apparatus. *I fix it myself and superintend the first sitting*, and if the materials are not at hand I do not leave the patient until they are obtained. The ages of my patients ranged from three years up to thirty years. The last was a colored man in my employ, and was the worst case of croupous diphtheria I ever saw recover. A pearly gray, thick, cartilaginous-looking membrane, extended from the very gums, covered the roof of the mouth, the pharynx and tonsils, down to the windpipe (rimaglottis.) I put him under treatment on a Sunday, and the following Saturday he was enabled to return to his home, some three miles distant. A few days after, negro like, he went to a camp-meeting, suffered a relapse nearly as bad as the original attack, which again speedily yielded to the same treatment. A girl about eight years old, whose diphtheria extended from the pharynx to the larynx, had been sick quite a week before I saw her. Her voice was completely extinct, and her breathing quick and oppressed, but she rapidly recovered on the application of the steam. Oertel says that astringents, germicides, antiseptics, and caustics will not only fail to penetrate and destroy the membrane, but by their *irritating properties* will increase its growth by increasing the multiplication of micrococci and bacteria termo; that nature effects a cure by setting up a profuse suppuration, and thereby permits the detachment and expulsion of false membrane, and that this suppuration also forms an impermeable layer on the affected tissues, which prevents the ingress of poisonous masses into the system, and that in using steam we are merely imitating nature. This seems reasonable, and every physician has applied this principle in the treatment of other diseases. How impossible it is to apply, with any chance of success, soothing, astringent, or alterative lotions to rupia, ecthyma, or milk-crust, unless the impermeable crusts are first removed by poulticing. After these are removed our way is clear enough.

I have foreborne, thus far, to make any reference to the constitutional treatment of diphtheria, and will add, in conclusion, that I regard it as equally important as the local treatment. As we seldom see a case until the constitution is affected, and the prolonged continuation of the disease is bound to set up blood-poison; and as the local disease reacts upon the constitution, and the constitution in turn keeps up and increases the local trouble, the patient early demands the free and prompt use of brandy in large doses, milk, beef tea, soup and other liquid nourishment, administered day and night, and the use of quinine, muriated tincture of iron and chlorate of potass ; and special indications are to be met by their appropriate remedies.

DICUSSION ON DR. PIPER'S PAPER.

At the conclusion of Dr. Piper's paper, Prof. A. B. Arnold said:—"I wish briefly to mention a case of diphtheria successfully treated by the process first set forth in the excellent paper of Dr. Piper. I was called some years ago to see a case—a little girl of eight years of age—and found the patient suffering with diphtheria. I at once applied steam by inhalation. I requested, however, a consultation, and an eminent surgeon was called, and arrived two hours after the steam had been persistently applied. He advised tracheotomy, but I was unwilling to have the operation performed at once. It was agreed between us that he should return in two and a half hours, and in the meantime that the use of the steam should be continued, and if, on his return, he still advised the operation I would consent. At the time fixed he returned prepared to operate, but the use of the steam had so checked the disease that an operation was no longer deemed necessary, and the child speedily recovered."

Dr. John Morris.—"We are under great obligations to Dr. Piper for his excellent paper, but I would take exception to one statement. I contend that there are no known prophylactic *remedial* agents that will prevent the disease. The hygienic agent *cleanliness,* is the only preventive. I do not consider chlorate of potash a preventive agent, but I regard it as a dangerous drug. I have seen many cases of poisoning from its use."

Dr. Piper:—"I entirely agree with Dr. Morris in all that he says about chlorate of potash. I know it to be a dangerous drug, when improperly used, and the best thing we can do is to teach the public this fact. Dr. Jacobi also regards it as a dangerous drug in the hands of the inexperienced. The salicilic acid is comparatively new, and is used by some physicians, but if it is an efficient remedy, I am very anxious to know the fact."

Dr. James A. Stewart:—"I wish to ask Dr. Piper one question. When you spoke of twenty grains of chlorate of potash for an infant, and two drams for an adult, you meant, I suppose, that these quantities were to be given during twenty-four hours?"

Dr. Piper:—Certainly, sir. I am much obliged to you for calling attention to the matter."

Dr. Chambers:—"I should like to know the age of the patients successfully treated with steam? I have not found that children under three years of age can be subjected to the use of steam, and without it they seldom recover. In my judgment, the only safeguard for children three years of age is *not to have the disease.* I would here sound a note of warning. Where there are several children in a family, the eldest is most likely to contract the disease first; and the mother should be warned that if the younger children, not yet affected, require her attention, she should refrain from coming into contact with the sick child; she should isolate both herself and the smaller children, lest the disease be communicated to them."

Dr. Piper:—"I do not recall any case younger than three years; but several of the age of four years were successfully treated."

After the conclusion of the discussion on Dr. Piper's paper, the following resolution was was offered and adopted:

"*Resolved*, That all papers read before this Convention be submitted to the State Board of Health for publication in the next bi-ennial report of the Board."

President Carroll announced that the next business in order was the reading of a paper by Prof. George H. Rohe, of Baltimore.

DANGERS IN FOOD.

By George H. Rohe, M. D., Professor of Hygiene and Clinical Dermatology, College of Physicians and Surgeons, Baltimore; Member of the American Public Health Association, etc.

[Read before the Second Sanitary Council of Md.]

That "man must eat to live" is an axiom, that has never, I believe, been disputed by even the most transcendental philosophers. Experimental physiology, as well as the collective observation of mankind, have shown that organic and inorganic matters in certain proportions and quantities are necessary to the preservation of health. It is also a matter of observation that under certain peculiar conditions, articles of food, ordinarily wholesome, may become unfit to fulfill their function of nutrition or may be, if consumed, the source of disease and death. By the invitation, and at the suggestion of the Secretary of the State Board of Health, I shall endeavor to indicate as briefly as I can, the conditions under which certain articles of food in constant use may become dangerous to the health and life of the consumer, and point out the general and individual measures necessary to avert such consequences.

The most important single article of food is

MILK.

It is the one perfect food found in nature. It is not merely the normal aliment for young infants, but human beings, of all ages, may under its exclusive use preserve life and strength. You can realize, therefore, how important it is that this food should always be pure, unadulterated and free from all deleterious admixtures or modifications.

Leaving out of consideration the intentional poisoning of milk with criminal intent, with which we are not concerned in our present discussion, milk may be rendered unwholesome, first, by becoming impregnated with the germs of various diseases, from without; and secondly, in consequence of some disease or poisoning of the animal from which the milk is derived.

It has been abundantly proven that some of the most fatal contagious or infectious diseases that afflict the human race may be spread by milk to which the germs of such diseases have gained access. Mr. Ernest Hart, a distinguished English medical writer, has collected reliable evidence showing that up to 1881, fifty outbreaks of typhoid fever, fifteen of scarlet fever and seven of diphtheria had been observed, in which the origin of the outbreak had been traced to the use of milk into which the germs of these diseases had been introduced.

At the time of writing (September 11th) one of the Baltimore newspapers contains a brief report of an investigation into the causes of a local epidemic of typhoid fever at Elkton, in this State. The conclusion reached by Dr. Chancellor, the Secretary of the State Board of Health, is to the effect that the disease has been spread by infected milk. I understand that Dr. C. will give an account of his investigation before this Council.

The manner in which these disease germs gain access to the milk has been in most instances traced to the admixture of polluted water with the milk. It is not necessary to assume that the water is added with fraudulent intent, for the water used in cleaning the milk cans, pails and other utensils employed about the dairy may be—and probably is—the medium through which the poison is conveyed to the milk. It is well known that most of the water for drinking and domestic purposes in this country is derived from shallow wells, which are often in close proximity to cess-pools, and thus liable to infection with disease germs. You can readily see how easily the milk can be contaminated by the accidental or intentional admixture of such water.

It is also stated by some authorities that milk exposed to an atmosphere containing the germs of typhoid or scarlet fevers, or diphtheria, may become infected. Cases are on record which seemingly leave no room for any other conclusion. Persons recovering from scarlet fever or diphtheria are not infrequently employed about dairies. It is not improbable that of the multitudes of fine scales thrown off from the surface of the body in convalescence from the former disease, some may gain access to the milk. The same may happen with the secretions from the throats of diphtheritic persons.

The milk of animals suffering from certain diseases, is likewise often dangerous to health. In some of the Western and Southern United States cows are not infrequently attacked by an acute febrile disease called "the trembles," from one of the prominent symptoms. The milk of cows suffering from this disease produces severe gastro intestinal disorder, collapse, fever, etc., in the consumer. This disease, called "milk sickness" is fatal in a pretty large proportion of cases. It is said that the flesh of animals with "the trembles," will, if eaten, produce similar dangerous effects. A late writer (Dr. Beach, of Ohio), estimates that 25 per cent. of the Western pioneers and their families died of this disease.

A disease identical with pulmonary consumption in man frequently attacks cows that are kept in dark, damp and ill-ventilated stables. It has been asserted with apparently good reason, (although it must be stated that the assertion has been denied), that the milk of animals affected with this bovine tuberculosis may communicate the disease to human beings using it as food. If there is such danger it is evident that the source of milk used as food for children should be very carefully examined. The objections that have lately been urged against the use of milk from cows fed upon swill, brewers' grains, or distillery slops are based upon this danger, for it is a notorious fact that the majority of swill-fed cows are stall-fed cows, and such are in very many instances the subjects of bovine tuberculosis. In my opinion, the milk of swill or slop-fed cows may be as rich and wholesome as any other milk, provided the cows are housed in clean, dry and well-ventilated stables, and often turned out to pasture. The danger does not lie in the food of the animal, but in the character of the animal's surroundings. If our city or surburban dairymen could be made to understand the importance of this, the outcry against "swill milk" would soon lose its effect. As things are at present, it is based upon a real danger.

The milk of cows suffering from the so-called cattle plague, contagious pleuro-pneumonia, or foot-and-mouth disease is also said to produce illness when drunk. The symptoms are generally referred to the gastro-intestinal tract.

Butter and cheese, or ice-cream, made from diseased milk, may take on a like poisonous character. I am not aware whether the recently observed cases of ice-cream poisoning in Brooklyn, N. Y., were due to diseased milk, or to the accidental or intentional admixture of a poison.

CHEESE

has often caused serious illness in people who have partaken of certain samples. Very recently an outbreak occurred in the State of Michigan. About one hundred and sixty-four persons who had eaten of certain cheese, were taken ill with pain and burning sensation in the stomach, intense vomiting and purging, feeble pulse, cold extremities and tendency to collapse. All finally recovered. When the cheese was cut or broken, a whitish liquid oozed from the pores, and in the liquid microscopic organisms were found. The liquid was very strongly acid. Dr. V. C. Vaughan, of the Michigan State Board of Health, who made an analysis of the poisonous cheese, gives the following easily applied test of good cheese. He says: "Much has been written on the subject [of cheese poisoning] and many investigations carried on, especially in Germany. It has been variously ascribed to diseased milk, decomposition, and the development of fatty acids, etc., but we do not yet know what makes the cheese poison. Good cheese is only very slightly acid, and slowly reddens blue litmus paper. *The poisonous cheese was intensely acid, intensely reddening blue litmus when the paper was applied to the freshly cut surface.* This test for poisonous cheese appears to be practicable. The blue litmus paper could be applied by any grocer to each freshly cut cheese. If the litmus paper is instantly turned red by the liquid which oozes into the pores, the cheese is to be suspected as poisonous."

The poison may sometimes even be transmitted to nursing infants. Husemann refers to the case of a woman, who, while suffering from an attack of cheese-poisoning, nursed her child, which was also attacked by choleric symptoms.

UNWHOLESOME MEAT.

It is a serious problem of public hygiene to determine to what extent diseases of animals render their flesh unfit for use as food, There seems no room to doubt that the flesh of animals suffering at the time of death from splenic fever, foot-and-mouth disease, symptomatic anthrax, and contagious pleuro-pneumonia will, if consumed, produce serious or fatal diseases in the consumer. It is well-known that the use of meat containing animal parasites, such as trichinæ spiralis, echinococcus or crysticercus, will often result in very grave affections in persons eating such meat, especially if not properly cooked.

It has been shown beyond question that the flesh of beeves suffering when killed from splenic fever, will produce this disease in the human subject.

In 1874 an extensive and violent outbreak of an acute disease characterized by vomiting and purging, fever and dizziness, occurred at Middleburg in Holland. Three hundred and forty-nine persons were attacked, of whom six died. The outbreak was traced to eating liver-sausage (Leberwurst), in which the characteristic bacillus of splenic fever was found on microscopic examination. In July 1877, an outbreak of choleric disease, from eating carbuncular meat occurred in the town of Wurzen. In the latter epidemic the bacillus of splenic fever (*bacillus anthracis*) was found in the intestinal canal and in the blood of those attacked.

In Detmold, in Germany, an outbreak of violent gastro-intestinal inflammation, accompanied by high fever, occurred. Among the one hundred and fifty persons attacked three died. The disease was traced to eating the meat of a cow suffering before death from pleurisy, (probably pleuro-pneumonia). In view of the somewhat extensive prevalence or this disease among cattle in this country at the present time, the record of this outbreak may suggest to sanitary authorities some measures for the prevention of similar epidemics on this side of the Atlantic.

In July, 1880, seventy-two persons who had eaten of certain beef and ham sandwiches in Welbeck, England, were attacked by choleric diarrhœa. Four of the cases died. Inflammations of the lungs and small intestines were the most prominent pathological conditions found *post-mortem*. The smaller blood-vessels of the kidneys were filled with finger-shaped bacilli, which, when cultivated and inoculated into guinea pigs, rats, and white mice, produced similar pathological conditions. At Nottingham, England, in 1881, a number of persons were attacked by a similar train of symptoms after eating baked pork. One case terminated fatally out of the fifteen attacked. It is uncertain whether the meat in these two instances was from diseased animals, or whether it had undergone partial decomposition. The former is the more probable supposition, although the organisms found were neither those of splenic fever or swine plague, but resembled those of symptomatic anthrax (black leg, or black quarter).

Whether the flesh of tuberculous animals can communicate tuberculosis to the consumer is still an unsettled question. Foreign veterinarians and hygienists incline to the view that there is danger of such transmission. At the International Sanitary Congress of 1883 at Brussels, the subject was discussed, and M. Lydtin, the chief veterinary surgeon of the Grand Duchy of Baden, submitted the following propositions, which were adopted by the Congress.

1. That the flesh and viscera of tuberculous animals may be used as food, provided the disease is only commencing, the lesions extending but to a small part of the body, the lymphatic glands being still healthy; provided the tubercle centres have not unergone softening, and provided the carcass is well nourished, and the flesh presents the characters of meat of the first quality. 2. That the flesh of animals showing very pronounced tuberculous infection should be saturated with pretroleum, and afterward burnt under the direction of the police. 3. That the milk from cows affected with pulmonary phthisis, or suspected of having it, should not be consumed by man or other animals, and the sale of it should be strictly prohibited.

Within in the past year the trichinosis question has occupied a considerable share of the attention of the public. The press has given pretty detailed accounts of the formidable outbreak of the disease in the town of Emersleben, Saxony, and vicinity, about a year ago. Three hundred and seventy-six persons who ate pork bought of a certain butcher, fell ill of trichinosis, and fifty-three died. The commercial and political complications arising out of this epidemic will readily be remembered. The statements in the American newspapers were calculated to leave the impression on the public mind, that trichinosis is a practically unknown disease in this country. This is decidedly erroneous. A considerable number of cases of trichinosis in man are on record in American medical and sanitary literature. The fact that American pork is not rarely infected with trichinæ has also been abundantly established. Dr. F. S. Billings, a veterinary surgeon of Boston, reports having personally examined 2,701 hogs, and claims that he found 150, or 5.7 per cent. of them trichinous. In a recent report from the Illinois State Board of Health (*Medical Chronicle*, March, 1884), three limited outbreaks of the disease which occurred in November and December, 1883, in Illinois, are recorded. Three of the patients died of the disease. Dr. Rauch, the Secretary of the Board, states that since 1866, sixteen deaths from trichinosis have occurred in that

State. In July of the present year, twelve cases of trichinosis, with two deaths, occurred at Arietta in the State of New York. (*Medical Annals*, August, 1884). All of these patients had eaten raw ham, which it was afterward ascertained, was packed and shipped in Chicago. Microscopic examination showed the presence of the trichinæ in the muscles of one of the fatal cases. These brief references are sufficient to establish the fact that American pork is sometimes trichinous, and that it may communicate trichinosis to persons eating it, if proper measures of prevention are not taken.

Cysticercus cellulosa, the transition form of one variety of tape-worm, and which is the parasite in measly pork, may also gain entrance to the human body, and, failing to undergo development, cause very serious lesions of various organs and tissues. The frequency of tape-worm is evidence that pork is often thus diseased.

The use of partially decayed meat or fish, has often been the cause of serious or fatal illness. Sometimes the illness partakes of the character of septic infection. In these cases it is probable that the morbid process is due to the action of the organisms of putrefaction. In other cases, the symptoms are widely different. These cases have been the source of much perplexity to physicians and toxicologists until very recently. Within the past six years, however, Selmi, Husemann, Brouardel, Casali and others have drawn attention to certain intensely poisonous chemical compounds found in decomposing flesh, and which have been named by Selmi, *ptomaines*. While there is still much uncertainty concerning the nature of these compounds, it seems pretty well established that when flesh undergoes decomposition, in the absence of oxygen, certain unstable chemical combinations are formed which act as violent poisons. Selmi, followed by most toxicologists, believes these compounds to be alkaloids, analogous to the vegetable alkaloids, such as morphine, atropine, etc. Casali, on the other hand, disagrees with this opinion and believes the ptomaines to be amido-compounds. Husemann regards Casali's hypothesis as plausible, inasmuch as the formation of amido-compounds in animal and vegetable bodies, and during decomposition, is well established.

The form of poisoning due to the organisms of putrefaction is not infrequent. An extensive outbreak of this nature occurred at Andelfingen in Switzerland, in 1839. A musical festival was held at which there were over seven hundred persons present. Out of these, four hundred and forty-four were suddenly attacked by violent gastro-enteric and nervous symptoms. Ten of the patients died. The illness was traced to roast veal, which had been keen kept in a warm place for two days after roasting, and which was probably in a state of partial decomposition.

The class of cases which seem more probably due to the action of ptomaines or related poisons, have been frequently observed after eating sausages, or canned meats. Sausage poisoning is not rarely observed in Germany. It has been ascertained that the internal portions of the sausage are the most poisonous. It is supposed that the ptomaines which are formed in the absence of oxygen are the active agents in the production of the train of symptoms. Poisoning by canned meats seems to be due to a similar poison.

Fish, oysters, crabs and lobsters, frequently give rise to symptoms of poisoning. In most of these cases the poisoning is probably due to partial decomposition, but it is a well-known fact that oysters and crabs are unfit for food at certain seasons. Some persons, however, are subjects of a peculiar idiosyncrasy, in consequence of which, shell-fish always produce certain unpleasant symptoms, among which nettle rash and a choleric attack are most prominent.

That form of fish-poisoning known among the Spaniards, in the West Indies, as *siguatera* is, however, very grave. The mortality is large, and in many cases, death succeeds rapidly upon the attack. The symptoms are as follows: Sometimes suddenly, sometimes preceded by dizziness and indistinct vision, great prostration and paralysis occur. Often death follows the onset of the symptoms in two or three hours; exceptionally in less than twenty minutes. In most cases consciousness is totally lost; in others, it persists, with interruptions, until death. Sensation and the powers of speech and deglutition fail. The jaw muscles become paralyzed, the pulse is slowed, and the temperature diminished. There is sometimes vomiting, but no purging. The secretion of the kidneys is also checked. The President of the State Board of Health, Dr. McSherry, states (*Health and How to Promote It*, p. 143,) that he has seen all the gastro-enteric and nervous symptoms of siguatera produced by eating oysters, lobsters and crabs unseasonably.

In Russia, a form of poisoning has often been observed which results from eating salted sturgeon. In the fresh state these fish are perfectly wholesome, but when salted and eaten raw they produce a very fatal illness. The mortality is said to reach fifty per cent. of those attacked. So far as I am aware no cases traceable to this cause have been observed in this country.

CANNED FOODS.

The vast importance of the canning industry in its various branches in this State, renders it unnecessary to tender an apology for dwelling a few moments upon the relations of canned foods to health. The charge has frequently been made of late that canned vegetables and fruits often contained poisonous salts of lead or tin. Mr. A. Winter Blyth, an English sanitary officer, reports having made analyses of twenty-three samples of canned fruits, including apricots, tomatoes, pine-apples and cranberries. In two samples of the apricots, tin was found in the proportion of 11.05 grains to the pound. The smallest quantity found was 1.58 grains, in a can of the tomatoes. Dr. Henry Leffmann, of Philadelphia, has also found tin in canned peaches analysed by him. The proportions were quite small, and in all cases the fruits were over a year old. Drs. Unger and Bodlander have made similar analyses of canned fruits and vegetables in Germany, and found tin in every sample examined. The metal was, however, in very small protion, not exceeding 1-25th of 1 per cent. in any case. Following this, however, comes Prof. Attfield, a distinguished London chemist, who states that he has frequently examined canned foods during the last fifteen years. He has found tin, at times, but the quantity was too small to deserve notice. His results seems to agree with those of the authors last quoted. In his opinion "given after all evidence hitherto forthcoming, the public have not the faintest cause for alarm respecting the occurrence of tin, lead, or any other metal in canned goods."

Opposed to this, however, is the testimony of Dr. Jno. G. Johnson, a practising physician of Brooklyn, N. Y., who reports, (*Sanitarian, June* 1884), six cases of "corrosive poisoning from eating canned tomatoes." Dr. Johnson thinks the poisoning in his cases was from muriate of zinc and muriate of tin resulting from using muriate of zinc as a flux in soldering the cans. These cases, however, are of no value in helping us to a conclusion, because no chemical examination was made of the supposed poisonous food, or of the matters discharged from the stomach and bowels of the patients. This writer makes a statement which requires notice here. Quoting the New York *Herald* of April 18th, 1883, as authority, he says the "State of Maryland has a law prohibiting the use of the muriate of zinc flux." I have not been able to obtain any confirmation of the statement from canners of Baltimore. If such a law exists here, however, it is daily violated. Thus, it will be seen that there is very little definite knowledge in our possession upon the relations of canned foods to health. The following may be stated as facts.

1. Competent chemists have found tin, in suspiciously large quantities, in cans of preserved food.
2. Cases of poisoning, apparently due to some corrosive agent, have been noted after eating canned food.
3. Cases of poisoning after eating canned food, apparently due to partial decomposition of such food, have been frequently observed.

PREVENTIVE MEASURES.

After the recital of these facts, I think it needs no argument to prove that preventive measures should be instituted against the sale and use of poisonous food. Individual measures of prophylaxis will not suffice; a collective effort on the part or the State must be made. Maryland has passed laws in the interest of the consumer looking to the detection and prevention of fraud in the sale of food. The compulsory inspection of canned oysters, is one of these beneficent acts. There is, however, no provision in the statutes, so far as I am aware, which protects the consumer against diseased or tainted meats, adulterated or diseased milk, or poisonous canned food. It seems to me, this Council should take cognizance of this defect in our State laws, and urge the subject upon the attention of the people. Laws will only be made when they are demanded by public opinion. To create and foster an intelligent public opinion concerning public health is one of the duties of an organization like this. If judicious action is taken, success will follow.

The question will be asked: What is the character of the measures to be taken by the State, and by individuals to prevent the dangers referred to. I shall endeavor to answer as briefly as possible. The State must inspect, through competent agents, all articles sold as food, which are liable to produce disease. The milk, cheese, meat and fish must be regularly inspected before being offered for sale. All food animals must be inspected both before and after slaughter, and the sale of all diseased meat strictly prohibited

Splenic fever, contagious pleuro-pneumonia, foot-and-mouth disease, cattle, or swine plague can be detected in animals suffering from these diseases. After death the gross and microscopic pathological conditions will give similar information. Pork should always be examined microscopically for evidences of trichinæ and cysticerci. It is manifest that such inspection cannot be carried out in a city unless the slaughtering is done at a limited number of places. A centralization of the slaughtering business will be necessary. Boston, New York, New Orleans, Chicago, Philadelphia, Cincinnati, Pittsburg, and Jersey City have solved this problem by the erection of the public abattoirs, resulting in the abolition of the private slaughterhouse, with its manifold outrages against decency and public health. Are we willing to allow these communities to maintain the advantage they have already gained over us? I trust not.

The sanitary inspector of food should ascertain the conditions under which milk-giving animals are housed and cared for, and whether care is taken to prevent infection of milk by the germs of specific diseases. The mere physico-chemical examination of milk, as practiced in some cities can only prevent fraud, but is no safeguard against diseased milk.

It is clearly evident that a person competent to intelligently perform the duties required of the official here denominated the inspector of food, cannot be found among those who seek positions merely as a reward for party service, or because they have political influence. The inspector must not only be a physician or veterinarian, but he must be familiar with the principles and practice of preventive medicine, and must possess above all else, common sense and sound judgment.

But the mere inspection of food will not be sufficient to prevent the dangers which exist. Power must be given the health authorities to take such action as is necessary to protect the public. If loss results to individuals through no fault of theirs, the state must reimburse them. Vested rights must be respected and legitimate business must not be obstructed or otherwise injured. If anyone, however, wants to prosper at the expense of the health of his fellow man, let him suffer a just penalty.

Respecting the relations of the canning industry and of canned foods to the public health, I venture to suggest that this Council can in no single act better signalize its usefulness than by the appointment of a commission, either from among its own membership, or outside of it, whose duty it shall be to thoroughly study the question in all its phases and bearings. The scope of such an inquiry will suggest itself.

Among the individual prophylactic measures against unwholesome food, the first is to reject all articles which from their appearance, taste or *price*, are open to suspicion. Uncleanliness, beginning decomposition, unusual taste, odor, or appearance of food should be sufficient reason for avoiding its use. Pork should always be thoroughly cooked in order to destroy the life of trichinæ or other parasites, and this procedure will likewise render poisoning by diseased meat of other kinds less likely to happen. Milk infected by the germs of various diseases will probably lose its infective character after thorough boiling, although too much confidence must not be placed upon this. In selecting canned foods, those cans which are swelled out at the ends, showing partial decomposition of the contents, or which exhibit evidence of having been re-processed, which is easily detected by the presence of a second sealed vent in the cap, should be rejected. It would also be safer to avoid the use of any canned goods which have been put up longer than one year. There seems good reason to believe, that most cases of poisoning by canned foods have resulted from articles which had been packed a long time.

Any personal idiosyncrasy concerning an article of food, should be sufficient to enjoin its use. Shell fish should not be eaten out of season.

At the conclusion of Prof. Rohe's paper, the Council adjouned 9.45, p. m., to meet Thursday morning, the 18th inst., at 10 o'clock.

SECOND DAY—Morning Session.

President Carroll in the chair. The Session was open with prayer by Rev. George Armistead Leakin, of Baltimore.

The Secretary read the following letters:

"LETTER OF HON. ERASTUS BROOKS, OF N. Y.

"STATE BOARD OF HEALTH OF NEW YORK,
Staten Island, Sept. 14, 1885.

"DR. C. W. CHANCELLOR,
Secretary State Board of Health of Maryland:

"My Dear Sir:—Your letter has just come to hand. I am much obliged by your cordial invitation to be present at your annual meeting on the 17th, 18th and 19th insts. I fear I shall not be able to be present, as our Board meets the same week, and the absence of the Secretary in Europe makes it necessary, as Chairman of the Executive and Finance Committee, that I should be present.

"Your Board is engaged in a most important public work, and deserves what I hope it receives, the cordial support of the people of the State. It would, if possible, give me sincere pleasure to witness and participate in your deliberations.

"I am very fraternally yours,
ERASTUS BROOKS."

LETTER OF R. H. THOMAS, ESQ.
Secretary of the Pennsylvania State Grange, and Editor of the "Farmers Friend."

"MECHANICSBURG, PA., Sept. 15. 1884.
"C. W. CHANCELLOR, M. D.,
"*Secretary State Board of Health of Maryland:*

"Dear Sir:—I am in receipt of your kind invitation to attend your Sanitary Council at Blue Mountain House. I am in strong sympathy with the object of the meeting and will, if at all possible, endeavor to be with you. I would like to see our agricultural classes wake up to the importance of this matter, and will do anything I can to advance the good work in which you are engaged.

"Thanking you for your kind invitation, I am,
"Very truly yours,
"R. H. THOMAS."

LETTER OF GENL. HENRY S. TAYLOR,
President of the Maryland Hospital for the Insane.

"OFFICE MARYLAND HOSPITAL FOR THE INSANE,
"*Baltimore, Sept.* 12, 1885.
"DR. C. W. CHANCELLOR:

"My Dear Doctor—I am glad to see the continued interest you take in sanitary reform in this State. Such action ought to awaken a general interest with our people, which, I trust, may be reflected on the next Legislature.

"I hope to be able to accept your invitation, and be at the 'Sanitary Council' at Blue Mountain House next week.

"Very truly yours,
"HENRY S. TAYLOR,
"President."

A number of other letters from prominent sanitarians and citizens of this and other States, were read, after which President Carroll announced that the reading of papers was the next order of business, and introduced Dr. John Morris, of Baltimore.

THE NECESSITY FOR A MORGUE, AND THE PROPER DISPOSAL OF THE DEAD IN THE CITY OF BALTIMORE.

BY JOHN MORRIS, M. D.

In an enlightened community, in the nineteenth century, it may appear to be a work of supererogation to present an argument urging the neces-ity of a morgue in a city of three hundred and sixty thousand inhabitants; yet so great have been the neglect, indifference, or ignorance of the municipal authorities of Baltimore in the past, that such an argument is not only necessary, but really imperative. The subject of a morgue in Baltimore is not a new one. Time and again it has been urged upon the councils of the city by the health authorities and by writers through the public press. Feeble and half-hearted measures have been devised at different times, but all legislation looking to the desired object has so far proved an utter failure. Men who would cheerfully vote for or sign bills appropriating two and a half millions of the people's money to aid a railroad corporation in another State, have haggled over the petty appropriation of one thousand dollars to erect a building demanded by the requirements of decency, justice, and civilization. Baltimore is perhaps the only large city in the country without an institution to protect the bodies of the unknown and unclaimed dead. Small communities of twenty and twenty-five thousand inhabitants, in the Western and Northwestern States of the Union, have, by their action in this respect, reflected lasting shame upon her citizens. These communities have been settled by enlightened men from the New England States and European countries—men who recognize the true principles of human progress.

Many persons die yearly from accident or by suicide in Baltimore, and are interred without identification.— Frequently the bodies have to be exhumed for purposes of identification. In one instance, a highly respected gentleman from one of the counties of the State, who was not recognized by any of the citizens, was buried in Potter's field, and when search was made by sorrowing friends, the body was found in the dissecting room of a medical college, undergoing mutilation in the interest of science. A few weeks ago a poor laborer was crushed in the Union tunnel, and nearly a week transpired before any one came forward to claim relationship with the dead man. The station-houses of the city are the only places provided for the reception of the bodies of unknown persons dying by violence or accident. Station-houses are for the living and not for the dead. Bodies are kept at these police stations for a brief season, without any measures being taken for their preservation or proper disposition. This condition of things is not only a gross violation of decency, but may lead at times to the obstruction of justice; and as the city increases from year to year, this evil will grow in magnitude.

Two years ago, after the shocking disaster at Tivoli, the bodies of the dead were exposed on the deck of a steamboat at the wharf for hours, blistering in the sun, a bloated, disfigured, lifeless mass. At the spectacle all men cried shame—but there was no shame. A morgue could be erected at a very trifling expenditure. Two years ago, I submitted through the columns of the Baltimore "Sun," to the city authorities, a plan by which a suitable building might be constructed at a very small cost. I proposed utilizing a lot belonging to the city. This lot fronts about forty feet on Pratt street, between Commerce and South streets. It extends back towards the dock, running up between the two last mentioned streets about fifteen feet; but as there is no unloading of vessels at this point a building erected on it could be extended any distance that might be required. Here the authorities could place a morgue which would prove an ornament to this part of the city. The front should be ornamental in character and in the best style of modern architecture. There is sufficient room for a gateway, or *porte cochere*. The bodies of drowned persons could be brought up the dock in boats, in the rear, without observation or excitement. After providing for a gateway and a morgue proper, two fine offices could be fitted up on the first floor, which would serve as a central office for the coroners, and also, as a depot for all the morbid machinery, so to speak, of the city. Telephonic and telegraphic communication could be established with the health office and police stations. The second floor of this building could be divided into four offices, which could be used for other municipal purposes. This plan would secure to the city a beautiful and ornamental public edifice. The situation is everything that could be desired; it is central, and yet removed from the crowded thoroughfare; it is near the water and approachable by boats, thus securing both privacy and decency. The lot itself belongs to the city, and has been lying unoccupied for many years, a useless and unsightly reproach to the neighborhood. This plan may not meet with acceptance, but a morgue of some kind must be secured, even if it be but a covered shelter, so that humanity may be respected and the fair name of the city preserved. At the meeting of the Sanitary Convention, held in November last, a resolution was unanimously passed, urging the city authorities to action in this matter. This resolution was placed before the Mayor and Councils, and the Health Committees of the Councils were waited on by members of that convention. Notwithstanding these efforts, no practical steps have yet been taken. It is to be hoped that a stronger resolution will be passed by this Convention, and that a committee be appointed to urge prompt action in this most vital matter.

The proper disposal of the dead in a large city like Baltimore, is also a subject of great moment in a sanitary point of view. The arrangements for the funerals of all persons dying from contagious or infectious diseases should be placed under the control of the health authorities. All persons, save the immediate family of the deceased, should be debarred from visiting the dead body, and only the pall-bearers and near relatives be permitted to attend the funeral. Proper and thorough disinfection should be afterwards employed to render the carriages safe for future use. The disposition of the dead is a subject which at this time occupies very largely the attention of educated men throughout the world, and will, no doubt, claim much greater consideration in the future. Cremation, as a sanitary measure, is unquestionably the most efficient means of disposal, but, as the prejudices of the day will prevent its adoption, proper earth burial must still be practiced. To secure proper earth burial the health authorities should have controlling power in the selection of the ground to be used for graveyards or cemeteries. In England, where the people are far in advance of us in matters of this nature, this power is vested in the home office. Intramural burial should not be tolerated, and the places of burial should be as far removed from the city as possible. A hard, stiff, clay soil is not fit for the absorption of the body, nor is a water bearing stratum, in rock, suitable for this purpose. As an evidence of the manner in which living things may be preserved in the soil, I will cite an incident that occurred at Norfolk, in the year 1855, during the epidemic of yellow fever which prevailed that year. My friend, Dr. Robert Thompson, a volunteer physician from Baltimore, fell a victim to the disease after a very short illness. His body was placed in an iron casket, and buried in a shallow grave. Fourteen months afterwards, when the grave was opened for the purpose of removing the remains to Baltimore, a number of "plague flies" that had been entombed with him were found living and active in the grave. This plague fly was a hybrid form of fly, which appeared for a short period during the epidemic. If cemeteries or graveyards are to be surrounded with houses, as will shortly be the case with our Greenmount and Cathedral cemeteries, hillsides are not proper locations on account of the drainage and washing away of the soil. The case of the celebrated Enon Chapel graveyard, in London, exemplifies the necessity of this precaution. This famous old graveyard was purchased by Doctor Walker ("Graveyard Walker," as he was termed,) and among the thousands of bodies exhumed, a large number were found in the various stages of putrefaction and decay. Caskets, lead coffins, even simple pine boxes, are a hindrance to the great purposes of nature. Bodies should be placed *immediately* in contact with the soil, and only covered by the simplest light vestment or shroud, so that the earth may speedily fulfil the great office of decomposition and redistribution. Vaults are of all places the most objectionable, and their erection should be prohibited by legal enactment. They are a feeble and vulgar imitation of the sarcophagi of the Egyptians. The scientific methods employed, however, by the ancients (the knowledge of which has been lost) rendered the dead body innocuous; but by burials in vaults, as with us, the dead are made the enemies and destroyers of the living.

This whole subject is a vital one in all of its bearings, and should claim the serious attention of every one interested in the progress and welfare of man.

When Dr. Morris had concluded the reading of his paper, which elicited much interest. Dr. J. A. Steuart moved that a Committee of five, with Dr. Morris Chairman, be appointed to call the attention of the city authorities to the necessity of erecting a morgue. He referred to his efforts as Health Commissioner in trying to have a morgue erected. He said that after having bills twice passed for the erection of a morgue, they were both times vetoed by the Mayor, who at one time excused his vote by saying it was a luxury, and not a necessity. Dr. Steuart said, though disgusted at this proceeding, he hoped yet to have a morgue.

Dr. A. B. Arnold seconded the motion, and said it would meet with the general approbation of the medical profession. The motion was carried, and ex-Governor Carroll, the President, appointed as the Committee Drs. John Morris, James A. Steuart, C. W. Chancellor, A. B. Arnold and George H. Rohe.

TYPHOID FEVER AT ELKTON.

The next paper read, was an abstract of a Sanitary Inspection of Elkton, Cecil county, Maryland, made with reference to the incidence of Typhoid Fever.

BY C. W. CHANCELLOR, M. D.,

Secretary of the State Board of Health of Md.

On the 2d of September, 1884, I received a request from the town authorities of Elkton, Md., to visit the place and inquire into the causes of a prevailing epidemic of typhoid fever. Arriving in the town on the 4th inst., I immediately proceeded to the investigation, assisted by Mayor Jones and the physicians of the place.

Elkton is on the P., W. & B. R. R., 52 miles from Baltimore and 46 miles from Philadelphia. It is situated at the head of Elk river, a small stream with a mean tide of about 12 inches, and navigable only for the smallest crafts. The town has a population of 2,000, and some manufacturing interests. It is in the midst of a fertile and well-cultivated country, the soil of which is a light loam. A few feet beneath this loamy surface is a stratum of tenaceous clay, underlaid by gravel and sand. On sinking down through these various strata, potable water is met with abundantly, at depths ranging from 15 to 20 feet. It is into a formation of this character that nearly all the wells which furnish the water supply of the town are sunk.

Skirting the town to the south is a considerable marsh, which was formerly subject to regular inundations by refluent tides, and is still liable to periodical overflows. The water-shed is towards this marsh; consequently it receives nearly all the drainage of the place, including the drainage from pig-pens, slaughtering establishments, and a number of privies located on or near its immediate border. It is also the receptacle for quantities of *debris*—vegetable and animal impurities—all of which tend to render it a fruitful and certain source of disease. With the exception of this marsh, fringed as it is with a reeking cess-pool along the border adjoining the town and the pig-pens, Elkton may be represented to be in better sanitary condition than many other towns of the same size in other parts of the State, for the reason that the streets, back-yards, and cellars are kept reasonably clean, and some care is exercised in the disposal of excretal sewage, which, in most instances, is covered with dry earth or ashes and removed at such intervals as may be found necessary. There are no foul cess-pits to pollute the soil and poison the water supply by soakage or direct flow through underground channels.

In an inquiry into an epidemic such as this, where the cases of the disease are distributed generally over the town, there are four sources which are ordinarily looked to as those whence the contagion or infection of the disease is most likely to have proceeded and by the medium of which it may have been distributed, viz:

1. A common source of water supply, such as some particular well or stream, or the mains of a system of public supply, in which case infection or pollution of the water, either at its source or in its progress of distribution, may result in the distribution with it of an infective material.

2. A common system of drainage, in which case a sewer becoming infected may be the means of distributing through the medium of sewer air, infective matter to the houses in relation with such sewer air.

3. Where there is no common water supply and no common system of drainage to account for a wide distribution offered, the cause of the spread may be found in the progressive infection of independent privies; and by soakage from them into independent wells or other supplies of water; or (4) the cause of the spread may be found in the distribution over the town or district of some particular article of food, such as milk, which has become infected.

With a view to a full understanding of the present case it will be well to consider these ordinary sources of infection severally, and I shall do so in the order in which they have been mentioned.

1. There is no common water supply in the sense in which I have used the term, to the town or to the

houses that were invaded. The drinking water of the town and of all the houses invaded is derived from wells close to the houses, and most of them are sunk into and gather their water below the stratum of clay mentioned as underlying the loamy soil on which the houses are built; and it will be one of the inferences of my argument (subsequent indeed, and incidental to the main contention) that the water in this layer having become infected might have been the medium of infecting one particular well. Similarly, it might might be argued, other wells drawing upon the same water layer might have become infected, and in this way the disease have been spread through the town. I am not prepared to deny the possibility of such an occurrence, but that it was not the main cause of the spread of the fever in Elkton, and could have had, at the most, but a very small influence over it, is proved by the fact to be presently pointed out, that, even assuming all the houses invaded to have drawn well water from this layer (which was not the case), very few of the whole number were attacked, while among those that were invaded there was something else in common and differentiating those houses from others that took water from the same source. To attribute the spread of the fever to this cause would, under the peculiar circumstances of the case, be almost as reasonable as to attribute it to the general atmosphere which the population breathed in common.

2. There is no common system of drainage in the town, so that this source of infection must at once be eliminated from consideration.

3. The third ordinary mode of spread of infection may also be eliminated so far as the relation of the mode of disposal of excretal matter to the water supply for drinking purposes is concerned, inasmuch as the disposal is by the pail system and not into cess-pits. Throughout the town, however, there are sanitary defects of the kind, too commonly found in small towns and rural districts, which defects might, under certain circumstances, aid in spreading the disease, but not probably so in the present instance. These sanitary defects have reference to the existence of pig-pens in dangerous proximity to dwellings, and to the disposal of the house refuse and garbage The pig-pens are in some instances, exceptionally filthy, and the house slops are either at once thrown upon the ground, or being fed to the pigs, ultimately soak into the ground and find their way into the wells through the highly permeable

soil. Indeed, the water in most of the wells on the premises where the fever prevailed, was found to be more or less contaminated, probably ·by such soakage and the animal life, such as worms, snails, toad-frogs, &c., which usually finds its way through the lining and coaping of wells not properly cemented; but in no single instance was the impurity found sufficient to account for the existence of the fever in question. Against these sanitary defects as the cause upon which the epidemic's spread depended, there are these considerations, viz:

a. That the condition of things described as respects garbage and drinking water had been in existence many years; and, although by importation or otherwise, cases of fever had now and then occurred in the town, the disease had, notwithstanding, never before in the experience of the oldest medical practitioner there, spread epidemically.

b. That in many instances the houses invaded, following the chronological order of their invasion, were situated at a long distance from one another, and that in very few instances indeed, even in the case of invaded houses situated near each other, was I able to discover any communication of any kind between their inmates, and especially of such a kind as would lead to any probability of persons attacked with the disease having infected the premises of any houses subsequently invaded.

c. That on the other hand, in the few instances where communication between the occupants of houses, one of which had been invaded, was of ordinary occurrence, or of more or less probable occurrence, and where, therefore, it was possible that the premises and well of one house might have been infected by the garbage and soakage from the premises of another house invaded, the disease did not spread from the one house to the other.

Lastly, apart from any question of infection of premises, or houses from some previous case, it is a notable fact that the disease, in very few instances, existed in adjoining houses, or in houses very near each other. Nor did the sanitary condition of any house or premises appear to have had any influence upon the spread of the disease. Almost without exception the cases occurred in houses the sanitary arrangement of which, although not always unexceptionable, were far superior to those of houses occupied by a large part of the population who yet escaped the fever.

With respect to the fourth ordinary cause of the epidemic spread of fever, viz., the distribution of some particular article of food which has become infected or polluted, a fact which had attracted attention before my visit remains to be accounted for, which is that the families invaded were almost exclusively those supplied with milk from one particular dairy farm. The *prima-facie* case against this milk supply is a strong one, inasmuch as it appeared that all the families invaded, except one, where the patient had been in Philadelphia and returned home sick, were supplied with milk from this particular farm; and furthermore, in the families invaded, it appears that only those who drank the milk suffered from an attack of the disease.

Of the ten or fifteen families invaded, it is stated that all were supplied with milk from this farm at the time of the invasion, and, with one exception (the case imported from Philadelphia), these families had been supplied for some weeks previously from this source.

Prima facie, then, there appears a strong probability that the prevalence of typhoid fever in Elkton was associated, as cause and effect, with the milk supply from this particular dairy, and this *prima-facie* evidence turns out to be strengthened by more particular inquiry.

Looking now to special cases as illustrating what so far appears accusatory of the suspected milk supply, the following facts are noteworthy.

This dairy is situated less than half a mile from the town. The barn and cow yards are located some 500 yards from the dwelling of the dairyman, who was himself first attacked with the prevailing fever. The history of the case, as derived from his physician, is as follows. He was taken sick about the 20th of July, with a fever somewhat remittent in character. In a few days he appeared better, but grew worse on the 7th August, and the fever continued, in spite of large doses of quinine until the latter part of August, when he began to convalesce. His physician, Dr. H. H. Mitchell, informed me that he could not define the exact nature of the illness, but he did not, in the absence of "spots" and metiorism, regard the case as one of enteric or typhoid fever. I have not, therefore, felt justified in including this and two other similar cases in the same house (the son and daughter of the dairyman) attacked respectively on the 20th of August and 1st of September, in my list of such cases. In a house on the opposite side of the road to that of the dairyman, a case of sickness has recently appeared in the person of a youth who drank milk from the suspected dairy, and this case Dr. Mitchell thinks presents more of the characteristics of typhoid fever than either of the other cases above referred to.

The following cases, in the order in which they were visited by me, have been under the professional care of Dr. Charles M. Ellis, who is very decided in the opinion that they are unequivocal typhoid fever. I was kindly invited by Dr. Ellis to visit and examine several of these cases, which he considered typical cases of typhoid fever, and I quite agree with him that they presented every indication, objective and subjective, of genuine typhoid fever. The following is a brief history of the cases under Dr. Ellis's professional care.

Case 1. H. H. age 13, sick upwards of three weeks, milk supply from the suspected dairy. The patient is the only member of the family who had drank milk previous to his attack. The milk supply had been changed soon after the patient was taken ill, and no other case of fever or illness had occurred in the house.

Case 2. Miss A. M. was taken sick about the 20th of August with the fever, was still ill at the date of my visit Sept. 4th. The family drew their milk supply from the suspected dairy.

Cases 3, 4 and 5 occurred in the family of Mr. R., Bow street—they are all young ladies, ranging in age from 12 to 25 years. The first case occurred about the 1st of August. At the time of the invasion, and until the occurrence of the second case, the milk supply had been obtained from the suspected dairy. It is proper to state that the third or last case, is not regarded as typhoid fever.

Case 6. Mrs. A, age 19, returned home from Philadelphia, sick with fever, about the 20th August. No other member of the family has been sick. Milk supply from a different source to that of the other cases, and not suspected.

Case 7. F. K., Main street, age 15, 21 days sick—still very ill. Milk supply from suspected dairy.

Case 8. Robert C., age 17, has been ill 16 days with continuous fever, very high temperature, almost constant delirium. The milk supply is obtained from the particular dairy suspected, and Robert was the only member of the family who used milk in an uncooked condition; he is said to have consumed it freely with fruits.

Other cases are reported, and in every family invaded, the milk supply is said to have been derived from the same polluted source.

The facts which I have detailed can leave, I think, no doubt upon the mind that the use of the milk distributed from the suspected farm was in some way directly associated, as cause and effect, with the origin and spread of the fever which exists in Elkton. It is no valid objection to this inference to say that many families to which this milk was distributed have hitherto escaped invasion, and that one party who used milk from another source suffered similarly from fever. The obvious reply to the first of the objections is, that in no milk epidemic hitherto investigated, has more than a fraction (although usually a large fraction) of the families using the infected milk been invaded; and to the second objection, that the operation of one predominating cause of an epidemic of fever by no means precludes the operation of other causes concurrently existent.

I have already suggested that the single case which existed in a family that did not use the suspected milk was an imported case, as the lady was already sick, when she arrived in the town from Philadelphia. It is highly probable that the various sanitary defects heretofore referred to, would be more or less operative in spreading the epidemic in an atmosphere already poisoned, as it were, by the existence of the disease. While any one of these defects might give rise to *dyscrasies* and distempers, not one, however, nor all together, would suffice to account for the entire epidemic—its origin, scope and progress.

In discussing the causes of the epidemic, it is proper to take all these circumstances into consideration, and to show how they may be regarded as limiting and reducing the direct influence of the milk supply in its causation. But, while making every possible allowance for the operation of these circumstances, there still stands prominently out from all of them the one fact, that nine-tenths—nay nineteen-twentieths of the persons attacked were persons using milk from the suspected dairy-farm.

In referring to the circumstances connected with this dairy as affording opportunities for contamination of milk with "filth," it is necessary first to give a brief description of the premises, and the arrangements under which the business there was conducted.

The farm adjoins the town on its northern side, and

the dwelling consists of an isolated house, less than half a mile from the corporate limits. Distant from this house, about 500 yards is the farm-yard and sheds where the cows are fed and milked. The yard is not paved, but the middle of it is depressed into a very filthy cess-pool, which catches the water that drains from the roof of the sheds, and from the surface of the yard, occupied over a large space by an accumulation of cow manure and other offensive decomposing matters. Adjoining this filthy yard, and very near the cess-pool, is a well which furnishes water for the use of the cattle; for cleansing the milk vessels and for other purposes known to dairymen.

It may be that water is sometimes used for diluting milk, but I have no evidence that the milk from this vachery was thus tampered with; if, however, this were the case, it is not improbable that the water from the well above referred to was used for the purpose, and this water I have since found by chemical tests to be largely contaminated by sewage matter which has soaked into it from the cow-yard. It contained very marked evidences of organic pollution, in the shape of free and albuminoid ammonia, nitrates, and an unusually large amount of chlorine, which pointed conclusively to sewage or animal refuse as the source of contamination.

The above account of the slovenly arrangements under which the dairy business was conducted will indicate very clearly the way in which the milk may have, and doubtless did, become polluted. It is obvious that the vessels in which the milk was drawn were liable every day or any day to befoulment, even during the process of cleansing. The water used for rinsing the cans was, as is clearly manifest from the sample here exhibited, a dangerous water for use, being befouled from the soakage of filth into the well from the manure-heap and cess-pool. In addition to this fruitful and certain source of contamination, the milk, when being drawn, was liable to pollution from the emanation of the foul yard in which the cows were penned and milked.

I have specially mentioned the circumstances under which the water used may have introduced a filth pollution into the milk by merely rinsing the cans with it, because former experiences of milk epidemics of fever have demonstrated that using an infected water, the small quantity of such water that may hang about a milk vessel after rinsing with it, is amply sufficient to infect the milk subsequently put in. The infection of milk by an infected water by no means implies fraudulent dilution of the milk with the water.

It is very important that attention should be specially drawn to the fact that befoulment of the milk cans in the way indicated would be a particularly dangerous kind of befoulment, inasmuch as the pollution of the water in the well is an excremental pollution by soakage from the manure heap.

There is now a considerable class of persons, among whom are many highly distinguished medical men, who do not longer contend for the necessity of a pre-existing case to explain the local origin and spread of typhoid fever. To all this I may add that there is an accidental way in which filth may gain access to milk, which should not be overlooked, and that is from the hands of the milker.

In giving evidence of the opportunities for contamination of milk with filth, and particularly with excremental filth, the necessary proof has been afforded of the sufficiency of the alleged main cause of the epidemic in Elkton, and the inquiry may here be brought to a close.

In concluding this paper it may not be amiss to refer very briefly to the dangerous impurities sometimes contained in drinking water.

Prof. Chandler states that organic matter of a purely vegetable origin, such as occurs to the extent of one, two, or three grains per gallon, in country springs and wells, or in ponds and rivers, even when it contributes a tint of yellow to the water, is entirely harmless and unobjectionable. The nitrates, nitrites and ammonia salts found in wells in densely peopled towns, are themselves harmless, but their presence proves the contamination of the water with the products of decomposition of animal refuse, and should always be viewed in the light of a warning of the presence of impending danger.

The products of the decomposition of animal matter in water, is, however, by far the most objectionable impurity. Organic matters, produced by the decomposition of vegetable substances, are not especially dangerous, but the products of decomposing animal substances are highly dangerous, even when in minute quantities. These impurities do not make themselves apparent to the taste. On the contrary, such waters are frequently considered unusually fine in flavor, and persons go a great distance to procure them, nevertheless, they contain an active poison. Many diseases of the most fatal character are now traced to the use of water poisoned with the soakage from soils charged with sewage and excremental matters. Sudden outbreaks of disease, are often caused by an eruption of sewage into wells, either from a break in the sewer or cess-pool, or from soakage, or from some peculiarity of the season. Such contamination of water is not indicated by any perceptable change in the appearance of the water. The filtered sewage, clear and transparent, carries with it the germs or causes of disease. At a convent in Munich, thirty-one, out of one hundred and twenty-one inmates, were affected with typhoid fever. It was found upon investigation that the well was polluted by sewage, and the disease disappeared as soon as the proper repairs were made.

At Pittsfield, Mass., the typhoid fever suddenly broke out in a large boarding school for young ladies. The water was found to be contaminated with sewage, owing to leakage from the cess-pool. A similar occurrence took place two years at Princeton College, New Jersey.

At Edgwood, on Staten Island, in 1866, the inmates of a small block of houses were affected with typhoid fever, several deaths occurring. On making investigation it was found that a neighbor, through whose land the underground drain passed, had taken the liberty of closing up the drain, thus sending its contents back upon this block of houses, contaminating the wells and thus murdering the unfortunate victims with sewer poison. (Foot note.—Chancellor upon the sanitary chemistry of water.)

Illustrations might be multiplied without end, of cases in which diseases have been directly traced to impure water. Cholera, though it does not originate from polluted water, is disseminated chiefly by the aid of wells and other impure water supplies.

From these facts, it is seen that water aids in disseminating either directly or indirectly, two of the most fatal diseases which affect the human race; the typhoid fever and the cholera. This poisoning by bad water is therefore fully established, and should awaken communities to the vital importance of securing a pure and unfailing supply of this indispensable beverage.

NOTE—Dr. Chancellor exhibited a specimen of water taken from the infected well referred in his paper, which he stated was, when first drawn, limpid and sparkling, and pleasant to the taste, but when tested chemically, showed a large amount of decomposed organic matter, or excretal poison, which had soaked into the well from the adjoining cow yard. The greenish, yellow precipitated by chemical agents was quite sufficient, without further analysis, to condemn the water as unsafe to use for any domestic purpose.

DISCUSSION ON DR. CHANCELLOR'S PAPER.

Dr. Ward: "I remember an outbreak of typhoid fever which occurred in several houses, near London, England. The physicians found that only persons were affected who drank milk from a particular dairy. I examined the cows at this dairy and found them in a healthy condition. Upon careful examination by the Board of Health, it was discovered that it was the habit of the dairyman, before sending the milk to market, to stand it outside his dairy, in the cans in which it was shipped; they further found, that near the dairy a sewer had burst, and for some days the sewage matter flowed down a gutter, passing by where the cans stood, and that the milk had thus absorbed disease germs."

Dr. Rohe: "Dr. Chancellor did not call attention to the fact that some water may be apparently pure and yet dangerous, and other water may *look* very impure and yet be harmless. I do not think that chemical examination of water can at all times be relied upon, because the quantity of impure matter which is capable of causing disease is so minute that it cannot be detected. I would like to ask Mr. Brewer to give the convention an account of an epidemic of fever which he related to me this morning."

Mr. Brewer: "I can only speak of what I have read. The cases I spoke of did not come under my personal observation. At a summer resort near New York, which had always been considered a very healthy place, typhoid fever broke out. The Health Department of New York sent an officer to investigate its cause. He found that all the cases attacked had taken milk from one dairy. The daughter of the dairyman also had the disease. The case is very similar, in many of its features, to the Elkton outbreak, so carefully and intelligently investigated and reported by Dr. Chancellor."

Dr. Miller: "This investigation is certainly very important in its relations to the public health, and demonstrates, incontestably, the value and necessity of maintaining an efficient State health organization, upon which the people may call for aid in just such emergencies."

The discussion on the Elkton epidemic was followed by the reading of a paper on

THE RELATIONS OF THE DISEASES OF DOMESTIC ANIMALS TO THE HUMAN RACE.

By Dr. Robert Ward,
F. R. C. V. S. of England.

Whatever conduces to the welfare of mankind must surely at all times become a subject of deep interest to society. Therefore, in introducing the subject of this paper, no words will be needed by way of preface.

The importance or magnitude of the subject is at once realized, and so impressed was I of this importance that I hesitated some time before I could reconcile myself to grasp a subject of such vast importance. Some philosopher has said that the increase of the population is the increase of the wealth of nations, and justly so. Public health is a great subject, for if it means anything it means national prosperity, wealth, power, and character. Sanitary science is the most important department of social science, an upon its teachings depends the well-being of the masses—*i. e.*, the public health.

To become thoroughly conversant with this science, the scientist has to draw upon many branches of human learning, especially that branch of medical science, comparative pathology, a branch of medical study and research, which has only in very recent times received the attention of medical men in Europe, and now just beginning to engage the attention of those of this country.

I think that much might be done in this direction if the State government would do something to foster and encourage the younger, yet important profession, the veterinary art, and I am sure the medical profession here will assert, as it did of yore, in the old world.

The two professions are so closely allied that in the interests of humanity they should be no longer separated, but the latter fostered until it reaches the mental standpoint of the former. Then, and then only, can the relations of the diseases of the domesticated animals to the human race be properly grasped and understood.

There is nothing that can offer for the medical student a more brilliant future or more useful career than the study of Comparative Pathology; a broad field of truly scientific research, hitherto almost entirely unexplored, offering as it does, material for truly scientific work, *ad lib et ad infin*, which if properly undertaken must in the near future tend to settle those biological etiological questions which at this present disturbs the mind of the scientific world.

At a meeting of this kind it may be impolitic for me to fix my standpoint on truly scientific ground, but better for me to assume a more practical one, leaving the scientific aspects for some other occasion, when those of you who are more interested in the scientific are in the majority, and pass at once to the subject of my thesis, which really is: How far are the diseases of the human subject produced by or owe their origin to the consumption of diseased animal products or animal disease?

For some years men of science have been greatly exercising their minds anent the connection between diseases epizootic and epidemic—for certain it is that our knowledge respecting the transmission of diseases from one animal to another is marvelously little, in a scientific sense, leaving alone transmission from animals to man, and *vice versa*. Nevertheless, we have facts before us which must arouse suspicion, for it has proven beyond doubt that certain specific diseases have been traced from animals to man, I may mention glander or farcy—anthrax rabies—as of long standing so recognized, and now we have tuberculosis, diphtheria or diphtheritis enteric fever, and horse-pox as well as cow-pox, which yielded the variota vaccine of Jenner. Then we have several disorders due to animal or vegetable organisms—the list is rather formidable both in quantity and quality

With the little knowledge we possess, of a special nature, concerning the diseases of our domesticated animals, and the slight information we have respecting the coincident epidemics and epizootics, or of epidemics following or preceding epizootics, we are in a position to assert that several fatal diseases and troublesome disorders owe their origin to certain necessary changes—"metamorphosis of particular animal existences." These existences, previous to implantation in human organisms, having found a habitation in the bodies of those creatures with which we are more or less in contact in every-day life, and which extrinsically or intrinsically operate on our own organisms.

The introduction of these living entities, or, in other words, partially developed organisms, may occasionally occur indirectly through their having passed into other and different media; yet the ordinary and general introduction is through the direct passage of these entities, in definite stages, while located in particular tissues of such animals as are used for human food.

Doubtless many of these partially developed animal forms, from various causes, prove abortive on entering the human digestive organs, even to a moiety, whilst some thrive to maturity, perfect their existence, and pass away to continue the circle of existence, without temporary annoyance, much less serious disease, whilst others, during their development, prove to be the direct cause or factors of great disturbance or of serious disease.

In some instances this disturbance to health may be due to the direct agency of the immigrants themselves; at others, by their proving to be the developers of some material, or agency, which acts thus hurtfully. Sometimes the effects of these parasites presence in the animal economy is short, transient, only evidenced at a period of their growth, at others, impairment of function, and general disturbance continues during the stay of these organisms in the body.

These are not the only forms of disease producing influences emanating from animals to man, for we have those which operate otherwise than through the ingestion of animal tissue as food, by direct implantation of disease germs, whether these are organisms, living and particulate, or particles of specially formed animal tissues—bioplasen. This group of diseases is directly, or indirectly, implanted in human bodies, quite apart from the use of animal tissus as human food, and these diseases are capable of indefinite multiplication, and induce certain specific febrile disturbances. In this class or group we have glanders, farcy, diphtheria, and specific skin diseases.

Of all the malignant diseases to which animals and man are liable under this head, the fever of glander-farcy is the most terrible, communicable by direct and indirect contagion. The recorded evidence of its ravages among horses and men leaves undoubted evidence of the volatibility possessed by the virus, to make us suspicious of the congregation of human beings in dwellings in close proximity to stables, and this is a matter deserving our attentions, for this disease is in our midst, and it may make Baltimore like other large cities, one of its abiding habitations.

Although diseases of the dermal tissues are not dangerous, they are admitted to be very troublesome and a great inconvenience, and we have two authentic cases of the parasitic disease "ringworm," developing in a most severe form in two parishes directly traceable to a like uncared for condition in some young cattle.

Much inconvenience resulted from this outbreak, and

the proof was abundant to link the outbreak with the young cattle.

Men in daily contact with animals, and those whose trade or labor bring them in contact with animal products are exposed to these inoculable and contagious diseases, and become a media for propagation of disease unknowingly.

Of all diseases, diphtheria is the one probably most to be dreaded, and it has been clearly defined by the most careful investigators as due to a special parasitic vegetable organism, which can be cultivated artificially. Thanks to such men as Huter, Frendelenburg, Nasiloff Eberth and Talamon. The latter has, by experiments on rabbits, guinea-pigs, fowls and pigeons produced the characteristic pathological lesions, and in the pigeons false membranes. Diphtheritis in animals and in man has almost identical physical and pathological phases.

In man it is generally localized in the fauces or pharynx, the upper air passages, the spleen and kidneys less frequently, the peculiar greyish-white membrane or slough which marks the presence of the disease and which is closely adherent to the mucous membrane beneath, is found in the mouth or pharynx, *not beyond*, for when the larynx and trachea *are* involved, the pseudo membrane formed is of a croupous nature, easily detached.

Among poultry it is a most fatal disease, and generally appears among them in an epizootic form, after them the bovines suffer most frequently, then sheep, the pig, rabbit and the dog and cat, the horse being less liable.

Now, in animals as in man, the disease is ushered in by acute fever succeeded by prostration and rapid emaciation, and often collapse. The symptoms vary in individuals or species and in different outbreaks. The buccal, labial, lingual, pharyngeal and palative mucous membranes, as well as the nostrils and upper air passages, are swollen, congested, and covered in patches by greyish-yellow, tough fibrinous masses, which are with difficulty removed.

Diphtheric enterites is not uncommon nor yet diphtheric opthalemia, terminating in perforation of the cornea.

I have briefly dwelt on these symptoms that you may realize the lesions in animals and man. We will now consider the evidence of its transmission from animals to mankind, and this must interest us, seeing as we do the terrible fatality among the human race, and the mystery which surrounds the outbreaks. This should incite us to the utmost of our power to discover the source or origin, with the object of prevention—V. I. September '81.

The most interesting case on record is that of Prof. Dammann, director of the Hanover Veterinary School, published in the "Veterinary Pathological Journal" of that city in 1877.

The Veterinary Inspector of Ludwigsburg, reported that a number of young calves, about 20, had died very quickly of some throat affection, a *post-mortem* revealed those lesions I have before enumerated. Prof. Dammann performed several crucial tests and came to the conclusion it was diptheritis, the Professor placed a healthy calf with two sick ones and it sickened five days afterwards. It remained without treatment, on the second day micrococci and rods were found in the nasal discharge, microscopical examination of the deposits resulted in the discovery of numerous bright looking granules, scarcely tinted by carmine, nor were they soluble in chloroform, ether acids or alkalies, when isolated they showed decided movements—they were micrococci and rods.

The Veterinary Inspector was infected May 1st, and showed the usual severe symptoms; the dairyman was taken about the same time; the Professor on the 8th, and his assistant on the 11th.

It may be noted that antecedent to the outbreak among the calves the child of the coachman died of diphtheria but nothing clear could be defined.

In 1880, an outbreak of diptheria in the human species occurred at Kilburn, London, and it was suggested that it originated from a dairy of cows supplying milk in that locality. Now, if calves do suffer from this malady, and this disease is so highly infectious, are not the cows liable to be affected by the sucking of the calf? Or may it arise in the lacteal secretion of the parent and thus infect the calf in the first instance. I merely refer to this theory, because there are authorities who speak of infectious mamanites as affecting cows, among them Prof. Dieckerhoff, of the Berlin School, and Prof. Franck, of the Munich School.

Tuberculosis is another septic disease, and should engage our attention, for I opine its relations to mankind to be most marked, indeed, it is a disease of mankind as well as animals. The mortality among milch cows from tuberculosis is great.

Prof. Toussiant, of the Toulouse Veterinary School France, says a disease which kills one fifth of a species is certainly a disease of that species. Tuberculosis is really a disease of mankind, and when it is present in the form of germs in a good portion of the food which we consume, surely it does not savour of temerity to ask that sufficient hygiene conditions should be maintained to prevent this enormous mortality.

Tuberculosis of man is exactly the same as that of the ox and cow.

When it is conveyed to animals by inoculation, it produces absolutely the same kind of lesions, is capable of transmission to other animals and is constantly reproduced in the same form. * * * Of this I have assured myself, says Toussiant, by causing animals to eat tuberculous matter derived from man, or in inoculating them with his blood.

It is now generally admitted that consumption in man and tuberculosis in cattle are one and the same disease with all pathological analogy. Experiments have been instituted, in unlimited number, to prove this etiologically, and it now remains on record for legislative measures.

The flesh of tuberculous cattle and the milk of the tuberculous cows each contain the disease germ, and therefore the risk to human life must exhibit itself to any one interested in public health.

In the discussion on tuberculosis at the meeting of the National Veterinary Association, held in London, in May, 1883, Mr. Hopkins said: If we feed children on diseased meat, will it produce tuberculosis now, or ten years hence? I had an assistant who came to me from one of the islands of Scotland. The family from which he was derived was healthy and strong, but when two of his sisters were young, the herd of cattle became affected with tuberculosis. These two girls were fed upon the milk from these cattle. The two brothers were more fond of whiskey than milk; they are now healthy and hearty; the sisters are lying in their graves victims to tuberculosis.

There are so many difficulties in the way, to trace infection from animals to mankind, that the evidence is generally accepted as presumptive, but as I said in the forepart of my address, there are facts sufficient to arouse suspicion in many instances.

I will draw your attention to this fact, that in Vienna, New York, and elsewhere, efforts have been recently made to suppress the sale of milk from tuberculous cows.

I will not trespass with this subject any further, but will say that although I am unable to state to what extent this disease exists in this country, I do know that it does exist in this State to some extent, and as it is specially a disease of warm climates, I anticipate its existence in many other States, and from the death reports among our citizens, I find a fair percentage die of phthisis pulmonalis, and although the disease is one of the hereditary class, nevertheless, development *de novo*, may in many cases obtain.

As a duty I owe to my science and to the public I feel bound to speak with emphasis on this subject; and moreover, being the guardian of the animal wealth of this State, so far as sanitary science is concerned, and also, to some extent, of the public health, I feel that I should be open to a charge of neglect of duty if I spoke otherwise on this grave subject—"Tuberculosis" and its relation to the health of mankind.

This one important subject is at this present receiving the serious attention of the authorities on the European Continent, and on some future occasion I shall be pleased to open this subject again.

The lacteal secretion of the cow frequently has become the vehicle for transmission of disease germs from man to mankind, as was most clearly exemplified in an outbreak of scarlet fever in St. John's Wood and in the vicinity in 1879, and in the investigation of which I was professionally engaged.

The milk was traced to a farm at Thame, in Oxfordshire, and the dairyman who attended these cows had his wife and family down with scarlet fever in its worst form. This poor man was the nurse and doctor to his plague-stricken family, nursing them all night, then at early dawn rushing off to attend the dairy work, milking the cows in the same clothes, and doubtless with unwashed hands. Here, then, was the source of the outbreak in town, for it was only among the families consuming this identical milk that the fever developed itself, and with the sad result of several deaths.

I have referred to this one instance out of many, that I may direct attention to our local dairies.

That much feared porcine disease, trichinosis, is another addition to those seriously affecting mankind, but I am pleased to say that I have not observed a case in this State up to this present, but hog cholera is a disease of the same class or other infectious diseases, and certain it is that during its prevalence the health of man is in jeopardy if the flesh of hogs so affected finds its way to market as human food.

Our noble friend and slave the horse, comes in for his share in complicity for endangering the health of his master, otherwise than with the loathsome disease glanders-farcy.

The disease commonly known as pink-eye is scarlet fever, with all the usual physical indications and pathological lesions, and I have frequently noticed that the attendants have complained of throat trouble, febrile feelings and debility whilst attending the patients, and in some cases they have been laid up in consequences.

I might enlarge upon this subject to an unlimited extent, but think I have taken sufficient ground for one sitting, and for cogitation or reflection.

I will therefore close in the language of my friend, Dr. G. Fleming, in the introduction to his animal plagues.

To the medical philosopher who desires to see his science stand on the broadest basis, as well as the lover of his species, the study of diseases in animals cannot fail to be of much moment. The same class of causes which generate epidemic maladies are, we may be certain, fertile in including similar diseases in the lower animals and perhaps, also, in plants on which the human family so much depend.

It has been a matter of common observation from the earliest times, and our history will testify to its accuracy, that widespread pestilence in plants and murrain in cattle, have frequently, either preceded, accompanied, or followed closely on those visitations which caused mortality and mourning in the habitation of men; and when it is remembered that some of the animal plagues are readily transmissable to man, there is additional incitement to their study.

To the agriculturist and political economists a knowledge of the history of these affections must always be of pressing importance, as the science of comparative pathology has clearly shown that many of the diseases of animals which are indigenous to our soil, may be deprived of their generating causes, and thus altogether abolished.

To close, I will remark that it has afforded much pleasure to prepare this short paper on so important a subject, and if time had permitted I should have endeavored to have arranged something better for you, but my duties and practice fairly consume time, that leisure moments do not abound.

I am here among you, as a laborer in the broad field of practice and in the workshop of science, when time allows, always and at all times.

The paper was briefly discussed by Dr. Piper, in which he referred to the value of educated veterinarians and the necessity for veterinary schools in Maryland.

Dr. Ward followed in some supplementary remarks to his paper, in which he commented on the ignorance which he had witnessed among so-called veterinary doctors in the State.

DISCUSSION ON DR. WARD'S PAPER.

Dr. Piper: I think the subject of Dr. Ward's paper is of great importance to the medical profession. They do not like, as a rule, to recognize the "horse doctor," because he is usually an ignorant man. The interest of the State, requires that Veterinary Science should be cultivated. The health and life of many people are dependent upon the cow, and therefore, cows should be healthy. This cannot be accomplished without proper accommodations and proper care and treatment when they are sick.

I am a great advocate for giving children cow's milk when the mother cannot nurse them. I test the chemical proportions of the milk in a very simple way; of course children must not be given acid milk. I provide the mother with some blue litimus paper, and instruct her to test the milk with it; if acid, the paper will be turned red. Then lime-water must be added until the red color in the paper disappears, and it remains blue when immersed in the mixture. This kind of milk the children can take with impunity. How are we to come at these matters? how are we to improve the cows, or know when they are diseased or tell when milk is bad? I cannot see a remedy, unless this council recommend to the legislature the passage of some act, looking to the advancement of Veterinary Science in the State of Maryland.

After which the Council adjourned until 2.30, p. m.

SECOND DAY---Afternoon Session.

Dr. John Morris in the Chair.

Letters were read by the Secretary from Dr. Jas. E. Reeves, Secretary State Board of Health of West Virginia, and Dr. Willis, of Caroline county, Md., expressing regret that they were not able to be present and participate in the meeting.

The regular order of business was resumed, and the following paper was read:

THE CAUSES OF CHOLERA, AND SHALL WE HAVE THE DISEASE IN BALTIMORE.

BY JAMES A. STEUART, M. D.,

Health Commissioner of Baltimore City.

The time of this Council is entirely too limited to admit of any lengthy discussion of the subject of cholera, nor would it be appropriate to the occasion to enter upon more than a few brief remarks upon the theme of this paper. "Are we to have cholera, and how to prevent it," and how deal with it, if it come in spite of all our care to keep it out.

It has crossed the Atlantic and become epidemic in the United States quite a number of times in this century, the first and greatest epidemic being that of 1832, the second in 1849, again in 1854 and again 1866 and 1871. Even in the winter of 1872-73 it showed its head again at the harbors of New York and at New Orleans, where it was fortunately arrested through the knowledge of its existence and the excellent quarantine arrangements instituted at these ports.

The danger of the introduction of cholera is never so great when it comes openly and in an undisguised form. When a vessel for instance arrives from a port known to be infected, or with cases on board, or having occurred during the voyage, then the quarantine officers know how to deal with it, and have generally been successful. The following quotations from the report of the Cholera Epidemic Commission of 1873 will illustrate this fact:

"As early as August, 1871, cholera began to be exported from Hamburg, and in September infected vessels arrived at Amsterdam, in Holland, at Hull, Sunderland, and at Harttlepool in England, and at Cardiff, Wales. On the 6th of November of that year the steamship

Franklin put into Halifax, Nova Scotia, in distress. She had cleared from Stetting, October 10th, touching at Copenhagen on the 12th and at Christiansad on the 15th.

"On the 23d, eight days after leaving the last named port, the first death from cholera occurred, and, on her arrival at Halifax, there were twenty-eight deaths on board and two other fatal cases occurring while the ship was in harbor. The disease was carried on shore by two men who were employed in coaling and watering the vessel. Both were taken sick on the 13th of November, and one died after twelve hours illness, while the other carried the disease to his family, four of whom contracted the disease and two of them died. After coaling, the steamer proceeded on her voyage to New York, where she arrived November 12th, having lost eleven more of her passengers, making forty-one deaths in all during the voyage. Seventy-two cases were removed from her to the Quarantine Hospital, among which number there occurred twelve more deaths, making a total of fifty-three deaths out of her 611 steerage passengers. All the passengers were detained in quarantine about three weeks, or until the early part of December," all possible disinfecting measures having been of course used, "and no diffusion of the disease is known to have followed."

This is only one of many instances that might be quoted where effective quarantine controlled the disease when it came in this open form.

But it is from another source that real danger comes, namely, from passengers and their baggage or personal effects embarking from a non-infected port in a ship bearing a clean bill of health and having had no sickness on board during the voyage, but who come from infected interior places where cholera prevails.

"In 1873 three distinct outbreaks of the disease occurred at widely remote points in the United States from this poison packed and transported in the effects of emigrants from Holland, Sweden, and Russia. These people and the vessels in which they were carried, had been perfectly healthy, and the people remained so until their goods were unpacked at Carthage, Ohio, at Crow River, Minn., and at Yankton, Dak., respectively. Within twenty-four hours after the poison particles were liberated the first cases of the disease appeared, and the unfortunates were almost literally swept from the face of the earth.

"Those instances, which might be multiplied, sufficiently demonstrate that no amount or character of inspection of persons alone will suffice to prevent the importation of cholera to this country while the disease exists on the European Continent," nor are we safe as long as passengers may depart from European ports without such an examination as may be necessary to ascertain, not only their condition and health at that time, but also whether they or their baggage have been in contact with cholera anywhere from whence they may be proceeding.

This, I know, is a difficult task, but it does not lessen its importance or the truth of the assertion. Are we to conclude from the foregoing that quarantine, as a measure for protection for this country against cholera, is useless? By no means. The very success that I have quoted in the case of the steamer Franklin, at New York, and hundreds of others that might be cited (did time allow), all around our extended coast, demonstrates its essential value, and should cholera, notwithstanding the barriers we place in its path, leap over them, as it were, and show itself at some remote Western point, the vigilence of quarantine officers should not be questioned or condemned therefor. What is wanting is "prompt and accurate information to threatened ports of the shipment of passengers or goods from cholera-infected districts" by cable.

The recommendation of the above quoted report upon the cholera epidemic of 1873 is as follows: "That consular officers should place themselves in communication with the health authorities of their respective localities to advise promptly, by cable if necessary, of the outbreak of cholera (or other epidemic disease) at their ports, or in any section in communication therewith; to inspect all vessels clearing for the United States ports, with reference to the original and intermediate, as well as to the final points of departure of emigrants thereon; and to report, always by cable, the sailing and destination of any such vessel carrying infected or suspected passengers or goods," and also that "a medical officer, selected for his good judgment and attainments in sanitary science, should collate and digest the information thus obtained, and transmit direct to the threatened ports, as well as through the public press, the note of warning. Thus advised, the threatened community would have ample time for preparation, and the publicity given to the warning would be the most efficient means of insuring proper precautionary measures.

If the health officer of the port of New York, for instance, had been aware of the facts which were subsequently ascertained concerning the emigrants from Sweden, Holland, and Russia, there is no reason to doubt but that such measures would have been resorted to, on the arrival of these people, as would have effectually prevented the transportation of the cholera-poison in their effects half way across the Continent.

No one can answer the question, so often asked of health officers and others, "Do you think we will have cholera in this country," except by saying, "It is possible and even probable that we will have it sooner or later."

When we reflect upon the constant inter-communication between all parts of the world, (especially Europe) in this day of steamers and rapid transit, with this country, we may realize what the chances are in favor of cholera invading our shores. We have observed, and are now observing, its steady and rapid progress from one point to another in the South of Europe. It is true the conditions there are most favorable to its progress, for all travelers tell us of the filthy condition of these stricken cities; of the poverty and squallor of a large part of their inhabitants; of their utter ignorance and disregard of the commonest laws of hygiene, and of what in this instance is of the most vital importance, their total neglect of the sources and supply of drinking water. An eminent citizen of our own city told me only a few days ago that when he visited Naples, a very few years ago, he could not get a decent drink of water. Every one who could afford it they said—and, of course, a rich traveler could—drank wine, but as he did not like wine and would not drink it, he actually suffered for water, not being able to drink the vile stuff they called water.

And as to using water for personal or general cleanliness, that was looked upon as absurd and out of the question by most of the inhabitants. The poorest of these wretched people, being compelled to drink this poisoned water full of the cholera microbes, are, as our newspapers tell us, being carried of daily by hundreds.

We must be prepared, not only to meet it at the threshold and drive it back if we can, but also to deal with it should it obtain a foothold upon our soil.

I have sketched very briefly how the first danger, its introduction, may be warded off; what of the second? Sanitary science, the very subject we have convened at this place to discuss, teaches us that cleanliness, pure air, pure water, careful feeding and proper clothing constitute a barrier against disease under all circumstances and in all places. These are fundamental truths, and yet the microbe of cholera may defy them all.

The now celebrated Dr. Koch has demonstrated, what was theoretically known before, that the poison germ, which he calls a microbe, is propagated principally in water and in a warm moist atmosphere. That it requires a certain period of incubation and is favored or retarded in its development by certain conditions. He says it cannot develop without moisture and that certain precautions may protect those who strictly observe them.

His first recommendation is to boil every particle of water used for drinking or cooking immediately before using. Let it be borne in mind that no diarrhœa or looseness of the bowels is harmless during a cholera season. The excretions of cholera patients are always dangerous, and should be disinfected and removed immediately, taking care to burn all clothing or bedding which may have been soiled or touched by such excretions.

The fact also developed by Koch's investigations, that all the secretions of cholera patients show an alkaline reaction, strengthens and confirms the opinions of the best medical authorities, based upon experience, that acids, especially the mineral acids, the chief of which is sulphuric acid, are destructive to the cholera microbe.

One of the strongest among many evidences of this is the account, related by Dr. Curtin, of the epidemic of all cholera in the Pennsylvania Hospital for the Insane in 1866, when, after the trial of all other known modes of treatment, without success in staying the progress of the disease, the use of sulphuric acid in the strength of five drops to the ounce of water, he imitated lemonade by adding loaf sugar and lemons at once and effectually put a stop to the disease and cured every patient with whom it was used in time. This simple remedy was given to every person attacked or exposed with complete success.

Same principle applies in the treatment of all suspected goods, ships or apartments, by the soaking of such fabrics that we cannot afford to burn, for at least twenty-four hours, in acidulated water, or with acid gases, the best of which in my opinion is sulphurous acid gas—the fumes of burning sulphur. This can be applied to the hold or cabin or forecastle of any ship and to any room or ward of any building. Sulphurous acid gas has proven effectual when properly applied with yellow fever, typhus fever and other kindred diseases. It is cheap and expeditious.

But to return to our first question, and bring it nearer home, shall we have cholera in Baltimore? I may answer with confidence that the conditions which obtain in Baltimore are decidedly antagonistic to the development of a serious epidemic of cholera. With the exception of a few old pump-wells (a most pernicious remnant of antiquity,) which must be condemned and done away with in spite of the ignorant prejudice in their favor, the water supply of Baltimore is exceptionally pure and abundant, and coming as it does from a long distance through tight conduits, the chances of impurity are reduced to the minimum.

The habits of our people taken *en masse* are cleanly and our food supplies abundant and generally wholesome. The streets are clean and the removal of offal and excreta are well regulated. The undulating surface of our city facilitates rapid drainage, and the air in general is pure and healthful.

The quarantine department of Baltimore is second to none in the country—appropriately situated, completely equipped, and under the control of a capable and conscientious medical officer.

One word more and I have done. It has been observed in all epidemics of cholera that fear or panic enter largely as a factor into the elements of danger. This must, if possible, be counteracted. First, by precept, and secondly, by example. The constant reiteration of instructions through the public press and otherwise, and by the calm, intelligent and steady behavior of those who are looked up to by the ignorant and timid for aid, council and support.

"The true remedy against cholera is preventive medicine."

DISCUSSION ON DR. STEUARTS PAPER.

Dr. Piper: "I remember an instance in my early practice where two old people who lived in the country, entirely isolated from any direct contact with cholera, were suddenly attacked by the disease. It was discovered that their son had died a short time previously at the alms-house with cholera, and his clothes had been sent to his parents, and thus the disease had been communicated. This, I think, corroborates Dr. Steuart's views in regard to the contagious nature of the disease."

Dr. Chancellor; "I do not concur with the views entertained by the two last speakers. They are entirely at variance with the experience of Dr. Chamberlain, the Imperial Sanitary Commissioner of India, who affirms that cholera is not transmissable from person to person.

The old rags or old clothes theory errs in demanding a remedy for only one out of many sanitary defects, and is liable to give a false sense of security. As the very existence of the cholera germ has itself still to be established, as well as the opinion of my friend Dr. Piper, that it resides in the cast off clothing of a patient, not only is the chain of argument imperfect; but every important link in it seems to be wanting. The cause of cholera—what governs its distribution, and its relative incidence in different places—is still as inscrutable as when the disease first appeared; but it is well-known that when this cause or combination of causes is present, it is favored by filth, overcrowding, and every other condition adverse to health. *The practical work to be done is to remedy these conditions.*

[NOTE.—This discussion was continued by Prof. Arnold and others, but owing to the temporary absence of the stenographer their remarks were not reported.]

QUACKERY AND PATENT MEDICINES.

DR. EDWARD M. SCHAEFFER

Discussed at length, in an interesting paper, "The Twin Evils, Quackery and Patent Medicines."

He said that to enlighten the public on popular medical delusions is not easy, because persons fall into these delusions from an intrinsic proclivity thereto, and not as a result of investigation or a logical process of reasoning. There is no law regulating quackery, but the law rather favors it. A dyspeptic calls for a stomach bitters, a bilious man for a liver regulator and a jaded man for a brain food, and on the same principle he buys his wife a grease extractor or a universal polish. Why he does not call for a stimulating watch oil whenever "the wheels won't go round" instead of paying an experienced jeweler to repair the watch, is a problem for the student of the inconsistencies in life. Dyspepsias and neuralgias may arise from a dozen different causes.

Debility often requires abstinence from tonics. Apropos of druggists' advice, a knowledge of the properties of drugs is not a knowledge of when drugs are proper. Dr. Schaeffer read a death certificate of a child in Baltimore, signed by Dr. J. H. Smith, its medical attendant, which stated that death ensued after taking one dose of a patent medicine, according to directions on the bottle. The certificate is on record at the City Hall. Are the public and legislatures aware that they are offering a premium to infanticide? The opinion was expressed at the Baltimore health office that many of the infantile deaths reported as spasms are cases of infanticide, the parents using quack medicines to accomplish their purpose. The public can have no better test of the moral tone of a druggist than his attitude towards patent medicines. Most patent medicines, if efficacious, will prove to be old friends of the books or some good physician's prescription, masquerading under some druggist's guise. Five years ago I analyzed a popular neuralgia cure, selling at $1 per bottle, which turned out to be the well-known "iodide of potassium." He said, in conclusion, that seven years of investigation and analysis had settled the following points in his mind: 1. Quack medicine is the most expensive kind to the purchaser. A medicine selling for fifty cents and properly advertised, must not cost over ten cents to be profitable. 2. Successful nostrums are composed of well-known remedies, and are often stolen prescriptions. 3. It is almost impossible for anything new to be discovered outside the regular ranks. What quack found out vaccination or patented chloroform? He charged the clergy and religious press not to be the dupe of these ignorant pretenders, who value only too well the protection of a holy mantle. To the secular press he addressed the question: "Is it your function to encourage fraud?" There is no neutral ground here any more than in religion or politics. He strongly rebuked the action of certain firms in publishing fraudulent medical certificates and denounced the offer of percentages to reputable physicians, and the placing of whiskey to infant lips, that should know only a mother's breast.

[NOTE.—It is a matter of regret that Dr. Schaeffer's valuable paper cannot be given entire, as it was one of the most interesting read at the convention, but it does not appear among the other manuscript papers of the convention, and has, unluckily, been either mislaid or lost, and consequently the above imperfect abstract only can be given.]

THE RELATION OF THE MEDICAL PROFESSION TO SANITARY WORK.

BY PROF. A. B. ARNOLD, M. D.

The medical profession is greatly indebted to the impetus which sanitary investigations of recent date have given to the studies of hygiene and prophylaxis. These branches of medical science begin to assume an importance which properly belongs to them. Formerly they were but summarily treated in medical works, the facts and principles which underly them were left unsystematized, and little zeal was displayed to interest in their behalf the general public, much less the official authorities, that alone could give substantial support to carry out practical suggestions. Although the incalculable benefits of measures preventive of disease has at all times been acknowledged and advocated by the medical press, yet it was only when communities began to appreciate the philanthropic spirit, which animated those who applied themselves to sanitary work in earnest, that the whole subject took a more practical turn and indicated concerted action. Physicians would prove untrue to the traditional fame of composing a body of public-spirited men, if they did not contribute their knowledge and experience, and the full weight of their professional authority, to the cause of sanitation. It is, therefore, gratifying to witness that some of the best talent in the profession is now engaged in sanitary work in conjunction with many of their intelligent and generous fellow-citizens.

These are special considerations from a purely medical point of view, which strongly appeal to the sympathy and co-operation of the general practitioner to encourage the cultivation of sanitary science. I shall only touch, in a fragmentary manner, on a few points in connection with this subject. Etiology constitutes the profession and ably seconded by the medical press, most obscure chapter of medicine. With the exception of heredity and infection as etiological factors, we have only a very limited knowledge of the predisposing and exciting causes of disease. The contributions to morbid anatomy, thanks to improved methods of investigation, may be called satisfactory; diagnosis has acquired a high degree of certainty, and therapeutics, in these days, can boast of numerous and valuable accessions. The exceeding backwardness of etiology in comparison to departments of medical science, is undeniable, though this fact can be easily accounted for. Among the multitude of external influences to which the human organism is exposed, and which frequently assume a morbific character, there is only a small number to which we have any clue. Our knowledge of those subtle agencies which we designate as telluric, thermal and electric, is so extremely meagre that it hardly exceeds in extent and precision the popular notion of the common causes of disease. We still speak of the effects of catching cold, as a universal factor of disorders, although we cannot form a clear and distinct idea of what this expression implies. "Atmospheric or rheumatic influences," belong to the same catagory of etiological phrases which convey no definite meaning. An immense field of research lies thus open before us, barren and unbroken, that awaits the efforts of sanitary investigations to extract from it some useful information.

We are better prepared to judge of the nature of those disease producing agents that underlie infectious diseases and develope epidemics, though even here we cannot affirm anything more definite than that they act the role of morbid poisons in the form of animal or civic miasms. Although debarred from obtaining sufficient knowledge concerning the intrinsic nature of these so-called miasms, the study of the conditions and circumstances that favor their development and which are associated with their action on the human system has yielded admirable results. Sanitary science has got hold of some truths in reference to this subject which are of the highest importance, I have merely mentioned there patent facts in order to dwell particularly on the rare opportunities enjoyed by every practitioner in his own sphere of professional labor to ferret out these conditions and circumstances. To accomplish such a purpose is the very soul of sanitary science and affords the only guide for sanitary work. It may even be considered a bounden duty on the part of the family physician, to search without stint of time and effort for foci of infectious diseases in his immediate surroundings, especially those of scarletina and diphtheria. Although these scourges of infancy are classed among preventible diseases, they still prevail as frequently, and are as deadly as when they made their first appearance. According to published reports, the high rate of mortality of these acute infectious diseases, has not varied under different modes of treatment. Sporadic cases which continually appear in different sections of the country indicate the existence of fevers in certain localities that might possibly be stamped out. There is no other practicable way of carrying out such a design than for every practitioner to undertake the proper inquiry in every instance that comes under his direct notice. Our Health Officers in the City of Baltimore can bear witness to the willingness with which this duty is generally observed. Suppose that medical men everywhere would impose upon themselves this task so becoming the liberal and humane profession of which they are members, the beneficial consequences of this kind of sanitary work would be simply immense. Fortunately there is now a general disposition to constitute Boards of Health which take cognisance of these matters.

Who knows what may not be expected from the possibilities of hygiene in relation to large and important classes of diseases which up to this time have proved inevitably fatal in their tendency and continue to baffle the best directed medical skill. To this order of diseases belong all cases distinguished by structural changes of a chronic character. When we meet, for example, with cases of Brights disease, or paralytic dementia, which may be taken as representatives of these formidable organic diseases, we are aware that destructial processes have already done irreparable mischief. Their exciting causes seem to be involved in an impenetrable mystery, at least they offer peculiar difficulties and perplexities to the pathologist. That these diseases may spontaneously develop through some internal disturbance that gives rise to nutritive alterations is just possible, but evidence is wanting in support of the supposition. If there are disorders which more than any others evoke a strong desire for preventive measures they are of this description, and any hypothesis that would throw some light upon these pathogeneses would be welcome. In our present state of knowledge we cannot conceive of any other morbid influences that tend to the development of organic diseases than such which establish a vulnerability of certain anatomical structures, so that slight exciting causes that would otherwise prove innocuous, eventually lead to tissue changes. I have often thought, that if the past history of patients suffering from organic affections were better known in regard to their habits and modes of life, the hardships they had undergone, both mental and physical, or their violation of physiological and sanitary laws, etiolgy would receive important acquisitions and the insight it affords would render prophylaxis possible. There is no better proof of the injurious effects of bad hygiene in causing an abnormal nutrition of animal structures than the cases of children affected with rickets or scrofula. It may be fairly concluded, that the molecular and chemical processes in the adult organism, take on a faulty direction under similar circumstances, and no valid objection can be urged against the probability, that degenerative changes, apart from heredity may be due to the cumulative effects of the deleterious influences that have been mentioned. There is reason to believe that those undefined evidences of sickliness unusual susceptibilities or the acquired delicacy of the constitution depend upon such causes. The general character of such a state of health certainly indicates a lowered vitality and a weakened power of resistance. From all this, the relation existing between sanitary science and etiological studies becomes evident. To trace the origen of ideopathic diseases which are so little amenable to treatment is half the victory of lessening the frequency of their occurrence.

But this subject has another side, which intensifies its importance. General and long-continued injurious influences, from whatever source, produce, not only in a gradual and subtle manner, deterioration of animal textures, but we also know of no other causes that exert the faulty dynamic tendency which eventually becomes organized and lays the foundation of an hereditary tenet— the most potent etiological factor of numerous ills of body and mind. Thus a vicious circle of causes and effects is formed. It is perhaps not too much to say that it will be reserved for sanitary science of the future to diminish the dangers from such a source by emphasizing obedience to its laws.

Since the establishment of boards of health and sanitary commissions in every civilized country, the proper machinery has been set to work to procure extensive tables of morbility and mortality. Formerly we had to look to hospitals for such contributions to vital statistics, which, for obvious reasons, were insufficient for scientific and practical purposes. It is evident that statistical results gain in value in proportion to their number and accuracy. But even the compulsory ordinances of governments and municipalities fail to accomplish the intended object without the hearty and conscientious co-operation of the general practitioner. A vast amount of information of incalculable value would be obtained if some of his time and labor could be enlisted in collecting materials in relation to topography, climate, soil, variations of temperature, influence of the seasons, the effects of different occupations on health, and the like.

The general practitioner enjoys peculiar opportunities to correct popular prejudices in relation to sanitary rules. Among a large number of such erroneous beliefs, the dread of the night air calls for especial reproof, as it not only prevents proper ventilation, but it also discourages out-door life during that part of the 24 hours when most people can conveniently indulge in it.

The enormous abuse of cathartic medicines cannot be too much deprecated as an unsanitary habit. These remedies are swallowed for the most trifling ailments and not unfrequently from sheer apprehension of some imaginary disorder. Druggists sell tons of them over the counter, probably for the benefit of the market people. According to popular pathology nearly all diseases can be run off by the bowels. That the habit of immoderate purgation is harmful does not seem to enter the mind of unprofessional people. There are few physicians who cannot recall cases of typhoid fever that were greatly aggravated by the untimely purgation during its early stage.

There is a growing conviction among sanitarians that the protective effect of disinfectants is much overrated, and that more efficient means are often neglected through the illusory expectations to which they give rise. It has yet to be shown, that even the most thorough and extensive disinfection has ever obliterated sources of infectious disease. I recollect when a student, the breaking out of a virulent type of puerperal fever in a building attached to the Blokly Hospital in Philadelphia, which was used for lying-in women. After the removal of the patients, the wards were renovated in the completest manner and fumigation kept up for weeks; but every woman who was subsequently admitted took the fever. At last the authorities ordered the demolition of the building. I believe that I express the opinion of every experienced physician, that prolonged isolation constitutes the only reliable safeguard against the contagion of zymotic diseases, small-pox not excepted. It would certainly be desirable to record the experience of the general profession in relation to the reputed efficacy of disinfectants.

The showing of vital statistics leave no room for doubt that the rate of mortality during the last decades has been considerably reduced. That this evidence of the improved condition of the average health in modern times, is due in some measure to improved methods of treatment would be unfair to deny, but it is also a proper question to ask in what these superior methods of treatment consist. Strictly speaking, they are more of a negative than a positive character. Harsh and spiculative measures have been abandoned, and a rational therapeutics has found favor which has cut itself loose from the tyranny of dogma, and the fascination of glittering but baseless hypotheses. It must be conceded that the higher rate of longevity in modern times is greatly owing to the more equal distribution of the comforts of life; people in the average being now better fed, better clothed and better housed than formally. Owing to the more general diffusion of useful knowledge, there is a more general observance of hygienic and sanitary laws. The establishment of hospitals, asylums, foster homes and dispensaries are the order of the day. Governments begin to display a jealous care of the health of the people. Protection is extended to those who for reason of their occupations run particular risk of undermining their health. The humanitarian and religious spirit of the age is constantly engaged in attempts to lesson evils and to multiply institutions of active benevolence. That part of the population which is surely to suffer in disproportionate ratio, when disease stalks about, is no longer neglected. Sanitary work, which has already done so much for the common welfare, promises to do yet vastly more if it finds an adequate response to the general interest which it tries to invoke. While pain and suffering will always be the lot of poor mortality, and for that reason, the practice of the healing heart will ever be called upon to dispense its blessings, yet the crowning glory of the medical profession is its unceasing efforts to uncover the dark and hidden places where disease lurks and spreads its baneful influences, and to devise such ways and means that guard against the insidious inroads of sickness and the surprises of death.

DISCUSSION ON PROFESSOR ARNOLD'S PAPER.

Dr. Steiner:—"I differ with Professor Arnold in regard to disinfectants, I must believe that such agents are often very valuable in restricting disease. Lime is a good disinfectant, but it should be freely used, and not, as is generally the case, sprinkled in very small quantities along the gutters of cities and towns. To get the desired effect use disinfectants in proper quantities."

Dr. McShane:—"After four years experience I have found that water is the very best disinfectant for street gutters. I have used barrels of lime, sulphur, &c., but flushing copiously with water is the best of all disinfectants."

Dr. Steuart:—"I concur with Dr. Steiner, that disinfectants are of great value. I could cite cases of the beneficial results from the use of sulphurous acid gas as a destroyer of bacteria in yellow-fever. It destroys all vital organisms."

SECOND DAY—Evening Session.

Rev. E. K. Miller, of Cecil county, presiding.

The following resolution was adopted:

"*Resolved*, That a committee of five be appointed to inquire the effects of improper or poisoned food upon the public health, and report at the next meeting of the Sanitary Council what legislation is necessary to protect the people of the State against this source of disease, especially with reference to canned fruits."

The Chair named the committee, under the foregoing resolution, as follows: "Prof. Geo. H. Rohe, of Baltimore; Dr. R. Ward, of Baltimore county; Dr. W. Stump Forward, of Harford county; Dr. W. Frank Hines, of Kent county, and Hon. Henry C. Hallowell, of Montgomery county.

Col. Jas. R. Brewer, editor of the Baltimore "Evening News," addressed the Convention on—

THE RELATIONS OF THE PRESS TO SANITARY WORK.

Mr. President and Gentlemen:—The very polite invitation of your Secretary came to me a few days ago and had I obeyed my first impulse or the pressing demands of business I should have promptly declined the task of furnishing a paper upon "the relation of the press to sanitary work." I realized at the first moment my inability to do justice to such a theme or to contribute anything of substantial value to the objects of this important convention. But I recognized and realized also the high personal duty devolving upon me and upon every citizen of flinching from no task that involved so great a public obligation as this occasion presents. Your profession is one involving great self-sacrifice and in convening for an interchange of opinions you are entitled, by right of valuable services to your fellow-creatures, to all the ready assistance, effort and compliance that any layman at your demand can render.

There is nothing so valuable to the individual or the community as health. Wealth cannot compensate for it, regrets cannot re-call it when lost. Life is a barren, a dreary possession without it. The grandest palace and the most luxurious appointments are shadowy mockeries, and the home of beauty and affection and all that makes earth elysian grow cheerless and sad with pain and sickness there. With health the humblest cot and the plainest fare are transformed; work and worry and care grow light; poverty is rich while enjoying it, and the cabin eclipses the castle in its exhilaration. Health and happiness go hand in hand; disease and misery are inseparable companions. There is nothing we prize so much when we want it; there is nothing we regard so little while possessing it. Hence individuals and cities and States can invest in no richer mine than in general sanitation, in securing and keeping a physical condition and the essentials to it that comport with the fullest freedom from physical ills. To contribute to this is the noblest work of the scientist and should be the willing effort of the journalist. Therefore it is that I recognize the duty and the privilege of the press to co-operate as freely and intimately as may be with your intelligent body, and therefore it is that I will strive to put plainly under a few brief heads the relation of my profession to your present subject:

1st. Newspapers are bound in morals and duty to do everything possible to advance the best interests of the public, which supports them. To the public there is nothing more precious and important than health. It is, therefore, as much our bounden duty to instruct in regard to the best methods of preserving the public health and to expose all that conflicts with it as to furnish information of the world's doings or the condition of the world's markets.

2d. They are selfishly interested in all questions of hygiene, since their offices are located in the hearts of cities where pulses of trade and the struggles of human energies are centred, and where the atmosphere is most apt to be polluted—spots furthest removed from the salubrious conditions that bless the residential selections. Large companies of men, employed in the various departments, constitute an aggregation in one building which demands the fullest attention to methods of ventilation and disinfection—questions intimately connected with your professional duties and study.

3d. Stretching forth their Briarean arms to every section, the newspapers touch every epidemic through their reporters and meet every plague and disease in its strongholds. Like the doctors, the newspaper men are heroes in times of pestilence, as well as war. They dare not shrink from duty. The world wants the news; the suffering and famished must appeal to mankind, and the stricken community must make known its wants and condition, and the press is its dependence. The latter has never yet flinched from duty, and as an aid to the medical profession, it has been invaluable. Every scientific explorer into the realms of disease finds an eager patron in the press, and the news-gatherers do not hesitate to stand with the scientist beside the bedside or the dissecting table to give immediately to the skilled of all nations the fullest description of discoveries made, or the promptest warnings of dangers threatened. The experiments of Pasteur and the researches of Koch are caught up and published, and the telegraph puts them at once before the civilized world for the information and guidance of you here and your co-workers everywhere. When yellow fever spread through the South, when small-pox scourged our cities, we had striking instances of professional heroism in our offices as well as in yours. The doctor administered relief and the reporter described the suffering and made vocal the famished cry for help and the prayer from fevered lips for assistance. And even now, while the plague that has ravaged the East is eating its way into the body of Europe, we have the newspaper men, sentinels on the line of danger, warning the menaced of every State and standing within the doomed circle calling for help for the afflicted and deserted.

4th. It is the mission and duty of the press to study sanitation side by side with the medical profession, and to assist it intelligently by pointing out the hot-beds where disease may find birth or be transplanted. To arouse the public to a sense and appreciation of its danger from neglect and dirt, and to convey to it the first and fullest information, as to the best means to avoid and escape disease, to explain the proper methods of ventilating buildings, and describe the newest discoveries, inventions, remedies, or suggestions in that direction, constitute the philanthropic and dutiful provinces of journalism, which responsible men in the profession readily recognize and adopt.

5th. No source of public affliction is more prolific of evil than that of adulteration. The greed of modern competition has become so great and prevalent that everything is adulterated—not only the beverages we drink and the food we eat, but the four elements themselves, the air above, the earth beneath and the waters that are under the earth—even fire, which we thought could not be contaminated, has been spoiled with bad kerosene. Many newspaper items are furnished through the attempts of foolish people to stimulate a blaze with the oil can, and the hospital is reinforced constantly with victims to these experiments, insurance companies are despoiled through them and newspapers supplied with material so plentiful that familiarity often degenerates into levity. The adulterated air is poisoned with mephitic ordors from refuse matter in cities; the adulterated earth has become, especially in thickly settled sections, surcharged with the fetid exhalations of cess-pools, and as to the water we drink, it has long ago entirely forfeited our confidence and respect. We have been told that it is the principal vehicle of cholera germs, and, in fact, all other diseases. The most eminent of investigators have given it out that the cholera microbe finds its favorite channel to the human body in the drinking water, and that it thrives in damp places. That which we have always been taught to regard as the most innocent of beverages has become to us a source of deadly disease. And, since the learned Secretary of the State Board of Health (Dr. Chancellor) pronounced our Baltimore drinking water to be inhabited by Algæ, a number of scientific and professional gentlemen have taken a turn at it and each has found in it his own peculiar, private and favorite brand of animalculæ. God only knows what our drinking water does contain, for each new professor finds a a new reptile engaged principally in breeding with the utmost industry and propagating its kind with great enthusiasm. One professor found cyclops—a horribly suggestive name—another fungi, until four or five different creatures with formidable titles were dislodged, when the stately John Hopkins University solemnly sailed in, examined for itself, and proclaimed the presence of rotifers also, said our drinking water was full of them, so, full that they gave it a bad odor in the spring. After such an authority had spoken, no prudent citizen ventured for a long time to approach his hydrant without a gun.

But if the earth is thus saturated with the germs of disease and the air permeated with the seeds of distempers and the waters inhabited by such terrible organisms and even the fire itself—which no one would have imagined could be adulterated—spoiled or intoxicated with such a villainous stimulant as coal oil, what may we expect from the other and purely artificial articles which enter into human consumption? There was a story, somewhat antiquated when I was a boy, of a deacon who was quoted as calling his servant early in the morning and bidding him "water the whisky, sand the sugar, gravel the coffee and then come in to prayers." Whether the prayers were adulterated also or only diluted by the addition of the servant I do not know. But that old deacon would have had no show in these competitive days. He would have been discounted badly. With a handful of chemicals and the city water supply at his back his neighbor would manufacture more whisky before breakfast than the deacon could find storage room for. Nor is dirt in sugar or gravel in coffee the limit of adulteration. A depraved ingenuity has found means to adulterate and vitiate almost everything we eat and to color dangerously all we wear. To show up this wickedness and to thereby restrain it has been a part of the courageous and enterprising mission of the press, and in this respect it has walked arm in arm with your profession in the service of the public health.

There are many less important and striking ways in which the press can and should and is willing to give efficient aid to public sanitation. To instruct, inform, warn and guide is its duty, and in no direction can it render such valuable service to the community as when enlisted in behalf of the public health. From denouncing loose dealing in poisons to advocating the purification of the streets; from warning against the approach of an epidemic to directing where aid is necessary for the helpless and starving; from recommending and explaining the best means of ventilation to exposing criminal neglect and pointing out the lurking places of disease; from exploding mephitic politics to proscribing indigestible food; in all of these the press has a mission certainly akin to that noble one to which you have devoted your lives.

In behalf of the press, a profession I have the honor so poorly to represent, a profession than which none displays more public spirit or a higher sense of duty at all times, I can assure this learned body that whatever you may do or suggest that will contribute to the high and holy object you have in view, you will find the press co-operating heartily and earnestly to the fullest extent of the light vouchsafed it. As health to man is a most precious boon, so health to communities is a priceless acquisition. The most useful life is blighted by its absence and without it the grandest metropolis tumbles to desolation and decay. In pursuit of such a public possession permit me to assure you that the press will second, sustain and help you with its most effective enginery now and in the future.

Following Col. Brewer's address, an interesting paper was read on

THE RELATION OF PHARMACY TO SANITARY SCIENCE.

BY J. F. HANCOCK, PH. D.

Modern pharmacy is a special and distinct branch of the medical science, with a sufficient range of research and practical work to engage all the time and attention of a single individual.

When medicine was an art unaided by science, the practice of physic, as it was anciently termed, included therapeutics, surgery and pharmacy. Hippocrates proclaimed it the most honorable of all arts.

Dr. Daniel LeClerc, in his admirable "History of Physic, or an account of the rise and progress of the art, and the several discoveries therein, from age to age, with remarks on the lives of the most eminent physicians," in his unsuccessful effort to identify the originator or inventor of physics, concludes:

"Let the knowledge have come through chance or reason, it does not exclude the concurrence of Providence, for it will always be true that physic is the gift of God, in the sense that we derive all our other blessings from the same source."

These words of the doctor remind us that all good comes from God, and our experience reminds us that all good gifts in this world, so far as we can judge, are more or less associated with evil, and it would seem that the great mission of man is to disassociate these two conditions peculiar to our being, as far as possible. This can be accomplished only through the agency of knowledge, moral force and systematic effort.

The most sacred institutions that God has planted on earth are subject to the abuse of man, and by him they are abused.

The art, (now a science,) which the great physician declared to be "the most honorable of all arts whatsoever," under our laws in the most part, is as much the privilege of the *quack* as it is of the physician and pharmacist.

Until the supreme authority of the people can be educated to a proper knowledge of the needs of the public, and shall command through the law-makers a better protection to society, *sanitary science* will be a failure to a large extent.

Under the influence of enlightened religious institutions and the increase of knowledge in the natural sciences man has much cause to hope for improvement. But since the majority of mankind have not the moral courage to embrace the former, or the intelligence to be benefited by the latter, the task must fall heavily upon the minority.

Under the best influences nine-tenths of the human race move and act under the influence of the one-tenth of thoughtful leaders. In this the work of sanitary regulation becomes more difficult in a country like ours, in which the majority rule.

In this land of boasted freedom the pauper who is influenced in his vote by kind words and strong drink, so far as voting goes, has as much weight in the political balance as the vote of the largest property-holder or the man of most extensive knowledge and moral worth.

This condition of government imposes upon the sanitarian a difficult labor, by rendering it impossible in many cases to apply sanitary regulations to the common wants of life.

As a rule, public officers do not represent the best class of citizens, and when the rule has its exceptions the individuals are frequently under obligations, and to a measure, in servitude to the political machinery by which they have been placed in power. This is another serious impediment to progress in sanitary science.

We will dismiss political causes of failure, and make a casual survey of trades, arts, sciences, and mercantile pursuits. In all these branches of human enterprise we find unworthy members, who, through ignorance and an intense selfishness, retard the march of improvement, and have their weight of influence against sanitary measures in the attempt to advance individual interests.

Human credulity, controlled by empirical influence is another enemy to progress and improvement in al true science, but perhaps more so in medicine than in any other, and since sanitary science is intimately blended with medicine in its varied application, it must be expected to meet with many enemies in the various branches of medical practice.

To deal with pharmacy as a special branch of medicine it is proper to observe that until scientific chemistry exploded the fallacious ideas of the Alchemists, there was not any need to divorce pharmacy from therapeutics but under the new dispensation of scientific medicine, with chemistry as its strong foundation, it became an absolute necessity to establish pharmacy as an independent pursuit, but to be intimately associated and identified with therapeutics and surgery.

For many ages the duties of pharmacy devolved upon the students and servants of physicians and the manipulations were crudely conducted on the premises.

In the course of time, some of the medical students established themselves as apothecaries, and in addition to the preparation of drugs and medicines for general sale, would prescribe for those of the sick who would repair to their shops. This class of medical practitioners have always held a subordinate position in the medical ranks and has been well described by Shakespear. From this humble origin has issued the class now known as pharmacists.

The first Pharmacopœia of the U. S., 1820, was entirely the work of physicians. The last edition, 1880, was almost entirely the work of pharmacists, the medical profession having only a consultant interest in the execution of the work. We now have Colleges of Pharmacy in several of the large cities, some of them having been in successful operation for a good many years. In 1851 the New York College of Pharmacy, through the intelligent eye of some of its members, issued a call for delegates from the other colleges of pharmacy. In response to that call delegates from the colleges of pharmacy of New York, Boston and Philadelphia met on October 15th, 1851, at 511 Broadway, New York.

The President-elect, Dr. C. B. Guthrie, of New York, on taking the chair, explained that the object of the convention was to adopt a series of standards for the use of the drug inspectors at our different ports, whereby their action might be rendered more uniform and satisfactory, as well as the proposal of any measure that might tend to elevate the profession and promote their interests throughout the country. Two sessions were held, during which the subject of pharmaceutical education was discussed, and it was resolved to adjourn to meet in Philadelphia the following year.

Another convention, more largely attended and representing a large number of colleges, met in Philadelphia October 6th, 1852.

From these two conventions pharmaceutical legislation assumed definite shape, and in the following year the American Pharmaceutical Association was organized, the membership of which at the present, though representing a small number of the pharmacists and druggists throughout the country, numbers 1,379 active and 29 honorary members. It includes in its membership the best element of pharmacy, and is doing a valuable work.

The standing and special committees on drug-market adulteration and sophistication, legislation, sale of poisons, furnish valuable literature each year, while the report on the progress of pharmacy notes all of special interest during the past year. This Association is growing in importance from year to year, and has done much to stimulate the colleges of pharmacy and to assist in the organization of State pharmaceutical associations. Several of these associations are in active operation and are working in harmony with the National Association. Through these influences drug laws have been enacted in several States, regulating the qualifications of those who sell drugs, and to regulate the sale of poisons. In most part the laws are in operation only in the large cities. In some cases these laws are inoperative because of constitutional defects, and in others not as stringent as they should be. The latter is the case in the good City of Baltimore. These defects exist in most cases through opposition to them on the part of mercantile pharmacists and druggists and the large number of grocers and dealers in general merchandise who are largely engaged in the sale of medical preparations.

In the midst of these difficulties the representative, or more professional pharmacists, who are in the minority, are persistently working in harmony with the better element of the medical profession, gradually elevating pharmacy to the ranks of a learned science, and thus to promote the public good. In this regard pharmacy is a valuable adjunct in the promotion of sanitary science.

To this end the National Association, colleges of pharmacy and State associations, through their standing and special committees and individual contributions, are noting ignorance, fraud and imposition from every standpoint, and exposing the same with every opportunity.

The frauds thus exposed include drugs, medicines, cosmetics, food and beverages—those things in common use in most every household. Through this influence pharmaceutical literature, in the past unknown as the work of pharmacists, is being diffused throughout the land and improving in character and quantity with each year.

All this is in the interest of sanitary science, which means not only to cure but also to prevent diseases. But all this is the work of the comparative few.

Running parallel with these earnest workers in the cause of sanitary science, and vastly outnumbering them, are those who have adopted pharmacy as a business—who place a money valuation on health and life, and depend upon patronizing manners and cheap prices as the best means to secure trade.

With these cheap dealers, or as they are now termed, cutters, the lower the prices the higher the profits.

The wholsale druggists being only merchants, will supply their customers with qualities in accordance with the prices they are willing to pay.

In many cases pharmacists seek to increase prescription trade, by advertising their establishments as cheap places where to buy the leading nostrums—a nauseous bait for an observant person, but very tempting to the nine-tenths of pharmacy customers.

Another influence to win trade resorted to by the majority in which the minority is compelled to yield, is the giving of illustrated cards advertising Mrs. Winslow's Soothing Syrup or similar nostrums, or the gratuitous distribution of illustrated almanacs, in which every amusing story and weather prognostication is followed by the advice to use somebody's *cure all*; never known to fail.

Sometimes soda-water tickets are given with each prescription dispensed, and in all cases there must be given a piece of licorice-root to each child coming in the store, on the principle that you can catch more flies with molasses than with vinegar.

Such public servants in matters of professional diversion have pharmacists become, that they have much of their time employed in matters of mere accommodation. Telephones are provided for public accommodation, and the time of the dispense frequently given with it. Directories are kept for the accommodation of the public, and much time given gratis in connection with them. Postage stamps are sold in large numbers, with the polite *I thank you, miss,* as the pay is tendered.

The neighborhood is supplied with the time of day, at every hour and fraction thereof, the departure and arrival of railroad trains, and a hundred other questions daily answered—all free to the public.

It is good to be accommodating, and a real pleasure to do a favor for one who appreciates it; but the question is, and it is a serious [query: should the pharmacist, charged with responsible duties, the reputation of physicians and lives of the people, even of a sacred character, have his time and attention so much divided by unimportant details entirely foreign to his legitimate duties?

Should the sick be kept in waiting while the healthy public are receiving accommodations? The answer comes from the *trade* pharmacist, it draws trade; the reply from the public, oh, he is so very accommodating; he is so polite, and we must patronize him for our drugs and prescriptions. The question is not often asked, is he qualified; is he correct in the discharge of his duties; is his character above reproach? No; these are unimportant questions to ask, the very fact of being in a pharmacy is a guarantee of qualification.

Let us consider the progressive pharmacist, who is ever busy and anxious to increase his stock of useful knowledge by utilizing leisure moments, under the present condition of trade. A lull comes in business. He meditates. He concludes to use his leisure moments in writing an article for the pharmaceutical journal, giving his experience on some subject connected with his business. This must be done between times, his hours of business are long, extending from 7 a. m., to 11 p. m. Trade profits will not allow a large force of assistants.

After a little thought he selects a topic and his mind moves under the inspiration of its importance; perhaps it may be a sanitary question he is discussing. In comes an urchin and posts himself near the door, the writer arises and approaches his customer with the familiar query "Well, Sonny, what will you have?" the answer—"Mr. please give me a picture card."

The dignity of his position would not allow him to swear, and prudence forbids, for should he *cuss* the little fellow, he would go home and tell his Ma and she would never again buy a postage-stamp from that rude druggist. So from prudential considerations, he gives the little fellow a card from his large store of such trash. Quiet is again restored and after a little effort the mind is put in motion and the pen glides rapidly over the paper as if to make up for lost time. Another interruption—this time a sweet little Miss; the spell is again broken—he meets her with a smile, (perhaps it is put on.) "Well, Sissy, what can I do for you?" "Mr. please put a stamp on this letter." Of course, the request is complied with, and the happy child departs, but she leaves no happiness behind. You may imagine the character of the article after it has been written. All we have to say is, that we would not like to listen to a sermon prepared under such disadvantagous circumstances.

Only this week, while the writer was endeavoring to prepare this essay, under somewhat similar circumstances, a stranger entered the pharmacy and took his stand near the door; on approaching him, he pulled from his pocket a watch, which he handed to us with the request that we would be kind enough to wind it up. Had it been any place but a pharmacy the fellow would have been wound up, but the dignity of the position would not allow anything rude, so the effort was made to wind up the watch. But fortunately we had no key to fit, so our friend was compelled to depart timeless. These facts are mentioned to show how perplexing it is to be a pharmacist with laudable ambition to serve the best public interests.

To indicate what is being done by the American Pharmaceutical Association, to advance sanitary regulations, the following remarks are taken from the report of the committee on adulterations and sophistications, 1874:

"The following report, on comparing it with the one of last year, will be found to be much smaller and apparently defective, by ignoring many important drugs. The reasons for this are mainly the following. In the first place, the previous report comprised all facts which were accessible to the committee, extending over the period from Sept., 1871, to Sept., 1873, while the present one embraces only the experience of one year; second, it was thought to be sufficient to state that, as far as is known, many of the statements made in the last report still hold true, and therefore make a repetition unnecessary. Finally, it turned out that the committee had to confine itself to whatever information could be gleaned from published papers, and a few stray items of personal observation; for, although the chairman of the committee had invited communications and contributions by sending out circulars all over the country, he is grieved to say, that, outside of the committee, he has received only one contribution.

"If the Association desires to obtain merely a report of such facts as have been published, it would be much preferable to appoint one man, who might be called 'reporter on adulterations.' But it is believed the association desires more than this. It should be its aim to stand guard over the quality of all substances relating to pharmacy, and to seek out and to denounce all frauds. To do this properly, a committee should not only gather all information obtainable from others, but should especially direct their attention to some prominent staple articles, obtaining samples at various places, and carefully examining or analyzing them. This suggestion has already been made by your committee last year, but the drawbacks connected with it were not then mentioned.

"We could undoubtedly have obtained all the samples required by asking for them over our signature, but those are not the kind we would wish.

"To represent the actual state of the market they should be purchased anonymously by a confidential and discreet agent, appointed for a certain district, say one for each State, who might send the samples to the committee.

"The want of acquaintance with members living at a distance, and the expense of procuring such samples will generally be found to be a serious drawback.

"The plan mentioned here is doubtless capable of much improvement, but, if carried out, would in course of time develop a central bureau for the detection of adulterations, with a museum and all facilities for carrying out all experiments, and furnishing in a great measure to the whole country, a portion of the benefits which England derives from its 'Adulteration Act.'

"The report is divided under three heads, embracing,

"1st. Crude drugs and commercial products.

"2d. Chemicals and pharmaceutical preparations.

"3d. Miscellaneous substances.

"Under the first head the committee report twenty-six substances impure and below the standard; under the second twenty-three preparations are reported, and under the third head ten are reported, in which are included the common necessaries of life, not strictly belonging to pharmacy. Of these, butter was found to be adulterated with lard drippings, tallow, and palm oil. Mustard was found to vary all the way from a mustard flavored with flour to flour flavored with mustard.

"Flour and bread were found to contain alum. Fifty grains of redlead were found in a can of extract of meat. Port wine was found to contain copper. Cream of tartar was was found adulterated with carbonate of magnesium, chloride of sodium, and starch; rhubarb with tumeric, &c., &c."

The same committee reported about one hundred adulterated and sophisticated articles at the meeting of the association held in Philadelphia in 1876—the centennial year.

In the report the committee say:

"We would call particular attention to the outrageous frauds practiced in the adulteration of spices and cream of tartar, the former having such a degree that the demand for worthless mixtures, with which the adulterations are made, has led to a distinct branch of industry, in which unprincipled speculators have invested their capital for the sake of gain by defrauding the public.

"When we consider that these mixtures are almost exclusively used for culinary purposes, passing from the hands of the grocer, and even a large number of dealers in drugs, who have no means, or are unable to test them, into the hands of the public, for prices which are far above their real value, we deem it high time that these vile swindlers engaged in this disreputable business, on par with a counterfeiter, should also be treated to a similar punishment, or, to say the least, be obliged to label their packages, giving composition of their contents, and that steps ought to be taken to accelerate the establishment of a central bureau for detection of adulterations, as proposed by your committee in 1874."

In this report are two articles extensively employed for table use. 1st. A fine lot of honey of fine color and flavor, styled "boxwood flowers," proved on examination to be a fine specimen of syrup made from corn starch. 2nd. Chocolate mixed with bean starch and with animal fat.

Pharmaceutical journals, of which several are published in this country, frequently expose frauds, but the facts are scarcely ever given to the public. Only this season an article appeared in the "Pharmaceutical Record" of New York, exposing the character of the soda-water and other beverages as sold by street corner dealers, and others who are ignorant of the danger to which their patrons are exposed. So pointed was this article that the Board of Health took the subject under consideration and produced what is termed in New York the Soda-water scare.

DISCUSSION ON DR. HANCOCK'S PAPER.

Dr. Schaeffer :—"I have been strongly impressed with the fact, since preparing my own paper and hearing that of Dr. Hancock, that the medical profession is largely responsible for the present relation of druggists to quackery and patent medicines. The druggist is the physicians right hand man, yet our profession extends to him no act of fellowship. We meet his efforts to protect our professional reputations and interests by leaving him to compete with others who have disgraced their calling and become mere representatives of quackery. I for one, shall use my influence to bring about the necessary and proper discrimination."

THIRD DAY---Morning Session.

C. Ridgley Goodwin, Esq., in the chair.

Prayer by Rev. Wm. F. Gardner.

The session of the third day of the Sanitary Council opened with an humorous address by the Hon. John L. Thomas, of Baltimore:

ADDRESS.

Ladies and Gentlemen : When Dr. Chancellor, Secretary of the State Board of Healh, invited me to address you to-day, I asked him what I should talk about. He said anything would do, only not to encroach on the special subjects selected by the council. He then presented me with the Fifth Biennial Report of the State Board of Health, containing the proceedings of your last year's convention, remarking, "here is something that will give you an idea of what we are driving at, and I would advise you to read it." I have read the Report, including that highly interesting portion, entitled "Vital Statistics," and I must say I was amazed, not to say paralyzed, at the astounding revelations contained in the pamphlet. I found that at least one-third of all the deaths that occur in this State in a year, could have been prevented, had proper steps been taken to check the causes that produce disease.

I thought to myself, if this is so, and I have no reason to doubt the statement, why is it our authorities do not devise a remedy to uproot and prevent these deadly diseases. The pamphlet does not so state, but I take it from reading other portions of the report, that the greatest mortality of this one-third arises from malaria and its kindred diseases.

It is stated as a fact that the industrial interests of Maryland are injured every year to the extent of over one million of dollars by malaria alone, and that the bulk of this loss is on the Eastern Shore and Southern Maryland. Two per cent. of our population, it is stated, suffer annually with some form of malaria, and one out of fifty attacked dies.

These statements are as important as they are astounding, and call for the same energetic action in removing the causes that produce them, that a conflagration would in tearing down a burning dwelling in order to save adjoining property. I was aware that the Eastern Shore had been afflicted with dumb ague some twenty-five or thirty years ago, but of late years I understood from some very reliable Eastern-Shore farmers that the dumb ague had entirely disappeared and was now sojourning in Delaware and the peninsula counties of Virginia. I know myself that Eastern Shoremen do not look as yellow as they used to, and are more sprightly in our State conventions and in our Legislatures than they used to be, and until I read this report I had it in my mind to buy a peach farm somewhere on the Choptank or the Wicomico or the Pokomoke, but as I have no very great desire to be one of the two per cent. who suffer annually from this disease, and am not particularly anxious to be one of the fifty that die annually, I have concluded to continue to buy my peaches on Light-street wharf, or from that persistent and enterprising class of individuals called "street arabs," who break more door-bells in their efforts to arouse the slumbering inmates of our dwellings, to buy their wares, than a whole peach-orchard would be worth. I have not been to the Eastern Shore for some time, but the last time I was there I noticed a raw-boned, yellow-tinted inhabitant sitting on a log fishing. He shook so much that not only the rod, but the log kept incessantly in motion. After giving him some distilled peaches that I happened to have along with me, I asked him if there was such a thing as chills and fever in that section. "N-o-o-t on this si-d-d-e the b-a-a-y," he replied through his chattering teeth, "but if you're an-x-ious to find some, I guess you can come across 'em over thar." Not being a member of the State Board of Health, I was not very anxious to come across this peculiar species of disease, but I left the Eastern Shoreman impressed with the conviction that nothing short of a health board would be able to find a dumb ague in that locality. I am glad the board has discovered a lot of it, and as a private citizen, I am in favor of draining the land and filling up the marshes so as to prevent it in the future.

I learned further from this report that the object of this society is to make men "happier, healthier and wiser." Whether men can be made happier or wiser by making them healthier, is a proposition open to discussion. Some men can never be made wise, I care not how healthy they may be, and others will never be made happy, however much they may possess of wisdom. The average healthy man ought to be happy, but unfortunately, health is not appreciated at its full value until one loses it, then the happy possessor of it becomes miserable because he cannot regain it.

But however, this may be the plan hit upon to make men happy, healthy and wise; to purify the air we breathe, the water we drink, and the food we eat. The discussion of these subjects involves many interesting and intricate points, which, although highly scientific, are of great practical value to every man, woman and child in the State. I am sorry to say, however, that the great mass of the people seem to care very little about the kind of air they breathe, and are not over scrupulous as to the kind of food they eat; and as to the water, they drink this beverage so seldom that they are not particular whether it is pure or impure. This class of men belongs to the unthinking portion of every community, but they can be taught to know what is hurtful and what is not, and as soon as they are convinced that foul air or decayed food, or food that is not properly cooked, is likely to shorten their lives, you will find that they will be as eager to follow the rules prescribed by this board, as the most scientific man amongst you.

The air we breathe, the food we eat, and the water we

drink involve questions of far more importance to us than to our grandfathers and grandmothers of sixty or eighty years ago, because the air that our grandfathers inhaled was freer and purer, the food was more plain and simple, and the water was sweeter, because it came from the babbling brook or the purling spring. Our forefathers lived in a style entirely different from us. They did not build tenement-houses for three or four hundred women and children to be huddled together like swine or cattle. There were no French flats, with bath-rooms and all the modern improvements, reaching from the ground floor up to the tenth story; but they lived in long two-story houses, with no cess-pool or sewer inside of the house. Every room had a fireplace, and none of them were heated with a furnace or steam pipes. There was plenty of yard-room, and the air had as free a circulation as it has on the top of this mountain. They did not cook their food or eat it either as we do. They had three substantial meals a day, and when they sat down to a meal they did not bolt it, but took their time to it. We take our meals whenever we can get them. Sometimes we take all three at once, and if we think we can make a few dollars by it, we do not take any until the next day.

Our hotels are not like the old-time inns and taverns, but are so large as to be good-sized villages in the number of people they hold, whilst the quantity of gas-pipe, sewer-pipe, and water-pipe they contain would reach for miles.

Then, again, people travel more than they used to in old times, and they travel fast—as they live—in the fast line or lightning express style.

Our ocean steamers are floating palaces, super-heated with steam from the engine room, and though an ocean trip may be made from eight to ten days, by the time you land on either side of the ocean you can be truly served up as fried, roasted or stewed. The old Baltimore Clipper was not so fast, but more roomy and breezy, and the ocean air untainted with coal-oil, grease and the sulphur from the smoke-stacks. Travel by rail is superb, but whilst the distance is shortened between place and place, the risk to life and limb, and the general impairment of health, is multiplied in proportion to the rate of miles traveled per hour.

I mention these things not as a complaint, because we live in a different age of the world; things and the condition of things have changed, and as we do not live as our fathers did, we must expect new responsibilities for these luxuries we enjoy, and it is the duty of every man, not only to himself but to his fellow man, to find out wherein we are deficient, and by legislation and otherwise, to supply a remedy that will cure the evils that we have brought on ourselves, and avert and prevent disaster, disease and death in our household and our neighborhood.

The day was in Baltimore when we had no waterworks, but wells, springs and pumps. The streets went up hill, then down, and were neither straight, crooked or circular, but all three. The rains descended and the floods came, and the water ran off into Jones' Falls, or the basin, just as God directed it. But modern innovation has come in and man has endeavored to improve on nature. The wells have been filled up and the springs have been walled in, and the old pump is only seen in the museum as a relic of the past. Streets have been cut down and graded, widened and straightened and lengthened. The water mounts up to the fourth and fifth stories of our houses, and this through pipes made especially to burst when the first cold snap comes on. The tallow-dip and the old fashioned oil lamp have given way to the gas chandelier and the Electric light, and the odor that permeates a neighborhood at times is as trying to the stomach as it is deleterious to health.

The question is: What are we going to do about it? Are we going to abandon all these new innovations and improvements and go back 25 or 50 years, or are we going to work to find out the causes that make our homes almost uninhabitable and our cities the abode of deadly fevers and pestilence and apply proper remedies to correct the abuses.

I say, as a landholder, as a citizen, as a humanitarian, we can't go back to olden times if we would, and we would not if we could, so that the proper thing to do is to stare stern facts in the face and grapple with the evils that threaten and have already been pointed out by scientific men who have made these matters their every day study.

The State Board of Health in conjunction with this Sanitary Convention has been organized for this purpose. These conventions are composed of men from every county in our State, who are well-known for their medical, scientific and practical attainments. The doctors make their living by giving men medicine when they are sick, but they come here without fee or reward to tell men how not to get sick, and thus voluntarily to yield up their living.

It looks to me as though the millennium was near at hand when doctors will thus assemble to tell people how not to get sick. The lawyers undertook years ago, to point out to the people how to avoid law-suits, but somehow or other, law is considered to be such a luxury that the more some people get of it, the more they want of it. But medicine is not a luxury, neither is sickness, and it is a great deal better, and safer, and cheaper not to run the risk of contracting disease, than to wait until it has come and then attempt to cure it. Hence, this is a noble work that the medical men of Maryland have entered upon, and the least the people of Maryland can do is to listen and hearken to them and help them. When you are sick you send for them and take their advice and their medicine. Why refuse their advice when you are well, and when they tell you how to keep well. If they are valuable in the one case, why not in the other?

The work the State Board of Health is engaged in, is one that is demanded by the necessities of the hour. It concerns every man, woman and child in the State, and should be countenanced and assisted by every individual, and by the State Government as a body politic.

The practical information and advice given by our State Board might have saved millions of dollars to the State and hundreds of lives, had it been taken, but our wise legislators took more interest in cattle than they did in human beings. They made large appropriations to prevent pleuro-pneumonia from infecting our cattle, but left every man, woman and child to take care of themselves. They protected the oyster beds because it provided some soft places in our Maryland navy for a favored few, but they failed to protect the oyster eaters from the cholera that is slowly but surely coming this way. In simple justice, they are the ones who should suffer when disease comes, but they never do. They are too hide-bound. Baltimore needs a new system of drainage and sewage, and this society has pointed out what ought to be done, but it is not done because it takes some money to do it. Malaria, in all of its deadly forms, lurks in the marshes and creeks, and even in some of the up counties, and this society has shown how these places can be made healthy and pure. But it is not done because it costs money to do it. Some people seem to leave every thing to God, and fold their arms and make no effort to do any thing. In other States they think that God helps them who try to help themselves, and hence they place power and money in the hands of their Health Boards to carry out the designs of the Almighty, to make man happy, virtuous and contented. Are we going to take the advice of these philanthropic men, or are we going to wait until pestilence and disease has invaded our homes, and death has carried off our loved ones, and then do what Memphis and other plague-stricken spots have been compelled to do.

Some people will say it costs too much money. Of course it costs money—everything costs money. You've got to pay to be born, and you've got to pay to live, and you've got to pay to die. You pay the doctor when you're sick; why not pay something not to get sick? I'd rather pay $100 a year for a guarantee health policy than $10 a year for a doctor, with the blue pills and castor oil thrown in. But you don't believe these things. Why don't you? You can't see that the air is impure, therefore you will not believe there is such a thing as impure air. You can smell the poison gas that comes from the sewer, the cess-pool, or the marsh, but you think it goes everywhere except into your lungs and blood. You drink water that comes out of an old well or that flows through a lead pipe, and because you connot taste the poison that is in it you drink it and think it is pure.

In this way you become a moral suicide, because people who know better tell you what the result is sure to be and how to avoid it, and because you do not believe it, or it costs something, you go on in your listless, careless way, until some day you die, and soon the balance of the family follow. Typhoid fever, scarlet fever, diphtheria, and all of their kindred are generated and diffused in this way.

Now, I say make a law to meet the necessities of to-day. Let a commission of scientific men be formed in every county in this State and the city of Baltimore, and let that commission be well paid, just as lawyers are paid for codifying our laws.

Let this commission report what ought to be done to give us pure air, water and wholesome food; what localities are infected and how the infection can be removed; to inspect our homes and tell us what alterations should be made to guarantee them from noxious gases and fetid odors; to look at our streets, and lanes and alleys, and tell us the best way to get rid of the dirt and filth that nearly half a million of human beings accumulate in a week. And when this commission has told us what to do, do not let us wait and ask our children to do it, but let us go to work and do it for them and for us. This generation of men has done great things, greater than any that ever preceded us. Do not let us stop here, but let us press on and keep doing. Our State is a garden spot; our city of Baltimore is the cheapest and best city in the land for an honest man to live in. Let us make them a sanitarium, where the rosy cheek, bright eye and the light step will give proof of vigor and health. Our Chesapeake bay brings to us every day the salt air of the ocean, whilst the Alleganies waft back into our faces their pure pine-ladened atmosphere. These are the gifts of God. Let us feel thankful for these inestimable blessings, and let us use the God-given talent of the State in devising methods of destroying disorders engendered by the trades, the traffics, the manufactories that have sprung up in our day. We receive the benefit of all these, and we must expect to pay for the evils that come with them. As the State is developed in its resources, new enterprises will spring up, and these in their turn will necessitate additional caution and remedies. If we attend to what is upon us, our children will imitate us in performing their part.

Let us not hesitate, then, to call upon the people to take this thing in hand, and the people will take up the work that you have started, and when our next Legislature meets you will find men there who have brains enough to comprehend the situation, and hearts enough, in providing for dumb brutes, to provide for man—the monarch over all. I thank you, gentlemen, for your kind attention, as well as for the honor of inviting me here. I wish you God-speed in your noble and charitable work, and trust that your society may increase in numbers and grow in usefulness, and that the people of the State may appreciate what you are doing before it is too late for anything to be done.

After Mr. Thomas' address, the following paper was read:

ASIATIC CHOLERA; ITS ORIGIN AND PROPAGATION.

BY C. H. OHR, M. D., CUMBERLAND, MD.

The recent irruption of the pestilence known as Asiatic cholera from its original habitat, and its lodgement on the western shore of the Eastern continent, has excited the anxious attention and interest of physicians, sanitarians and the general public. The fearful and sudden destruction of human life which has marked its previous history, affords ample reason for the great interest, not to say anxiety generally felt, and the apprehension as to its appearance on our continent. From what is known of its hitherto habits and progress, it must be admitted that its appearance in our midst sooner or later is not unlikely but highly probable. This fact imposes a weighty and solemn responsibility on sanitarians in and out of the medical profession, as it is no longer a matter of doubt that this pestilence is dependant on and propagated by a specific germ, the product more or less of unsanitary conditions. The time and mode of its origin is uncertain; the place of its origin and the circumstances of its development, unfortunately, are not so uncertain, although the peculiar conditions and modes of communication and spread are to a certain extent matters of speculation.

That it is a communicable disease is not a matter left in doubt by its history. How it is communicable is a matter undetermined after much debate, and the publication of many theories in regard to this point, which is one of great importance and demands earnest attention and examination on the part of sanitarians.

The object for which this convention is assembled is to devise and suggest the best means for the prevention, not for the cure of diseases, and therefore it is not an occasion for fine-spun theories and extensive displays of the literature published on this subject in regard to its pathology and therapeutics, but for the exhibition of facts the result of actual and careful observation as to its origin and propagation and thus affording legitimate data for the consideration and examination of others from which may result practical and efficient modes of prevention. To facilitate in obtaining these data it is important to have some knowledge as to the point of origin, the specific element, its apparent pabulum, the circumstances favoring its development, and its means or mode of progression of any particular disease. Upon the accuracy and completeness of this knowledge to a very great degree depends the efficiency of sanitary measures.

In regard to cholera, the time of its origin is involved in doubt and uncertainty. But fortunately for sanitary purposes, its age is of minor importance. Writers have endeavored to trace it back to the year 1629, and even to the remoter period of 1500. Others have placed it in the latter part of the eighteenth century. Whether it is entitled to an antiquity as great as either of these periods is a matter not demonstrated and can be of no importance in a sanitary point of view, as the brief and imperfect accounts of them furnish nothing which throws any light on the causes of its origin or proves them to be identical with the pestilence again threatening its march of devastation. The earliest and only reliable descriptions of this disease fix the date of its origin in the nineteenth century, (1817.) To that period we must look for our information and to the epidemics which have succeeded to it. The history of that period is from official sources, and is therefore the most reliable information obtainable.

The existence of this disease prior to 1817, may be considered as too indefinite and uncertain to be reliable, if it is not mythical. Its origin at that time with the history of its spread and devastations, then and subsequently, furnishes all the data to be relied upon, and on which must be based such measures of sanitation as can be devised by human knowledge and ingenuity for the prevention and mitigation of this pestilence.

What is known and reliable as to its origin, is that in 1817 it developed itself in the delta of the Ganges and made Calcutta its point of dissemination. From this point it spread in a northwest direction along the banks of the Ganges and reached the Caspian sea. It also descended southwest as far as the Island of Ceylon and southeast to the Straits of Malacca, and thence northeast into China. It proceeded to Bombay, southwest of Calcutta, from thence northwest to the Persian gulf and reached the shores of the Mediterranean sea. Such is a brief description of the routes it pursued in its march of destruction. Its manner or habit of migration and the time it occupied in arriving at the points named is important to a better understanding of its nature.

For this, as well as much other information on this subject, refer to the history given in the "Study of Medicine," by John Mason Good, written and published at the time of its irruption, from official reports. From this we learn that it "commenced its attack" at Icpore, in August, 1817, about one hundred miles to the northeast of Calcutta, situated at the head of the Bay of Bengal and the mouth of the western branch of the Ganges forming one side of the delta. From Icpore, "spreading from village to village, it reached Calcutta early in September, having destroyed thousands of inhabitants in its course. From Calcutta it extended to Behar, to Benares, Allahabad, Garuckpore, Lucknow, Cawnpore, Delhi, Agra, Mullra, Merat and Bavilla all suffered in succession, the pestilence not diffusing itself at once, but travelling by a chain of posts, attacking a second after it had ravaged the first." Marching all this time along the course of the Ganges "at length it reached the grand army and spread through its different divisions at Mundellah, Jubblepore and Saugor across the Deccan. It ravaged Hussingabad, when taking a course along the banks of the Nerbuddah it alighted at Tamnah. Having visited Arungabad and Ahmednugger, it spread to Poonah, and in the direction of the coast to Panwell, where it ramified north and south, crossed Salsette, and arrived at Bombay in the second week of September, 1818, twelve months after its appearance at Calcutta."

This history develops several points worthy of serious consideration. Notice its commencement in the Delta of the Ganges, in a hot and rainy season; note its adhesion to water lines; note its gradual and regular progress along these lines, leaving clear marks of its transportation from point to point along the banks of that river to and beyond Delhi; its march down along the coasts of the Bay of Bengal, southwest and southeast, to the Island of Ceylon on the west, and the Straits of Malacca on the east. In all this history three factors stand forth in bold and unmistakable prominence, to wit, *warmth, moisture and filth*. From this outbreak to the time of its great march beyond the country of its nativity in 1831 and 1832, even to the present time general attention has been led captive by the description of contagion or non-contagion; much learning has been displayed and strong evidence adduced to sustain both theories not to the determination and elucidation of the question, but to the obscuration of the important factor.

It is a communicable disease, but how communicable? There must exist an originating cause before a disease can be communicated. The most important inquiry then then is, what is that cause? The correct solution of that question may save the expenditure of much erudition and useless discussion on the less important questions of contagion or non-contagion. The cause must be ascertained by *observation* and *experience*. To observe is *to see* to experience is *to feel*. The intention of this paper is to discuss this subject from both observation and experience—I have *seen*, I have *felt*.

We have seen that the great outbreak of this disease commenced in the Delta of the Ganges in 1817, after a hot rainy season, amid filth and mud, these three seem to be essential to its production. It was, therefore, not an irrational conclusion which attributed its existence to a specific poison, and recent observations have demonstrated that the poison is dependent on a germ *sui generis*, or of a special character. We have not had sufficient observation and experiment to determine the chemical and other acts and agencies which produce or form this *germ* or poison further than that heat, moisture, and filth are essential to its generation. We have seen its predilection for water-courses, and at the same time pursuing them northwest along the banks of the Ganges, southwest and southeast along the coasts of the Bay of Bengal.

The recorded observations of that period are insufficient to determine that these movements were shaped or controlled by atmospheric currents. The evidence we have preponderates against the theory of its being controlled by atmospheric currents, though there is no room for doubt that the germ is conveyed from place to place. Personal observation is now called in for illustration.

On the 5th of July, 1853, a man appeared at my office, presenting a countenance forcibly reminding me of many I had seen twenty years before. A presentiment immediately made a strong lodgment in my mind that cholera would be epidemic in Cumberland. The man had cholera, and the next morning he was a corpse at the inlet lock of the canal. My observations in 1832 and 1833 had made me a decided antagonist to contagion and infection, my ideas on that subject remained unchanged, but the presentiment remained fixed.— Nothing more occurred for a month afterward, when another boatman came there with it. He lay in a "green grocery," near the junction of Will's Creek, on the Potomac river, on the west side of the creek. The building was a long, low, wooden barrack, half way below the level of the street, with an area about three feet wide between the sidewalk and the building.— About twelve feet from the gable end of the house was a pump, some twelve or fifteen feet deep, in a porous, loamy soil. This pump supplied the neighborhood with drinking and cooking water. The further progress of the disease will be continued by quoting from a paper published in the "American Journal of Medical Sciences" for January, 1854, merely stating first that this "green grocery" was kept and inhabited by a man named Hall:

"On the 6th of August a little girl living with Hall died, and on the 7th Hall also died of cholera. On the same day a boat-builder named Cooter was taken with the disease, and died in nine hours. He had been at Hall's part of the preceding day. He lived on the East side of Wills' Creek on Mechanic street, about a mile North of Hall's.* In the meantime several other deaths had occurred on Green street in the immediate neighborhood of Hall's place. On the 8th Kennedy and several of his family manifested the disease, they lived about fifty yards from Hall's and had had intercourse. On the night of the 9th Hazel Bell a watchman, was taken with the disease and lived until the 14th, he had been at Hall's and lived on North Mechanic street near Cooter. On the 12th Mrs. H. Beall was taken with the disease and died the same day. Four of their children were taken successively and some of them were carried into the adjoining house of Mrs. A. Simpkins, two of them died as did also Mrs. Simpkins and her child. On the 10th or 11th, Mrs. Nelson Beall went to Hazel's and assisted to move, she was taken with the disease went home and died. On the 13th her husband and two children were taken with the disease and died by the 19th. They lived out of town about a mile and a quarter South-east of Hazel Beall's on the Bedford road. No other persons in that neighborhood were taken with the disease and none of them entered the house from first to last. On 18th R. Sullivan was taken with the disease; he had been a day and night at Hazel Beall's, he lived on the Eastern Pike three-fourths of a mile from Hall's and a greater distance Southeast from Beall's. His mother and three children of a

*The Boat-yard in which Cooter worked was back of Hall's and not more than twenty yards distant therefrom, and obtained their drinking water from that pump, as did the whole neighborhood.

brother were successively taken, the mother and two of the children died. No other persons in that neighborhood were taken with the disease except two mulatto girls named Cole, both of whom had been assisting to take care of this family. During the interval from the 6th to the 18th a number of deaths had occurred along Green street, all passed off for cholera-morbus, a less number had occurred on different parts of Mechanic street and some other points. The disease had been gradually thickening, the warning voice had been raised and disregarded, the citizens generally disbelieved and most of the profession denied its existence. But the hideous fact stood at the door and would no longer be excluded. Blue Friday, the 19th, came and numbered thirteen victims, the panic became universal, the disease was diffused all over the town and consequently was no longer traceable."

In this narrative we have a local history which is a miniature picture of the general history quoted from Dr. Good. The intermediate and present history of this pestilence differ from them in no essential feature and contain lessons and instructions worthy of the best attention of sanitarians and humanitarians. It may be proper here to add another point of interest to the local history already given. The season at Cumberland had been dry and hot up to the 15th of August, when there came a very heavy rainfall during the night, flooding several of the principal streets and leaving them in the early morning covered with mud and rubbish, another of even greater magnitude followed on the evening of the 16th, which left our streets on the morning of the 17th in a much worse condition, and in two days after the epidemic had reached its climax and claimed its greatest number of victims.

From these histories, what facts are legitimately deducible as to the origin of Asiatic Cholera as we have it and as we know it? *First*, That there is one special and particular germ or bacillus, which alone can and does produce cholera, and no other disease. *Second*, That the bacillus of cholera is a native of the delta of the Ganges and does not originate anywhere else, and is the offspring of filth, warmth and moisture, with possibly certain atmospheric conditions, which favor the multiplication and development of this bacillus into an active poison detrimental to human life. *Third*, That these bacilli are capable under favoring circumstances of rapid and indefinite multiplication. Whether beyond these three factors, filth, moisture and warmth, there is any particular atmospheric condition or electric influence requisite to the development of this poison is unknown and unimportant to the sanitarian, because he has no means of combatting these latter, whilst he has the knowledge which enables him to meet successfully the former, and without their existence the germ cannot be detrimentally generated or developed. *Fourth,* That the disease is communicable by and through this bacillus only from person to person and from place to place.

The modes of communicability raises the question of contagion and non-contagion, infection and non-infection, which have largely engaged the inquiries and discussions of the medical profession, and to little profit. The *observations* of the writer have made him a decided non-contagionist, and for reasons which will subsequently appear. As to infection he was at the same time a non-infectionist, but his observations in 1853, changed him to an infectionist in the sense he shall describe it, and he prefers to use the word *communicable* as more accurate. Diseases known to be contagious, as well as those usually denominated infectious, are communicable, but the mode of communication differs. A contagious disease is communicated by the touch or contact; not so with infectious diseases. The idea has been, and yet to a great degree is, that to become infected with any disease it was only requisite to breathe the same atmosphere with the sick person; something more than mere inspiration is required to infect with cholera, the germ or bacillus must be conveyed into the stomach by swallowing it: in this way cholera is infectious or communicable.

The first case of cholera appeared in Cumberland on the 5th day of July, 1853. The subject of it lay and died out of doors on the green sward covering a small strip of land embraced within stone-walls filled up with clay, and spalls of stone used in building the locks. This afforded no nucleus for the development of the germ, the infection could not exist. A month later another case appeared, brought from a distant point, and had a more favorable location for incubation and development. In an old wooden building he lay, half buried beneath the level of the street, damp, ill ventilated and stored with bad whiskey, rotten cabbages and potatoes, mouldy codfish, &c., and the natural accumulation of filth incident to such a place, without the helpful hand of ordinary and female helpfulness. The bacillus found a congenial soil for development, and no one can say how far that pump served as a medium by which it was communicated to its victims. It incubated there, it was eaten and imbibed there, multiplied in the immediate vicinity; it was transported in the human system from that point; it was clearly traceable to that one point until it was epidemic or universally prevailing.

The infection must pass into the stomach by drink or food, or by swallowing the salivary secretion in which the bacillus has become entangled by inspiration. The bacillus may be deposited on the ground, and be conveyed by drainage into wells and fountains, and thus be imbibed into the stomach; it may float in an impure atmosphere and find lodgment upon or in food and drink, and thus be introduced into the stomach; its nucleus may temporarily be in articles of apparel, bedding, curtains, carpets and the like, materials remaining apparently inactive for a time until heat and moisture and untidiness or uncleanliness shall have *fermented* the bacillus into an all pervading, active and deadly poison. In this way it becomes an infectious epidemic.

The advance and researches of medical science have demonstrated that typhoid fever, scarlet fever, measles, diphtheria and other diseases called zymotic originate by, and are dependent on each, its own peculiar bacillus governed by its own peculiar laws. Each individual capable of unlimited development, under favorable circumstances producing its own peculiar form of disease as certainly and as surely as a grain of wheat or corn produces a stalk of wheat or corn, a peach-seed or apple-seed produces a peach or apple tree, and so each kind after its kind. The grain of wheat or corn must first find its genial nucleus before it can reproduce itself, must find heat and moisture to engender the fermentation which causes the proliferation of its cells, and thus forming its stalk, its blade, its ears and the grains which perpetuate its species. So it is with the peach, the apple, the melon and other varieties of vegetable and animal creation.

Perhaps a clearer view of this bacillus and developmental doctrine may be realized by introducing to your consideration a developed musical gentleman, who is by no means diffident or backward in introducing himself to your attention or blood. No doubt you recognize the mosquito, the offspring of rain-water and other stagnant water under favoring circumstances. You know him in his fully developed condition and able to draw your blood and poison your skin, but have you considered his origin and the mode thereof? Trace him back to his origin and observe his progress. Take a glass or pail of rain-water fresh from the clouds, having the appearance of being a clear, simple, and pure liquid, expose it for a few hours, or a day, to a hot sun and air and you will discover a minute organism developing into what is denominated a *wig-wag*, increasing in size and vigor. This organism has it laws, one of which is the law of limitation. When it has reached this it enters on a new development, and you will soon see a dark, double granular mass floating on top of the water with the empty shell or skin floating near it. The process of development goes on and clothes this mass with another form; you see body, legs and wings, and the sanguinary gentleman introduces himself with a song and manifests his affection for your blood, and gives you in exchange poison. Do you like him? I do not; but have further use for him.

You may conduct a portion of that same rain-water by filtration through a brick wall into an underground cistern from which sunlight, heat and air are excluded, and you will not find either wig-wag or mosquito! The purpose of this description is to pre-figure the origin, development and action of the cholera bacillus, and to this end it may not be inappropriate to recapitulate, in brief, the history of the disease in 1853.

It was brought by a boatman to Hall's, its place of incubation, and to Kennedy's family, on Water street; brought by Cooter and H. Bell to North Mechanic street; from them, through Beall's children, to Simpkins and several others in their immediate vicinity; to Nelson Beall, through his wife and himself; from the same place to Sullivan's. The drainage from N. Beall's was down Bedford and Frederick streets, reaching to Centre, Baltimore and Mechanic streets. From Sullivan's, the drainage was down the Eastern turnpike, to Decater, thence across the Baltimore & Ohio railroad track where it united with part of the flow from Bedford and Frederick streets, discharging itself on George, Centre, Liberty and Baltimore streets, to and beyond Mechanic street. After the deluge of the 15th, several deaths along George, Liberty and Baltimore sts. occurred on the 16th. On the evening of the next day another flood added an additional amount of filth on these streets, and the succeeding two days increased the number of deaths, which in three days (the 19th), reached their maximum; the disease continuing to claim its victims in a less but variable degree until the last of October, a period of more than eighty days. I have repeated this history and given it more in detail, because since writing what precedes it I have received and read the reports of Koch, Strauss and Roux. The observations and researches of these writers serve to confirm the convictions induced by my observations and *experience* in the epidemic of 1853, though our conclusions differ in some respects as to its origin and propagation as well as pathology.

Koch, Srauss and Roux have discovered and demonstrated the presence of bacillian organisms in the alimentary canal of cholera subjects in a manner to establish it as truth. They differ as to the individuality of this bacillian organism, both may be right and both may be wrong, but yet the labors of both are valuable and lead the way to truth. The terrors which surround cholera with so much mystery are not favorable to a speedy, clear and full discovery of the origin and nature of the cholera poison, consequently, the progress made in this direction is as yet imperfect and uncertain. The differences shown in the reports of Koch and Strauss are unimportant in a medical point of view, and the adoption of the views of either the one or the other have not much advanced, and will not retard the proper treatment of the developed disease. Not so, however, as to the condition of the sanitarian to whom it is a matter of the highest importance to have a true and full knowledge of the origin, habits and progression of the germ producing this terrible destroyer of the human race.

The investigations of Koch and his compeers have brought to light the existence of certain things suspected by some, but unknown to all, the existence of a bacillus—a discovery which is important. The error of Koch as appears from his report, was that he entered into the investigations of the subject with a mind trammelled by preconceived ideas, or not prepared to act on general principles or laws. He says, "he well knew the difficulties of the task before him, for hardly anything was known about the cholera poison or where it should be sought; whether it was to be found only in the intestinal canal, or in the blood, or elsewhere. Nor was it known whether it was of a bacterial nature, fungoid, or an animal parasite—*e. g.*, *an amœba*. But other difficulties appeared in an unexpected direction. From the accounts given in text-books, he had imagined that the cholera intestine would show very slight changes, and would be filled with clear (rice-water) fluid. From this statement it is evident that he entered upon this investigation, not with a *mind* free and desirous of finding the originating cause, but with an *imagination* beclouded with theories of the pathological changes to be found. He describes changes not found in the large majority of *post-mortems*, and not to be found generally, and not discoverable in true, unmixed cases of this disease. Had he a knowledge of the antecedents of any of his *post-mortem* subjects? Had he any assurance that they had not been previously victims of typhoid fever, or other enteric diseases not infrequent in that climate? If not, his pathological appearances must be taken with many grains of allowance. But he found the bacillus and cultivated it, and does not appear to have grasped the idea that his comma-bacillus is not the *fons et origo* of this destructive agent, a knowledge of which is the most important and and essential to enable us to stamp out this fearful pestilence. Despite the facts he elicited by his examinations and cultivations, he does not appear to have grasped fully the idea that it is a *developed* organism originating from a germ of lower condition, the germ produced by causes and circumstances not yet ascertained, but governed by its own laws of development.

Since writing the foregoing, and formulating the proposition immediately following, I have received and read in the "Medical News," an editorial account and criticism of the Berlin cholera conference, which places Koch's inferences and deductions in a more favorable light, more especially when we consider that he had to deal with second-hand manufacturers. The discoveries made by Koch and his colleagues are very important and will be used in support of the following propositions.

Epidemic, spasmodic, or Asiatic cholera is caused by a *germ* having its origin in, or being indigenous to the Delta of the Ganges; that this germ passes through various stages of development to the bacilian form, in which form it may be and has been found to exist in cholera subjects. That this germ, in its different stages of development may, and can be transported from the place of its nativity by human agency and atmospheric influence, the former being the most common, and perhaps the only mode. That this germ, developed or undeveloped, is introduced into the human system by the act of deglutition of food, drink, or the secretions of the mouth and throat. That under the favoring circumstances of filth, moisture and heat development goes on rapidly and virulently. That under the opposite conditions it is less rapid and severe. That this organism, after it has thus been introduced into the alimentary canal, communicates or injects into the tissues a poison of the most deadly nature, developing all the symptoms which constitute the disease known as cholera.

The difference between these propositions and those of Koch, is that they commence with his seventh proposition, or the original fountain and agent, tracing it through different stages of development, up to the condition of his comma-bacillus, according to the laws of development. The second and third of his propositions have no sanitary importance, and in this respect his fourth is incomplete. His fifth is very important and demands a further and more particular investigation and demonstration before it is permitted to be accepted in a sanitary point of view. That the comma-bacillus after it has performed instructive mission, may be like the butterfly or the locust after it had deposited its larva is possible, and would it not die without drying. But an all important question here suggests itself, for the consideration of the sanitarian; may there not be found in the dejecta and accompanying the bacillus as with the butterfly a larva capable of reproducing its progenitor and attendant evils? His sixth proposition may be true, but it is unsafe; under my observation beer, lemonade and vinegar have reproduced the disease in convalescents, and that the gastric juice destroys the baccillus, or its poison is a proposition that may well be questioned by any one who has had to deal with it as an epidemic. To *Virchoro's dictum* of "not proven" may be added *not to be proven*. If such were the fact, nine out of every ten who have the disease would escape unless this mode of destroying the bacillus sets free the poison which develops the disease, and lacto pepsin proves to be a most salutary agent. His seventh proposition is sustained by the entire history and observations of all writers on the subject. The eighth and last of his propositions is of the highest importance to the medical practitioner, and contains the all important fact on which to build up a successful plan of treatment in the stage of collapse and the one which deserves the most serious consideration of sanitarians, to wit, the generation or evolution of a *specific poison*.

It may be proper to say, that my first impressions in regard to cholera were based on reading an earlier edition of Good than the one quoted from, say 1822-23. In that edition were related some incidents important in this connection which have been omitted by the editor from the latter editions, and which, added to my observations in 1853 with subsequent reflection, induced the adoption of the theory contained in my seventh and last proposition, as also intimated in the eighth and last of Koch. The incidents referred to as related by Good are, that in one of the towns of its birth-place and in its first epidemic outbreak a tailor was found sitting cross-legged at his work dead; another, that a son of Crispin was found sitting, work in hand, dead on his bench. In 1853, during the cholera epidemic in Cumberland, several similar cases occurred, less sudden, but clearly indicating the same facts and resulting in death in less than two hours. One instance, only: Passing along Liberty street a man of stout, robust build, just about to enter his house, hailed me, said he was feeling very badly. He asserted there had not been either *ejecta* or *dejecta*, and yet the seal of Azrael was stamped on his brow in characters as unmistakable as I had ever seen. In an hour and a half he was dead. Reflecting on these incidents, the doctrine of poisonous causation was fixed on my mind, and the next day a plan of treatment based thereon was adopted in practice, and the success which attended it has, to my mind, settled the correctness of a poison as the causal factor. The experiments of Koch, in the cultivation of the bacillus in gelatine, indicate the action of a poisonous ferment on animal tissue. The fact that he was unable to communicate by inoculation with his comma-bacillus seems to indicate, also, that the factor is a poison evolved during the development of the germ.

The intent of this paper was not to treat this subject in a medical point of view, but to furnish the sanitarian with matters for investigation, which might result in ascertaining the cause, and to devise efficient means of prevention. The province of medication has not been invaded farther than was deemed requisite to deduce the points for sanitary investigation and practice, and will now be concluded by rehearsing the points deemed important in this respect, to wit: Cholera results from a germ indigenous to, and originating in, the Delta of the Ganges; this germ may be a cryptogam, an ameboid, bacteroid, or fungoid; that it is developed to a bacillian form; that during the period of this development it generates a specific poison deadly to the human system; that it is conveyed in some of its stages of development into the stomach by deglutition; that it is conveyed by human agency from the place of its nativity, and that filth, moisture, and warmth are essential to its development into activity.

I may not conclude without acknowledging my indebtedness to the kindness of Dr. J. M. Toner, of Washington, for furnishing me with the use of a copy of "Good's Study," and to Dr. F. S. Elder, of Indianapolis, for a copy of the second annual report of the Indiana State Board of Health, from both of which I have derived great "aid and comfort." That report shows an example of legislation worthy of the imitation of every State, and furnishes much matter worthy of the consideration of sanitarians.

THE DISPOSAL OF OUR DEAD.

BY ST. GEO. W. TEACKLE, M. D.,

Member of the State Board of Health.

The last breath has been drawn, and the spirit of the loved one has departed from its tabernacle of clay, and that which but a short while since was activity and motion now lies in the "profound, tranquil sleep of death." Here, then, seems to begin the final rest of the body, but, in reality, an activity of another character has already begun—sometimes even many hours before the spirit has departed. And what is this new activity and what its object? It is but one of the many examples of the economy of nature. The body having served as the abode of the spirit, and administered to its daily necessities, nature immediately commences to remove it. and at the same time to utilize it as food for the vegetable kingdom in the form of carbonic acid, gas, water, ammonia, and earthy elements. "This she does by chemical and physical agencies, resulting in decomposition and decay, with their repulsive and offensive attendant putrescence." To all of us, I admit, the hardest trial we have to endure is to give up our dear ones, and the first impulse is always to cling to the dead form, though in reality so little like the same in life; but the offensive results of decomposition compel our nature to assert itself, and every one cries out, "Remove my dead out of my sight."

All people, from the earliest history, have sought different means and devices to accomplish this purpose, and at the same time to protect them from wild beasts by putting their dead into caves and crevices of the rocks, and closing up the entrances with piles of stones. Some have tried to preserve the natural condition of the body as long as possible by mummifying and embalming, but what failures they proved, so far as retaining any personal resemblance to the deceased! Why, even a photograph taken immediately after death gives but a poor idea of the real appearance of the individual when alive. I will not shock the sensibilities of my hearers with the horrible and revolting details of the different stages the body undergoes before nature has accomplished her purpose of reducing it into its original elements. Any one who has curiosity upon the subject may easily be gratified by visiting any dissecting-room, or by viewing a *post mortem* a week or ten days after death. From a sanitary standpoint our present mode of disposing of our dead is absolutely defective. It is a well-established fact, which nobody, I think, will dispute, that localities in the immediate neighborhood of crowded cemeteries are unhealthful, and that the wells and springs flowing from burying-grounds have been frequently found absolutely dangerous for drinking purposes, and epidemics have been traced to the use of the same. I myself, for several seasons in the early spring months, have noticed a sickening and offensive odor in the neighborhood of one of our largest cemeteries, which odor has been investigated several times by both State and city authorities, and was supposed to have its origin in certain distilleries and factories in the vicinity, but which, though these establishments complied with the orders of the authorities, was only partially rectified.

The large mortality and sickness of armies during a campaign is undoubtedly due to the large amount of animal matter, in all stages of decomposition and putrescence, affecting both the air and water. This is also true when epidemics occur. A large number of persons are buried daily, and frequently, in fear of contagion, it is very imperfectly done, and it is a fact that earth has been taken from the top of a grave so thoroughly impregnated with noxious gases as to be absolutely dangerous. Two other objections I urge as against the present system. I refer to being buried alive (which I am happy to say must be very infrequent in ordinary times, but which does sometimes occur during great epidemics). Another, which I am led to believe is of a very much more frequent occurrence than any one supposes, is that of grave-robbing. This, I believe, is practiced not only in our potters' fields and asylum burying-grounds, but also in our best and wealthiest cemeteries, as proved by several cases reported in the daily papers during the last year or so. The plan is to ship the bodies stolen to other cities. The business is undoubtedly a lucrative one, judging from the high prices students have to pay for the bodies. "What, then, is it proposed to substitute for the custom of burial?" "The answer is easy and simple. Follow nature's indications, and do the work she does, but do it by the aid of science and education, more thoroughly, more rapidly, and without endangering the health of the survivors."

As an example of the practical and beneficial results of thus aiding nature, I have but to mention a case of severe frostbite; where, for instance, a foot has been entirely killed by extreme cold. Nature sets to work to get rid of the defunct member at once, by forming a line of demarcation between the dead and living flesh, but how slow the process, how offensive, and what a drain on the system of the individual, and how often it fails through blood-poisoning by absorption from the putrescent mass! The surgeon, by a few well-directed strokes of the knife, in as many minutes removes the dead and dangerous member and leaves nothing but healthy flesh and bone. The problem is this: "Given a dead body, to resolve it into carbonic acid gas, water, ammonia and its mineral elements rapidly, safely and not unpleasantly," and the answer is, "a well-constructed furnace, in which the body can be rapidly reduced to carbonic gas, water, ammonia and mineral elements; the fumes, being carried through another furnace, can be thoroughly eliminated of the disagreeable odor necessarily arising from burning flesh, and will soon be consumed by the vegetable kindom, and the remaining pure and inocuous residue may be disposed of according to the individual taste of the survivor." And here I would make the suggestion of two ways. First. The utilitarian.- Spread them on the ground, and thereby return to mother earth her due. Second. Or place them in a metallic box (which for the ashes of an ordinary body would only be 12 by 8 inches) and bury in cemeteries and erect tombs as now.

As for the practical working of cremation, I will state that Prof. Siemens has perfected a crematory furnace in which a body weighing 227 pounds has been reduced in fifty-five minutes, the residue weighing five pounds. I believe that there are many who, if they could be convinced of the fact that cremation is practical, would not hesitate to advocate it, and would prefer it if the necessary appliance were convenient to their homes. To show that it is thoroughly practicable I will read a letter kindly furnished me by Benj. F. Horwitz, Esq., giving a detailed account of the cremation of the body of his father-in-law, Prof. Gross, of Philadelphia, one of the noblest and most accomplished surgeons of the world.

37 LEXINGTON STREET, BALTIMORE, Sept. 16, 1884.

Dr. St. George W. Teackle,
Member of the State Board of Health:

My Dear Doctor: I willingly comply with your request that I should give you a detailed account of the cremation of the late Dr. Gross, of Philadelphia, at which I was present, and I do so in the hope that my account may tend, to some extent, to popularize cremation, which, in my judgment, is the only proper mode of disposing of a dead human being. I have often talked the subject over with Dr. Gross, and our conclusion was that, for every reason, sanitary as well as sentimental, the incineration of the body, so long practiced by the ancients, should be revived and generally adopted in this enlightened age. Many of these reasons are embodied in the valuable paper which you have prepared on the subject, and which, therefore, I will not here repeat. It can cause no surprise that Dr. Gross, who was as good as he was great, and who made the most tender humanity the handmaiden of the highest surgical skill, should have desired by his example to teach in death what he had so long advocated in life, and what seemed to his refined sensibility the only mode of disposing of the dead, which was not calculated to shock the living.

I had often promised Dr. Gross that if I outlived him, as, considering the disparity of our ages, it was likely I should, that I would accompany his remains to the Lemoyne Crematory, the only one at the time of Dr. Gross's death, and I believe now, in this country. Dr. Gross died on Tuesday, the 6th of May last. The funeral service of the Episcopal church, of which he was a member, was held at his residence, in Philadelphia, on Wednesday afternoon the 8th, and that night, at 9 o'clock, the little party, consisting, beside myself, of A.

Haller Gross, Esq., a son of the deceased, Medical Director P. J. Horwitz, United States Navy, Mr. Bringhurst the undertaker in charge, and Charles Draper, the faithful colored body servant of Dr. Gross, started for the crematory, which is located on the top of a beautiful elevation, not inaptly called Cremation Hill, lying a short distance beyond Washington, a flourishing town situate in a fertile valley of Western Pennsylvania, about thirty miles west of Pittsburgh. The next morning, Thursday, the 8th of May, at about 11 o'clock, we arrived at Washington, having been joined at Pittsburgh by my son, Eugene Horwitz, the grandson of Dr. Gross. We found everything in readiness for us at the depot; a hearse and two carriages awaited us. Dr. Gross' written instructions required that everything appertaining to his funeral should be conducted in the simplest and most unostentatious manner, and that only the members of his family should be present at his obsequies. Many persons, whom the ever busy telegraph had informed that Dr. Gross' remains were to arrive, some of them his former pupils, were at the depot for the purpose of showing their respect and joining the cortege. A little time was occupied in politely requesting those persons to withdraw. After this was accomplished we drove through the town, ascended the hill and found ourselves, at about noon, in front of the crematory, an unostentatious one-story building, surrounded by well-kept grounds and a neat railing. It was simply a perfect spring day; the sun shone brightly, the air was balmy, the birds were twittering in the trees and the lowing herds were grazing peacefully on the hill side. All nature, in fact, seemed to be imbued with the calm and benign spirit which had so recently left the body of the distinguished dead.

"The building was divided into two apartments, one a reception or rather preparation room and the other containing the furnace and retort. The coffin was taken from the hearse by Mr. Gross, Dr. Horwitz, my son and myself, acting as pall-bearers, and placed on a table arranged for its reception in the preparation room. Every one then withdrew except the undertaker and the body servant. The coffin was opened, the body taken out, disrobed and placed in a sheet saturated with a preparation of alum, intended to prevent the singeing or scorching of the body as it was placed in the oven. The body was then placed on what is called an iron crib, that is, an iron frame, with small bars about four inches apart running along its entire length, which is about seven feet, and it stands on feet about six inches high. The oven door was opened, the crib, with the body on it, was run in, the door closed and the process of incineration at once began. The Lemoyne Crematory, which is of rather a primitive character, costing for the building retort, furnace and everything complete, $1,500, requires twenty-four hours heating before it is in a condition for the incineration to properly begin; this, in Dr. Gross' case, had been attended to before our arrival, consequently there was no delay. The incineration began as soon as the door of the oven closed. About two hours and a half after the body had been placed in the oven Mr. Dyer, the superintendent, informed us that the incineration was complete. We looked through a small hole, placed in the door of the oven for the purpose of enabling the superintendent to watch the progress of the reduction to ashes, and found his report to be correct. There was not a vestige of the body to be seen. Mr. Dyer then informed us that it would require twelve hours for the furnace to become sufficiently cool to permit the removal of the crib and the gathering of the ashes. We were present, either in the building or in the grounds surrounding it, during the entire time occupied by the incineration, and there was not the least unpleasant odor, or anything calculated to shock, in the slightest degree, the tenderest sensibilities of the most refined human being. On the contrary everything passed off in such a way that death and burial seemed to be robbed of more than half their horrors. We left for Washington about 3 o'clock in the afternoon, after seeing the crematory locked, and giving instructions to the superintendent to permit no one to enter until our return the next (Friday) morning at 10 o'clock.

"We returned at the appointed time and found the furnace sufficiently cool. The crib was removed and then the ashes, which had fallen through it to the bottom (which is made of fire-bricks) of the oven, a distance of about six feet, were carefully gathered, placed in a metal receiver, which was then covered and carefully and firmly soldered. The ashes, which in fact were nothing but carbonate of lime, were of course as clean and nice as pebbles freshly gathered from the seaside, all impurity and everything calculated to make a dead body horrible and disgusting having been resolved into their original elements. Dr. Gross was a man six feet two inches in height and well proportioned; consequently his ashes weighed about seven pounds, the average weight being five pounds. We drove away with the precious ashes in charge, all thoroughly convinced that Dr. Gross had added another laurel to the chaplet which surrounded his brow, by his advocacy in life and example in death of the revival of cremation, and thoroughly determined that we would leave directions to have our bodies disposed of after death as we had just seen his. The ashes were afterwards placed in a handsome marble urn, which was placed by the side of the coffin containing the remains of Dr. Gross' wife in the family vault at Woodland Cemetery, Philadelphia.

"In discussing the subject of cremation, I have never heard a single objection urged which is entitled to the slightest consideration from a cultivated mind. To the ignorant it would seem to antagonize the religious dogma of the resurrection of the body; but the educated know that after the lapse of a hundred, or, at most, a hundred and fifty years, a human body buried in the earth is entirely resolved into its original elements, and there is, in fact, not a vestige of it left. The cremated ashes last for ages, as is shown by those more than eighteen hundred years old in the Columbaria at Rome. There would, therefore, as a matter of fact, be more left of a cremated body, when the last trump sounds, than of one buried in the earth, unless it should happen to be buried shortly before the final resurrection.

"Again, expressing the hope, my dear Doctor, that I may by this communication do something toward popularizing cremation, I am, very truly yours,
BENJ. F. HORWITZ."

DISCUSSION ON DR. TEACKLE'S PAPER.

Dr. Rohe: "I do not wish to argue against cremation, but simply to question certain statements made in the paper just read. I have no knowledge of the fact, and I believe there is no evidence that residence near a properly conducted cemetery is unhealthy, or that disease has ever been propagated in this way. Cremation is too slow and too expensive a process. The crematory must first be heated and after the incineration is complete, an equal time must be allowed for cooling. It is certainly not an economical method."

Dr. Stewart: There are cases on record where drinking wells near cemeteries have been polluted, notably one near Mecca, which was found to contain cholera microbes."

Dr. Teackle: "The expense attending the actual cremation of the body of Prof. Gross was $25."

Dr. Chancellor: "I am glad that my colleague, Dr. Teackle, has had the moral courage to 'speak out' on this subject. It cannot be denied that to bury the dead in or near a city is a serious evil, and one which has been a subject of sanitary regulation from the earliest times. The ceremonies of the Jews, the process of embalming practiced by the Egyptians, the burning of the dead by the Greeks and the Ethiopians, were but sanitary measures to escape the dangers arising from the process of putrefaction. Among the Romans the prohibition of inhumation in towns was fully established. '*Hominem mortuum in urbe ne sepelito neve urito,*" was a law renewed by each succeeding form of government. The Parliament of Paris in 1765, took a stand against the abuses of the then existing system of burying the dead, and in the preamble to their decree on the subject, it was asserted that 'daily complaints are made on the infectious effects of the parish cemeteries, especially when the heats of summer have increased the exhalations.'"

"We may endeavor to gratify personal feeling, prompted by affectionate remembrance, and try to keep together the frail fabric of the dead; we may swathe it in cerements, confine it in metal, wood or stone, build it into vaults and heap pyramids upon it, but all in vain. It is the law of nature that its elements shall pass again into the living world and so circulate forever. Our efforts, therefore, should be to expedite the processes of nature, not to check or retard them. There should be no burying in metallic cases or in vaults; all dead bodies should find a resting place *in the soil*, and a speedy intermixture with the earth, at such a distance from habitations that the putrefactive process of the grave may not exercise its baneful effects upon the living; *or they should be cremated at once.*"

The second paper of this session was entitled:

THE PLUMBER IN HIS RELATION TO SANITARY MATTERS.

BY JAMES MILLER, PLUMBER.

It is not our object to discuss the matter of plumbing and its sanitary objects and relations, but to enter a plea for the much abused plumber himself.

In no trade or profession, not excepting the medical profession, is there so much quackery or want of knowledge among its members as those professing to be plumbers, (as is now understood by that term.)

A plumber is entrusted with the important matter of the drainage and ventilation of modern dwelling-houses: This is a subject of the most vital importance to those who occupy them; work that should be done carefully by persons educated in the practical details of that branch of mechanics, as it is well known that many of the zymotic diseases are engendered by the contamination of the air of dwelling-houses by the escape of the gases generated by the decomposition of fecal and other organic matters, through the imperfect arrangement of the drainage system.

In order that the arrangement shall be made perfect it is necessary that the plumber should be familiar with the nature and mechanical action of those dangerous gases. It is not only necessary that he should have the requisite mechanical skill to put together the pipes used in the construction of the system of drainage but he should be sufficiently acquainted with natural laws to intelligently provide for the proper disposal of those gases to prevent the possibility of their contaminating the air of the dwelling.

A gentleman with his family occupies one of our modern dwellings, and one or more of its members is taken with typhoid, diphtheria or some disorder of this nature, which the physician, upon being called, is satisfied has been caused by impregnated air, water or improper circumstances of some nature; an inspection of the bath-room usually reveals at once to the olfactory organs that alterations or repairs are needed to the plumbing, the physician prescribes for the patient and recommends that the plumbing be looked to; the head of the family, if he be a tenant, notifies the owner of the premises, or his agent, and very often one of those cheap so-called plumbers is called upon to remedy the defects; he goes to the house, makes some trifling change, consumes some time and makes his charge, frequently without having accomplished any good whatever; if the complaint of the tenant is stopped for the time the landlord is satisfied. If it be a gentleman occupying his own fine residence the same case is frequently the result, except that he will employ an architect, whose profession it is to know everything connected with the proper construction of buildings, even to the minutest details of all the work. He will pro-reed to make plans and specifications for the improvements with the greatest care. It is the practice to call for bids for the work, based on these plans and specifications. Now the plumber who secures the job, even if he gets a price that will justify him in doing the work in a first-class manner, finds that he is hampered by the specifications of the architect which, as he gets into the details of the work, are found impracticable, for reasons not foreseen by the architect or even by himself; he goes to the architect and explains the difficulty, and for his pains is told to put the specifications in his pocket and see that he observes them. The result is *very* often *very* bad work. The moral of all this is that the competent and conscientious plumber is, by long observation and experience, the proper and only person to have charge of the drainage system of dwellings as it is not possible to formulate any fixed sanitary regulations that will be applicable in all cases and under all circumstances.

We must acknowledge, with a certain sense of humiliation, but nevertheless it is a fact, that the great majority of plumbers, so called, are men of not even ordinary intelligence, and yet those men are daily employed in the construction of the drainage system of your dwellings. And why is this so? It is due to the modern cheap style of constructing dwellings, and what would seem to be the indifference of the public to this important subject.

A capitalist wishes to improve an unproductive piece of ground; he employs an architect to make plans for one or a number of houses, the chief object being to make a paying investment. In order to do this, the houses must be erected at as cheap a rate as is consistent with the necessary ornamentation and display to make them saleable. The plans and specifications prepared by the architect are offered to contractors for competitive propositions, the lowest bidder usually securing the contract; naturally this contractor goes into the market to secure the lowest bids for sub-contracts for the details of work, including the plumbing, and, as a result, this most important work is done by incompetent, cheap labor, with imperfect, cheap material, no regard whatever being paid to the proper ventilation or sanitary features of the work, everything being glossed, as it were, on the outside—that important part of the work, the part hidden from view, being done in the most scamped manner possible. The result of this practice has entailed many annoyances and expenses on the unfortunate occupants of those houses, and the whole fraternity of plumbers have come in for a great amount of censure and abuse from the public.

A point that we wish to impress on your minds is: That there are responsible and conscientious plumbers, with a knowledge of their business which would not permit them, under any circumstances, to have such imperfect work done, but who have had to share in the general abuse heaped upon the craft by the public.

A little more than one year ago, in seeking for a remedy for this evil, certain members of the fraternity formed themselves into an association for the general improvement of the status of the plumbing business, to accomplish which it was deemed necessary to have a system of sanitary regulations adopted by the municipal governments and inspectors appointed to enforce a compliance with the same.

In order to make the system more effective, it was concluded to form a National Association, to which end a convention of delegates from local associations was held in New York one year ago last June, and means were there discussed for some protection to the legitimate members of the craft from the operations of the incompetent and unscrupulous men, generally not plumbers, but carrying on the plumbing business, who are the chief cause of the very imperfect work from which the public are suffering.

One of the methods adopted to accomplish this end was to institute a system of registration, meaning of course, that there should be some sort of an examination to test the competency of applicants, if this method was carried out there would be not more than about one-third as many members of the plumbers craft as there now are, which would be an abundantly sufficient number to do all the work to be done, but so far it seems to be impracticable to get a sufficiently stringent law for this purpose.

One object that has been accomplished has been the obtaining of a municipal law in most of the large cities for the appointment and maintenance of an inspector, who, though not properly backed with authority, is accomplishing a vast amount of good.

Though his powers are far too limited, yet the sanitary inspector of Baltimore has found in his official capacity, a great amount of work which he has been forced to condemn, as has been proven by occular demonstration here to-day, the exhibits being but a few of the many glaring defects met with in every day life by the plumber.

The work having been done without seemingly to have the slightest regard for the health, or even comfort of the occupants of the houses; indeed, in some instances even where fair prices were being paid for the work, the most lamentable ignorance of sanitary laws was displayed.

The necessity for the enactment of proper laws, and their rigid inspection and enforcement, is a matter, in our estimation, of the most vital importance.

VACCINATION AND RE-VACCINATION.

Dr. Connelly read an interesting paper on the above subject which elicited considerable discussion.

Dr. Piper moved that the paper be referred to the Committee on Legislative business, which motion prevailed and the paper was accordingly referred. Continuing, Dr. Piper called attention to the necessity of requiring all children entering public schools to exhibit unmistakable evidences of having been properly vaccinated. He thought there should be some legislative action in reference to the matter.

Dr. Scott, of Hagerstown, offered a resolution which was adopted thanking the State Board of Health for its efforts in behalf of the Public Health, and asking that the next Legislature will strengthen the hands of the Board so that it may take the necessary steps to secure further advancement of sanitary matters.

The chair appointed the following a committee to act with the State Board of Health in placing certain matters before the Legislature: Dr John Morris, Dr. Jackson Piper, Dr. Lewis H. Steiner, Dr. Charles A. Leas, Hon. Wm. Pinkney Whyte and Wm. Dannett.

The Convention took a recess of half an hour, and, on reassembling, was addressed by Mr. William Dunnett, plumber, of Baltimore.

Mr. Dunnett illustrated by diagrams defective methods of plumbing, and exhibited specimens of defective work. He remarked that there were quacks in his business, as well as in the medical profession, and that honest and capable plumbers had to contend with these ignorant people, who could afford, owing to their inferior work, to under-bid, and, as the public knew no better, they often employed these quacks, to the detriment of health and comfort.

Dr. Chancellor, in referring to Mr. Dunnett's address, said that, as a practical dissertation, it was second to no paper which had been read. It shows that the plumbers are not only desirous, but anxious, to render their part in the good work of sanitation, and they should be encouraged. He was very much obliged to Mr. Dunnett and other plumbers for coming to this meeting and showing such an interest in the proceedings.

Dr. Hancock asked Mr. Dunnett if he had found many water-closets imperfect.

Mr. Dunnett replied that he had frequently seen water-closets very defective, due either to the work of ignorant plumbers or to the fact that the owners of houses would not pay what was necessary to enable the plumber to do the work properly.

Following the discussion on Mr. Dunnett's remarks, a paper was read on:

IRRIGATION AS A PROCESS FOR PURIFYING SEWAGE.

BY GEO. E. WARING, JR., M. I. C. E., NEWPORT, R. I.

The occasion for the preparation of this paper was the publication by Dr. Chancellor, Secretary of the State Board of Health of Maryland, of a reply to a paper of my own read before this Convention in 1883.

I pass without comment all of Dr. Chancellor's references to myself, thanking him for his praise and disregarding his blame.

I pass unnoticed also the whole discussion concerning the Liernur system of sewerage. There is nothing connected with this system which to-day constitutes a live issue in American sanitary improvement.

I cannot pass without comment Dr. Chancellor's remarks concerning the purification of sewage by irrigation. The question of sewage disposal is one of the most important of all with which we now have to do. Boston, Philadelphia and Baltimore, together with many smaller cities, are confronted to-day by no such serious problem as that which relates to the ultimate disposal of the enormous flood of foul sewage by which they are pestered and whose volume and whose menace are increasing year by year. I have for many years given attention to the various suggestions as to the solution of this problem: I have tried to take nothing for granted; to accept no man's statement or theory without examination; and to verify for myself and on the ground the exact truth or falsity of the claims of those who have built the best works or have affirmed their success.

My first examinations were made in England in 1872. From that time to this, I have given unceasing, careful and conscientious attention to every fact or incident bearing on the question.

My general conclusion was stated in my former paper in the sentence which Dr. Chancellor makes the text of much of his comment. I said:

"The statement is made that an attempt has been made to remedy this evil in England by using sewage for the irrigation of land, or rather by using land as a means for the purification of sewage. This attempt has not only been made, it has been wonderfully successful wherever applied, and not only in England but on the Continent as well."

This was the deliberate conclusion of one who has had opportunities for obtaining information, who has used his opportunities faithfully, and who believes that so far as he is capable of looking at the facts and determining their bearing, his conclusion is the right one. I cannot allow a conclusion so formed, and of such importance to all who live in towns, to be set aside even by Dr. Chancellor, without making an effort to show that in this case he has exercised less than his usual perspicacity; without showing, if I can, that in this single instance, and by exception, his statements and his opinion are of value.

To tear down the fanciful barrier with which he has attempted to obstruct the path of sanitary progress, which he has thrown up and propped with a few lightly turned sentences, I must tax your patience with a somewhat full statement of the case, which, however, I shall try to make as short and interesting as I can.

The fundamental principle always to be borne in mind is this: Organic matter, however foul in kind or in condition, is destroyed as a source of impurity when reduced to inorganic compounds; the process of reduction is a process of oxidation or nitrification; in all forms of such reduction, except actual burning in a fire, it is probable that the most effective if not the only agents of these processes are the bacteria of decomposition which attack all destructible matter, and which work their end by a process of more or less active putrefaction, that these bacteria can work effectively, i. e., can be reproduced and live and die rapidly, only in the presence of free atmospheric air or oxygen, and that there is no better field for their work than in the interior of a porous soil containing organic matter. When we wish to destroy the organic parts of sewage and so to purify its water, our best means will be to pass the sewage through a filtering porous mass, to the surface of the particles of which its impurities will attach themselves, and where they will be attacked by destroying organisms, working under the influence of the air by which the moistened particles are constantly surrounded.

Or, to state the case more simply, the best way to purify sewage is to pour it upon, or introduce it into, the surface of a porous soil adequately drained at the bottom. The sewage will settle by gravity; its impurities will attach themselves to the surfaces of the particles of the soil; as the water falls away, air will enter and take possession of the spaces it has occupied; the bacteria, always active in a fertile soil, serve as the medium for the destruction of the organic matter by the oxygen of the air. They feed, that is, on the impurities presented to them, and the life that their feeding sustains involves the complete oxidation or nitrification of their food. As a result, the water of the sewage is purified by filtration, and the filth of the sewage is reduced to inoffensive and innocuous elements by decomposition.

The greatest good that can be done to the community in this connection, will be to secure the most rapid possible reduction of all the filth it produces to this condition of purity. If, incidentally, we can make the newly decomposed filth serve the purposes of agriculture—and we can—of course the beneficent result is so much the greater, but agricultural utilization is only a secondary incident. The vital thing is to get rid of the filth, and this, in a proper soil we may perfectly well do, whether vegetation be growing on that soil or not.

This is the proposition which Dr. Chancellor opposed. If you will give me your attention I shall hope to show that his position is not well founded.

Dr. Chancellor, writing from his sick-bed, and not able to consult authorities, says of the Berlin Irrigation Works: "I was not permitted to visit the 'fields' myself, the interdiction, so far as strangers are concerned, being preemptory on account, it is said, of their fearful unsanitary condition. They are, as I was credibly informed, already over-saturated, and the authorities, both city and State, are bestirring themselves as to what shall be done under the circumstances. I was also informed by prominent citizens of Berlin last summer that a pestilence was feared unless speedy relief was afforded, either by increasing the area of irrigable surface or adopting another system of sewerage, and several commissions have been appointed to look into the matter."

I visited these fields in September, 1881, and found everything connected with them in a most satisfactory condition. I could not believe that they could in so short a time have become so offensive and dangerous as Dr. Chancellor said *he was informed* that they had at the time of his visit.

I sent a copy of Dr. Chancellor's statement to Mr. James Hobrecht, the chief engineer of the Berlin works. The following is a translation of his reply:

"BERLIN, *Feb'y* 20, 1884.

"Dear Sir:—Your assumptions that it would be impossible that the Estate Rieselgut Osdorf, which you had seen in such excellent condition, should, in the course of one year, have fallen into utter decay and neglect, are entirely appropriate.

"I must confess that the assertions of C. W. Chancellor appear plausible to me only on the ground that no explanation or rectification of them is expected.

"When Mr. Chancellor says that it was refused him to visit the estate, and that this measure has been extended peremptorily to all strangers, owing to the dangerously unhealthy condition of the fields, then this assertion lacks correctness.

"Not mentioning the fact that a great number of public highways cross these fields, the travel on which can never be refused at any time, by day or night, the overseer of the estate takes great pleasure in permitting any one, at all times, and especially strangers, to enter the fields, and has, prompted by a feeling of pride, never failed to show the same to intelligent strangers, and to furnish wagons, plans, and guides free of charge, that they might show the efficiency of their management.

"After all this, it seems unnecessary for me to enter any further into the details of the report of Mr. Chancellor, who, as he says himself, has not personally seen the estate, but has acted from creditable information.

"I will say that the sanitary condition of the fields is an excellent one.

"I am, esteemed colleague,
"With great respect, yours,
(Signed) "HOBRECHT."

A very thorough examination of sewage disposal works has recently been made by Messrs. Saml. M. Gray and

Chas. H. Swan, members of the American Society of Civil Engineers, acting on behalf of Providence, R. I., of which Mr. Gray is the City Engineer. Mr. Hobrecht sends me a letter he has received from these gentlemen as follows:

"BERLIN, April 3rd, 1884.

"Dear Sir:—"We wish to express our acknowledgments for the very courteous manner with which we have been received, and to thank you for your kind assistance on our visit to the sewerage and irrigation works of Berlin. We have visited the works in the city and the irrigation fields, both on the South side and on the North side of the city. We have been received everywhere with marked attention. Every facility has been given to enable us to inspect the works in all their parts. All information necessary for a thorough understanding of the works and the method of operating them has been cheerfully given us.

"Any one at all familiar with the difficulties involved in the disposal of the sewage of a great city, cannot fail to be impressed with the high degree of success which has been attained at Berlin.

"Very truly yours,
"SAMUEL M. GRAY,
[Signed]   "CHARLES H. SWAN."

I have conversed with Mr. Gray on this subject and he fully confirms the opinion expressed in this letter, that the system at Berlin has attained a high degree of success.

Dr. Chancellor is still more surprised at my statement that I had visited the sewage irrigation works of Paris and found them also successful. He says:

"This statement is, if possible, more astounding, *me judice*, than his representations in regard to the Berlin irrigation fields, inasmuch as the latter, like those of Croydon, were *for a time* looked upon with some favor, whereas the Paris fields have been a source of nuisance from the time the first regulator was laid, up to the present time, and have never been regular as a success, except in so far as they served to divert the sewage flow from the Seine, which was simply transferring the evil from one locality to another, not curing it.

"The observations of Col. Waring in reference to these works certainly do not coincide with the experience of the municipal authorities of Paris and the communities in the midst of which these irrigation fields are located."

Dr. Chancellor seems in his paper to fortify his position by important quotations from three different French authorities, the translation being made by one who was probably not an expert. One is:—"Revue des deux Mondes, 1880;" another is, "The Sewerage of Paris, by M. Villet in Revue des deux Mondes;" another is. "M. Aubry." I find the origin of all of these quotations in a single article entitled "The Question of the Sewers" in the Revue des deux Mondes for October, 1880, by Aubry—Vitet, an article written in special advocacy of a particular method of chemical purification, confessing the success that was claimed for the irrigation works, but throwing doubt upon the possibility of a sufficient extension to secure the purification of all of the sewage of the city.

The first quotation, a remark of the Director of Works, is given accurately. It is a description of the well-known foul condition of the seine caused by the sewage, at that time only about one-eighth of the flow being treated by irrigation.

For the next quotation, I find the following basis: Speaking of what it was proposed by the engineers to do in the future on an arid and remote tract behind the forest of St. Germain, and describing the conditions that would there have to be met, Aubry-Vitet says, describing the reasoning of the engineers. "The cultivators cannot fail to contend among themselves for the elements of fortune that would be brought to them in a liquid form ; and the authors of the projects insisted not without good reason on the immense advantage to the public prosperity of the agricultural utilization of the sewage. But after all, this urgency might be less active than was fondly supposed. Then again, the cultivators—this must certainly be taken into consideration,—anxious before all for the good preparation of their ground and for the success of their crops, would without doubt abstain from taking any water on certain days, in certain months, even during certain seasons. The fifteen hundred hectares of the forest of St. Germain would be a safeguard in such cases. They would form an immense overflow field for the discharge according to circumstances of all or a part of the liquid manure." He then goes on to say that the suggestion of this project created an excitement among the people; that it was a country of *villegiature* (summer residents); that this opposition was found to be a serious obstacle and it was shown by quotation from the Director of the Works that he recognized the fact that this unfortunate condition of public sentiment was aggravated by the knowledge that a temporary rise of the subsoil water at Gennevilliers had led to a law-suit between the city of Paris and the commune of that district. He then says: "In the plain, sand quarries had to be abandoned and had, little by little, transformed themselves into ponds. In the village itself, even on the public square, a large number of cellars were perpetually invaded by the water rising to a height of from 20 to 30 centimetres (8 to 12 inches). Finally, at a large factory established for many years, a water basin of old origin had its level raised a metre and a half, so high that the water covered the hand rail around which previously there had been dry walking." He says: "The engineers affirmed, it is true, that this disastrous rise of the subterranean water had for its only cause a high flood of the Seine." This opinion, Aubry-Vitet questions, but it has been fully sustained by the effect of subsequent improvements in the subsoil drainage. He then says: "This is not all. The inhabitants of Gennevilliers still complain of certain widespread fevers very injurious to health if not mortal. In truth, the representatives of the city, after having contested the existence of these fevers, affirmed before the medical reporters that they had always occurred in the peninsula."

Probably, for the sake of brevity, but without the qualifying expressions and moderate temper of the special pleading quoted from, and without the scholarly accuracy which so generally distinguishes him, Dr. Chancellor gives us the following, in quotation marks, as a translation of consecutive sentences of the original, saying, it will be noted, that *they began to demand the cessation of the flow*, instead of saying, as the author did, speaking of a future contingency, that they *might abstain from taking* the flow,—

"At first the 'villegiature,' who owned, or occupied and cultivated the lands proposed to be utilized in irrigation, regarded the scheme as an element of certain fortune, relying upon the statement of the minister of public works that the land would be enhanced in value from one hundred and fifty to four hundred and fifty francs per hectare; but in a short time after the inauguration of the system they were overdosed by sewage, and began to demand, at first, the flow be stopped for one day, then for a week, and finally, for a month, and even longer periods, in order that the land might absorb that which was already upon it. As this could not be done, the lower lands were transformed into seas of sewage, and many cellars were overflowed by the filthy liquid, which on some of the farms even rose above the fences. A great deal of sickness was produced, and the peninsula of Gennevilliers is still plagued with fevers, which had been hitherto unknown. Such were the evils experienced, that public inquiry into the facts resulted in bringing to light an almost unanimous opposition to the system."

We have in the original no suggestion of "seas of sewage." The subsoil water that rose at Gennevilliers was perfectly pure. There was no filthy liquid in the cellars and no farm fences were submerged. The statement that the peninsula of Gennevilliers is still plagued with fevers is not true, nor was it true at the time, for fevers have always been rare and are now very exceptional.

Dr. Chancellor's third translation is correct, as a translation, but it is no more correct as a statement in the translation than in the original. That is, it is entirely incorrect.

Dr. Chancellor does not say that he visited these works himself and he makes it obvious to those who are familiar with them and with the literature concerning them that he has little familiarity with either. These works are located in the plain of Gennevilliers North of the city. As much of the outflow of the sewers as they are capable of receiving, the proportion increasing constantly as the irrigation works extend, is raised by force-pumps near the outlet and delivered by pipes to the irrigated area. These are much the most interesting and instructive sewerage works in the world, for the reason that they were instituted and for a long time were maintained as a field for investigation and experiment, later as a means of popular education, and finally as an important aid to profitable agriculture.— From the outset they have been carefully watched and accurately described, and they have given rise to some of the most curious and instructive experiments on processes of oxidation and on the action of the bacteria of putrefaction in the soil that have come to our knowledge.

It would be sufficient, as a mere answer to Dr. Chancellor, to say that he has been entirely misinformed on this subject, and that the single popular magazine article that he has read concerning it, while not so condemnatory as he conceived it to be, was, at the time he made use of it, and probably at the time when it was published, entirely obsolete as a valuable criticism of the work. It is not, however, sufficient to answer Dr. Chancellor. The question at issue lies at the very foundation of the most important problem connected with the future disposal of sewage.

I have already stated the general principles on which the success of purification by the soil is secured. The completeness with which it is secured seems to me to be remarkably well demonstrated at Berlin and at Paris, but it is substantially as well demonstrated all over England. One of the most conspicuous establishments of the sort in England is that near Croydon of which Dr Chancellor says that it was *for a time* looked upon with some favor. I know the Croydon irrigation fields from personal observation and from long and interested study of the varius publications concerning them. They are still looked upon with very great favor and they are a very great success. There is absolutely nothing connected with them, either in their appearance, their odor or their influence of any sort on the population living immediately about them, which is not altogether and completely satisfactory. If every place in the United State could be assured such a success as that, it need look no further for means of improvement. The sewage fields of Leavington are quite as successful from the purification point of view and are much more so from an economic point of view. The sewage farm there is a profitable one.

It would be interesting, had we time, to go over the voluminous documents which have appeared during the last twelve years concerning the irrigation fields at Gennevilliers. We should find in these the frankest possible statement of every obstacle that has been encountered, a description of the manner in which it has been overcome, and ample testimony of success.

At one time – due partly to a high stage of the Seine and partly to the establishment of a dam at Bezoins— the escape of subsoil-water was so obstructed that it rose into cellars, etc. It was not foul sewage, but clean water. It led to fear and discontent on the part of the people of the commune, and to a serious disturbance of their relations with the municipality of Paris. Suitable works of under-drainage being executed, this whole difficulty was overcome, and has never reappeared. The population of Gennevilliers, largely increased by the immigration of those coming there to carry on market-gardens with sewage manure, is substantially unanimous in favor of the work, and, in making its final concessions to the municipality of Paris, it exacted that the free and abundant supply of sewage should be continued for twelve years to come.

One of the strongest objections raised to the plan of delivering such an enormous amount of sewage on to these fields lay in the fear that the subsoil-water, and consequently the well-water, would be so fouled that it would be unfit to drink. Careful examinations and analyses have shown that this fear was unfounded. The average annual amount of sewage delivered on that land has been about four and a half million gallons per acre. Direct experiments were made as to the condition of the subsoil-water. Water was taken from wells in the midst of the irrigated lands which was found to be perfectly limpid, without special taste, and identical in appearance and flavor with the sulphurous waters of the subsoil which supplies all of the wells of the whole region in the plain. An analysis was made of the water of the under-drain in the experimental garden, which was found to be perfectly free from fermentable matters. "This water is purer than that of the Seine above the outlet of the sewer. * * * It is often better than water taken from the same level outside of the irrigated area."

Concerning Mr. Aubry-Vitet's fear that the land at St. Germain will be flooded with foul sewage (the translators "seas of sewage higher than the fences") Mr. Durand-Claye says: "There is no question, as Mr. Aubry would have us believe, and there never has been a question of drowning from three to four thousand acres under a layer of infective water more or less deep. It is a question of proceeding here as at Gennevilliers, as in sixty-four English cities, as at Berlin, Dantzig, Breslau, etc. That is to say, as is explained above, of cutting the land with trenches at greater or less distances to receive a stream of water. In winter, when cultivation shall have ceased, the soil alone, by the admirable oxidizing property so carefully studied by Messrs. Frankland and Schloesing, will transform the organic matters of the sewage into its absolutely inoffensive elements, the water thus purified will be partly evaporated and partly absorbed by the soil, that which may descend to the level of the subsoil water will in no respect taint its purity; at the drains constructed under the plan of Gennevilliers the inhabitants may be seen all through the winter coming with eagerness to seek this water of the subsoil which is so cool and clear that it is preferred to all other waters of the locality and of the neighborhood.

As to the fevers, Mr. Durand-Claye says: "Mr. Aubry raises, discreetly, it is true, the question of health. He speaks of fevers, etc. We refer him again to the official investigations made at Gennevilliers. This question was in fact raised about 1875; three persons at the cost of the opposers of irrigation, more numerous then than now, prepared a sort of memoir where cases were cited."

The investigation of these cases was not made in the presence of representatives of the administration. No complaint on the subject of the healthfulness of Gennevilliers had yet been made. It was decided to seek information. The case was submitted to a physician who was familiar with legal examinations. This developed at least a flagrant exaggeration in the report referred to. It was decided to give greater publicity to the facts as developed on one side and on the other. The names and the domicils of those who were reported to have had fevers were published, representatives of the medical profession and of scientific societies looked into the question and an exploration of the commune of Gennevilliers was made. The fevers disappeared as by enchantment. In 1878, only four cases were timidly suggested. Mr. Delpach and his colleagues went to the points indicated. In every case they found the house empty. The four patients had gone to the Universal Exposition. * * * And meanwhile the popularity of irrigation has not ceased for a single instant at Gennevilliers. Mr. Aubry speaks of less than 300 acres that received sewage in 1876. To-day, according to him, it reaches more than 750 acres. He is mistaken; the irrigated surface is more than 1,000 acres; and it is important to observe all of this irrigation is made without compulsion, on the land of the private owners, at their demand; and not only do they not complain of the excess of sewage, but we are often unable to satisfy them. In the place of from six to seven million cubic metres sent to the plain in 1874 and 1875, we have this year to the 1st of October, delivered about thirteen million cubic metres, always at the request and only at the request of those interested, who have united themselves into a syndic association."

The most interesting writer who has treated of the Gennevilliers works is Mr. Francisque Sarcey, who discusses the matter in a popular way in the Paris papers. He says: "As to odor, they say that the peninsula is infectious. I do not know how such false reports could have been put forth, when it is so easy to convince ourselves of their falsity. Gennevilliers is not far from Paris. Go there yourself; you will see, in fact, that if you hold your nose over the ditches they do exhale an odor, not infectious but stale, such as is known to those who have made the traditional visit to the sewers of Paris. Two metres away you smell nothing, nothing at all. * * *

"Paludal fevers! At this Latin word people tremble with fear. The truth is that the residents of the irrigated portion are perfectly well; (*se portent comme des charmes*;) that there has never been suspected in all this part of the peninsula the shadow of an epidemic or endemic disease; that they are mere stories, and that before crying 'fever,' as you would cry 'wolf,' we ought at least to have seen the tail of a wolf.

"It is true that the establishment of a dam at Bezoms had the temporary effect of raising the level of the subsoil-water which prevented the free percolation of the sewage; since then, works of drainage have remedied this temporary inconvenience; everything is restored to good order, and to use a familiar country expression, at this moment the country 'is sound as your eye.'"

He quotes from another official report: "After a profound examination of the various questions raised by the purification of sewage, the chief commission was of the *unanimous* opinion that the use of sewage for the irrigation of land constitutes, among the processes approved by use, the one which gives the best results whether in purification of the liquid or in the utilization of the fertilizing matters that it contains."

He describes a visit made to the proposed field of St. Germain by an official delegation of the municipal council to investigate the condition of affairs: "The account of this visit in the newspapers of the time is well remembered. From all the neighboring communes there came a flood of municipal councilors, armed with energetic protests; of peasants beside themselves with terror or furious with anger, who shook their fists at the engineers and threatened to smash the first irrigation pipe that they might lay.

"It was a universal outcry!

"The delegates of the municipal council of Paris did not know what to make of it. They stood stupefied by this violence, which appeared so unreasonable.

"They had just come from the peninsula of Gennevilliers; they had been shown the spectacle that I have described to you in the preceding chapters; they had been able to convince themselves, having like you and me, eyes and noses, that the sewage spread fertility, wealth and health over all the peninsula. They had even extended to themselves the courtesy, which is now one of the common ceremonies of a visit to Gennevilliers, of a drink of water from the outlet of the underdrains, being the same water, but purified, that they had seen five minutes before flowing out of the irrigation pipes black, foul, loaded with refuse and bad smelling. They had drank it, not without a slight grimace, and they had found it excellent. I drank it like the others; the people of Gennevilliers now prefer it for all domestic uses to the water of the Seine, and they are right, for it is not only agreeable to the taste, it meets all requirements of science; it has been analyzed by Mr. Pasteur, who found that no other is more wholesome, cleanly, or freer from microbes.

"The gentlemen had been delighted with all that had been shown them. You can fancy their astonishment on seeing this inexplicable effervescence of causeless opposition.

"'What!' said they. 'All these people live within three or four leagues of Gennevilliers! There is no one of them who might not in a half day have satisfied himself of the happy change effected in that country by the new system of purification; not one of them has taken the trouble; not one of them has studied, on the ground, a question which interests them so strongly; they only repeat the clamor that we heard sixteen years ago, before any experiment had been made. What a strange thing, this prejudice!

"If the engineers will allow me to tell them so, they know admirably well how to calculate natural forces; there is a force of which they have never measured the energy—that is, human stupidity. They do not take it into the account; they make a mistake.'

The last official publication on the subject that has come to my notice is the report of the technical commission on the sanitary improvement of Paris, published in 1883. It says:

"Numerous analyses of the subsoil-waters of Gennevilliers, made in the laboratory of the *Ponts et Chausee* and by Mr. Marie-Davy, have shown that the wells do not contain any considerable quantity of nitrogen, not more than is found in the drinking water of Paris. * * * Messrs. Marie-Davy and Miquel have made microscopic examinations of the effluent, and have counted the microbes, or living particles, found in a cubic centimetre of the water; thus, while a cubic centimetre of rainwater contains 35 microbes, the water of the Vanne* 62, the water of the Seine 1,200 and the sewage at the outlet of the great collector 20,000, the water of the drains at Gennevilliers contain only from 13 to 24. * * * Marie-Davy obtained another very interesting result: Of 24,000 cubic metres delivered on a hectare in a half year, only 1,600 reached a depth of 6 feet, and he concluded that in delivering on the ground from 5,000 to 6,000 cubic metres per month, that is to say, from 60,000 to 72,000 cubic metres annually, only one third of it would reach the water of the subsoil. [The surface of the ground and its crop would evaporate the remainder.] * * * At Gennevilliers, as we have already seen, the purification has been as satisfactory as possible. * * * There is, besides, no reason to fear that the soil will ever suffer from too great a proportion of organic matter. Subjected for several years to frequent irrigation, it preserves its filtering power and continues to perform its function of purification. * * * Messrs. Marie-Davy and Miquel have also shown that the micro-germs of bacteria or vibriones generally diminish in the atmosphere during periods of dampness.

"The dampness of the earth causes the vibriones to adhere more closely to the soil, and prevents the wind from displacing them with the dust that it raises. These observations are evidently very interesting, but for us physicians, although they explain the facts, they are much less important than the facts themselves. Now the facts are these: For some years there have been observed at Gennevilliers a greater number of cases of typhoid fever, of diphtheria and of intermittent fever than usual. In 1882 there were two deaths from typhoid fever and one from diphtheria. Since the drainage is properly carried out, *there are no more intermittent fevers.*

"This is established by official documents.

"It is shown also by other statistics communicated by the mayoralty of Gennevilliers that the death of infants under one year of age (twelve to sixteen per cent.) have not increased appreciably since 1870, the time when the irrigation experiment began.

"The averages are not founded on a sufficiently large basis to permit conclusions to be drawn. Nevertheless, if we consider the fact that the mortality of infants of this age over all France reaches an average figure of

---

*The best drinking water of Paris.

seventeen or eighteen per cent., it may certainly be admitted that the sanitary condition of Gennevilliers is not abnormal.

"In a word, the system of purification by the soil has not been invented to justify the projects of the city of Paris and to permit it to purify its sewage; it rests on the application of a natural law, that of the circulation of matter which has lived, toward living matter. The popularization of these ideas will overcome the last opposition to a project which marks a step forward in the sanitary improvement of cities.

"Now if, as Mr. Schloesing has shown, the soil of the peninsula of Gennevilliers combines in the highest degree the necessary conditions for the purification of sewage without injurious effect, have we not a perfect accord between the theory and the practical result everywhere obtained, and is not this result still further explained in the experiments of Mr. Marie-Davy on the destructive action exercised by the soil of Gennevilliers on the microbes of all sorts contained in the sewage?

"Everything seems to me, therefore, to militate in favor of the extension of the system of purification which has passed through its probation at Gennevilliers during a sufficient number of years to remove all possible doubt either of its advantages or its complete innoxiousness.

I have gone thus fully into the subject on this occasion, not because I desired to contradict Dr. Chancellor, but because of the vital importance of counteracting the effect on the public mind of the rash announcement, by a man of his position and influence, of conclusions which, had he studied the subject more fully, he could never have drawn. I do not advance the facts and opinions set forth as affecting the argument for nor against the Liernur system as a means of sanitary drainage, but only to uphold, as against the assaults of Liernur's adherents, the absolute safety and efficiency and economy of the well and long tried system of sewage irrigation.

I did not say unadvisedly in my first paper before this Society—and I repeat now advisedly and deliberately what I then said—that sewage purification by irrigation has been wonderfully successful wherever applied—nowhere, I believe, more so than at Paris, and at Berlin hardly less so. By this means "the question of the ultimate disposal of the noxious sewage *after it is out of the city* is perfectly solved." There is certainly no doubt that "the excessive influx of sewage matter will pollute and render noxious any harbor or stream into which it flows;" but before its inflow, it may, by the process described, be perfectly purified. The condition of the Seine, described by Dr. Chancellor as due to the matters discharged by the sewers of Paris will no longer exist after the whole outflow shall have been subjected to the treatment which is now applied to so large a proportion of it.

Dr. Chancellor refers us to the "Report of Privy Councillor Schultz, Chairman of the Berlin Sewerage Commission, giving an *expose* of the trouble and expense experienced with water carriage and irrigation at Berlin." This was published in 1880. I made my examination of the Berlin works a year later. I am sure that there then existed no ground for such serious criticism, and Messrs Gray and Swan found no ground for it in 1884.

DISCUSSION ON COL. WARING'S PAPER.

Dr. Chancellor said he was quite unprepared for the attack which had been made upon him by Col. Waring. He stated the ground of difference and discussion between Col. Waring and himself, which discussion had been conducted, on his part, with fairness and courtesy, but he regretted that Col. Waring had evinced a different spirit, and had even drifted into personalities. His paper, to which Col. Waring had first taken exceptions, was simply a detailed description of Liernur's pneumatic system of sewering cities, which he had ventured to speak of in terms of commendation. He conceived that he had an undoubted right to discuss matters of the kind, though he did not claim to be an engineer. Col. Waring seems to think differently. He (Dr. Chancellor) had stated, in a paper read before the State Medical Society of Maryland, in the spring of 1883, that in Europe the system of disposing of excretal and other household sewage by irrigation had proved a failure; and he now reiterated and reaffirmed that statement upon the authority of eminent European engineers. He did not claim to have personally observed *all the facts* given in that paper, but they were vouched for and are still vouched for by authorities quite as respectable as any cited by Col. Waring. His information as to the Berlin irrigation fields was obtained while on a visit to that city in the winter of 1882, and again in the fall of 1883, two years subsequent to the visit of Col. Waring, and he reaffirmed all that he had said in reference to the Berlin system, notwithstanding Mr. Hobrecht's denial. He thought Col. Waring's present position in reference to the purification of sewage water strangely inconsistent with his utterance one year ago, when he said that however much we may strain sewage or dilute urine they will become sources of offense. Col. Waring now declares that the water from wells in the midst of irrigated lands is purer than the water of the river Seine, above the City of Paris, and better than water taken from the same level outside the irrigation area— so cool and clear that it is preferred to all other water by the inhabitants for drinking purposes.

In concluding, Dr. Chancellor said he felt surprised and chagrined that Col. Waring should have seen fit to come to this meeting with an elaborately prepared paper intended to discredit him, (Dr. Chancellor) with his own friends and people; he regretted moreover that the discussion of an interesting scientific question should have degenerated into personal criticisms. He would not trespass upon the patience of the convention by replying at this time to Col. Waring, but as the correctness of his statements had been questioned, he would conclude by saying that Col. Waring should hear from him again. He could fully establish the accuracy of every statement made by him in reference to the Berlin irrigation fields, and he would do so.

Mr. Wm. H. Rothrock, of Baltimore, expressed his surprise at the statements made by Col. Waring. "How," he asked, "could it be that every well in Baltimore is polluted by seepage from privy-pits, if filtration through earth accomplished anything in the way of purification?" He criticised the paper read by Col. Waring and said he could not understand how the water from the irrigated grounds could be purer than the water in the natural sub-soil.

Mr. Dunnett, of Baltimore, called attention to the fact that cess-pools in the country frequently contaminated wells of drinking water and were a source of danger to the health of the neighborhood.

Col. Waring disclaimed any personality towards Dr. Chancellor. His paper, he said, was not a criticism of Dr. Chancellor, but of his position. He said he had made direct and incidental suggestions in reference to the agricultural disposition of sewage, and Dr. Chancellor had produced such statements in this connection as to astonish him, and he had to reply to them.

In reply to Mr. Rothrock, Col. Waring said, the filtering power of the irrigation fields of Paris was not at all similar to that of the soil of Baltimore. Abroad the process of the oxidation of the filth was perfected. In Baltimore there was only a bastard decomposition, which added to the malignity of the poison. In the country filth should not be poured on the ground too freely, lest the necessary oxidation be not attained. The out-cry in France was over what was proposed, not over what had been done.

After some further remarks upon the subject of Col. Waring's paper, the convention took a recess of fifteen minutes.

On re-assembling, the Chair announced the committees under the several resolutions passed.

The Secretary called attention to the next meeting of the American Public Health Association, which he stated would assemble in St. Louis, October 14th, proximo, and it was hoped there would be a large attendance from Maryland.

Dr. Frank Hines, of Chestertown, moved that the next meeting of the Council be held at some point on the Eastern Shore, to be fixed by the State Board of Health, which motion was adopted.

After a vote of thanks to the several railroad companies, the proprietors of the Blue Mountain House, and others who had extended hospitalities, the Council adjourned *sine die*.

SEWAGE DISPOSAL.

A Rejoinder to Col. George E. Waring.

(In Two Parts.)

BY C. W. CHANCELLOR, M. D.,

Secretary of the State Board of Health of Maryland.

PART I.

A COMPARATIVE VIEW OF THE LIERNUR AND WARING SYSTEMS.

"Irrigation as a Process for Purifying Sewage" is the title which Colonel Waring has thought proper to prefix to a paper read by him at the second Sanitary Council of Maryland, held September, 1884, and which, according to usual practice, will be published in the biennial report of the Maryland State Board of Health.

The title is undescriptive of the contents of the paper, which really pursues no inquiry whatever. It does not in any manner investigate the subject heretofore under discussion, but asserts, simply that the statements made by me in a paper published twelve months ago, in reply to Colonel Waring's attack upon the Liernur system of sewerage, are wholly incorrect, and assumes the point in dispute to have been proved without attempting to submit it to the test of evidence or of argument.

Colonel Waring's object has been, clearly, not to inquire into the merits of the Liernur system, which alone was under discussion, but to undermine and destroy it, by an assumption that "there is nothing connected with this system which to-day constitutes a live issue in American sanitary improvement."

If his paper had been truly entitled, it might have been called, after the style of De Foe, "The Shortest Way Out of a Difficulty;" or, in the manner of Swift, "A Protest for Preventing Obstructions to my Particular Schemes."

In reporting the proceedings of the Sanitary Council, the Baltimore *American* thus speaks of Colonel Waring's paper:

"Colonel George E. Waring, of Rhode Island, followed Colonel Thomas, with a paper on 'Irrigation as a Process for Purifying Sewage.' The paper was entirely a defence of his (Waring's) system of sewerage. Colonel Waring read a paper at the last Council fully explaining his system, which has been published. The document read to-day was a reply to Dr. C. W. Chancellor, who, in a paper published some time ago, brought out strong arguments to the effect that the system of disposing of sewage by irrigation, which has been in operation in some places in Europe, is a failure. This system consists in conveying sewage from the cities into the country and on land to irrigate it. Dr. Chancellor, upon his return from Europe, in the spring of 1883, declared (in a paper read before the Medical and Chirurgical Faculty of Maryland), that eminent authorities had stated that the system was a failure. It pollutes the water and creates a foul atmosphere, and the bed (irrigation fields) is converted into a bed of fermentation and infection. Colonel Waring declared Dr. Chancellor to be entirely wrong, and that water coming from the sewage-irrigated fields is perfectly pure, and that this disposal of the sewage is most perfect. The paper, as already stated, was entirely personal."

After such a statement from a public journal, it may be asked, why I think Colonel Waring's paper worthy of notice? Why I am induced to bestow attention upon a weak attempt to divert public attention from the main question, namely, the merits of the Liernur system? My answer is, that I consider the question of a proper disposal of sewage one of transcendent importance at this time, especially to the people of Maryland, many of whom would be injuriously affected, should Colonel Waring's project for sewering the city of Baltimore be adopted; and, furthermore, that the advantages which the pneumatic system of Liernur undoubtedly offer to the all-important end of getting rid of the excretal sewage of cities and towns, without offence to health or comfort, should not be swept away by the arbitrary determination of one man.

The minute details into which Col. Waring has entered to show that irrigation with sewage matter will convert a barren and unhealthy district into an "Elysian Field," and which he sets forth in such graphic and characteristic language, and with so much naivete and earnestness, is intended simply to draw attention from the real issue, viz: "The superiority of the Liernur system over that in which Colonel Waring himself holds proprietary rights. But I do not intend that the public mind shall be thus diverted.

The views which I advanced upon the question of irrigation, and supported by the best authorities, were only given incidentally, but they fell immediately and directly within the scope of my paper, which Colonel Waring has sought to discredit by a condensation of *ex parte* testimony collected from scattered and not easily accessible authorities, one of them being the engineer of the Berlin irrigation system, who is personally interested in denying what I said in reference to that system.

A certain author was once told that a book that he had published had been answered twenty years before the date of its publication, and a similar repulse might be offered to Colonel Waring's statement in regard to irrigation, taking away, however, a few years from the period of the anticipated disproof. But, before noticing in detail, Colonel Waring's plea in favor of irrigation as a means for purifying sewage, let us briefly consider whether there is anything connected with Liernur's pneumatic system which entitles it to be regarded as "a live issue in American sanitary improvement," in comparison with the so-called "Waring system."

For the sake of clearness, and in order not to encumber the argument by repetition, it will be useful to restate those propositions, which previous discussions and experiences have already established.

1. The removal of human excreta (fæces and urine,) without pollution of air, water or soil, can be accomplished by the pneumatic system of Liernur, but not by the Waring system.

2. The Liernur system, wherever introduced, unlike the Waring system, has done its work efficiently, and has given entire satisfaction.

3. It satisfies all claims whatever relating to the disposal of sewage, and is applicable to cities of every variety of local peculiarity in regard to formation of ground, extension of area, and number of inhabitants, and is in a high degree distinguished for ease of technical execution.

4. It allows equally well the use of water-closets and of privies without movable parts, and permits in both cases all water needed for cleanliness.

5. It prevents positively every pollution of the town air with sewer-gases, and of the soil with sewage matter.

6. It excludes from the sewers kitchen offal and waste products of manufactories, by means of arrangements which are simple to construct, convenient in use, and highly effective.

7. It converts the fecal matter, by means of a cheap and scentless process, into a dry manure powder of the quality of the best fertilizers in the market, enabling towns and cities to rid themselves of refuse, under conditions at once favorable to their own finances and the agricultural interests of the country.

8. Engineers of experience and reputation officially declare it to be easily constructed, and more economical, both as to first cost and working expenses, than water-carriage sewers which have been a source of much perplexity and trouble, besides being dangerous.

These are the principal peculiarities of the Liernur system, and in them will readily be recognized its great superiority over the Waring system, which of necessity must either pollute water or soil, according as the sewage is discharged into water-courses or upon the surface of the earth.

In the course of recent inquiries, I have obtained some facts concerning both the Liernur and Waring systems, in the shape of an open letter from Dr. V.

Ovenbeek de Meyer, Professor of Hygiene in the University of Utrecht, Holland, which I give in full, both on account of the opinions expressed by the distinguished author, and because the letter refutes certain charges which were unjustly preferred against me, in connection with statements unwittingly made by Professor de Meyer, in a pamphlet published in 1883 (Bailliere et fils de Paris).

LETTER OF PROF. DE MEYER TO COL. GEORGE E. WARING.

"UTRECHT, December 31, 1883.

"COL. GEORGE E. WARING, JR., M. I. C. E.,
Member of the National Board of Health,
U. S. A., Newport, R. I.

"DEAR SIR: I have read with great interest your kind letters of November 5th and 23d, 1883, denying some of the statements in my pamphlet, 'Les systemes d'evacuation des eaux et immondices d'une ville' (Paris: J. B. Bailliere et fils, 1883), and I am now fully prepared to answer, that I have been indeed, in some respects, as falsely informed about yourself as about the general disapprobation of your system.

"Having no other wish than to serve the truth and the science of hygiene *honestly*, I am very anxious to correct the unfounded parts of my statements, and to do what I can to give to these corrections the same circulation that my errors have had; and, therefore, I shall be much pleased by seeing this letter published in the American *Sanitary Engineer*, or in any other periodical which you might choose, but this only upon condition that the letter shall be printed *entire*, without the omission of a single word. I hope that you will find yourself in this way fully satisfied.

"My first correction relates to page 68 of my pamphlet, where I have called you an 'ancient negociant, plus tard lieutenant-colonel quartier-maitre (charge de l'approvisionnement des troupes) et actuellement ingenieur a Newport.' In giving your record, it was my intention to show that you are a self-made man, but as you think that the erroneous recital of your career might give a wrong impression as to your preparation for the engineering profession, I am quite disposed to state, according to your letter of October 4th, 1883, that you began the practice of engineering in 1855, and that you had served your country from 1861 till 1866 as major of infantry, major of cavalry, later as colonel, and commander of important military posts.

"My second correction relates to the statement which I have given on page 75 of my pamphlet, in these terms: 'Neanmoins, la bonne reputation du systeme Waring parait diminuer en Amerique. Je viens d'apprendre que la ville de Baltimore, avec 435,000 habitants, qui avait voula suivre l'exemple de Memphis, a abandonne ce project et a demande a M. Liernur un projet sur l'application de son systeme d'assainissement a tant la ville. Cette resolution a ete pris apres la discussion d'un rapport tres defavorable au systeme Waring, presente par M. le docteur Chancellor, Secretarie du State Board of Health of Maryland.'

"I feel myself obliged to recall this statement, and to quote the following sentences from two letters addressed to you, and now in my hands.

"*First.*—In a letter dated Buffalo, N. Y., October 18, 1883, Mr. William Henry Baldwin, civil and consulting engineer, has written: 'I do not know of a single serious objection that has been sustained by observation or practical experience. On the contrary, I have noticed that engineers formerly opposed to this (the Waring) system of drainage and sewerage are now beginning to adopt it in their own practice.'

"*Second.*—In a letter dated Baltimore, November 3, 1883, M. White, the Mayor of Baltimore, has written: 'Baltimore has taken no definite action on this subject, except to obtain from its special engineer, Charles H. Latrobe, Esq., a report in that connection, and to print one from a committee of the Council. No action of the corporation in favor of, or in opposition to, any system has been taken by any department of the city government, nor has the city asked M. Liernur for estimates. Although I have personally looked somewhat into the Liernur system for my own edification, I do not know of any other city official who has ever heard of him, and no one (connected with the city government) has been authorized to request of him a plan.'

"The conclusion, therefore, is that I have been misinformed on these two points. I state, moreover, that my informer was not Dr. Chancellor. But I must also state that my statement as to Captain Liernur having been consulted in reference to a plan for the sewerage of Baltimore is based upon *fact*. He has been so consulted by one who opposes the Waring system upon sanitary and financial gronnds, and who expresses him--

self strongly in favor of the Liernur system. Whether or not he was authorized to do so (by the city of Baltimore) is not for me to say.*

"With regard to the *sanitary* excellence of your system, I must, however, persist in all that I have said in my pamphlet on this point, notwithstanding the declaration of the health officer, named in your letter of November 25, 1883, who has said that all of my conclusions about your system are 'absurd.' Of course, I have no answer to such unseemly language; neither am I disposed to meddle with the so-called 'Sanitary Engineer' who wrote *anonymously* 'a very sharp criticism' of my pamphlet, probably for advertising purposes; but I refer only to *your* observations upon several points in my notice of your system.

"I must here declare it *impossible* that the deposits in the main sewers of Memphis 'contain no trace of animal matter.' The 'absence of odor' proves not at all the absence of germs of disease. You acknowledge yourself that there is a 'feeble sliming of some parts of the wall of the sewer, and that this sliming *decomposes* in the presence of ample, changing currents of air,' which statement is quite sufficient to condemn your system.— After the most careful examination of all that you have been so kind as to write me in your letters, there exists in my mind no doubt that your system is, in a *sanitary* point of view, *a bad one*, as it favors the propagation of pathogenic bacteria.

"I cannot agree with you in the opinion that Liernur's system does not *secure* such absolute *cleanliness* in house-

---

* The statements of Professor de Meyer are not without foundation in fact. In the winter of 1882 I met Captain Liernur in Berlin, and, being most favorably impressed with the working of his system in Amsterdam, I requested him to give me an approximate estimate for introducing it in Baltimore. This was done, not officially, but, nevertheless, with the view of utilizing the information in the interest of the City of Baltimore, if I should see fit to do so on my return to America. I also stated to Captain Liernur that an ordinance had been introduced in the City Council of Baltimore looking to the introduction of the Waring system of sewerage by a private corporation, but had failed to receive favorable consideration; that the increased mortality in Memphis since its introduction into that city in 1880 (being 42.1 per 1,000 for the year 1881, as against an average of 34 per 1,000, excluding the mortality from yellow fever, in the five years preceding the year 1880, in which the new sewers were constructed), was not a favorable exhibit in a sanitary point of view; and that the increased expenditure in providing manholes and other improvements, which were found to be necessary, rendered the economy of the system at least questionable.

The ordinance above referred to, which was "pigeon-holed" in the second branch of the City Council, was introduced prior to Mayor Whyte's term of office, and he, of course, was not aware of this fact when he wrote to Colonel Waring that "no action of the corporation in favor of, or *in opposition to, any system* has been taken by any department of the city government." But Colonel Waring was cognizant of the introduction of the ordinance and its subsequent fate.

Professor de Meyer is also correct in stating that "my (his) informer was not Dr. Chancellor," since I had never seen or heard of that gentleman until I received a note from Mayor Whyte, calling my attention to the paragraph quoted from page 75 of M. de Meyer's pamphlet.

The course of Mayor Whyte, in writing *directly* to me in reference to the matter, was in strong contrast with the unfriendly action of Colonel Waring, who jumped to a conclusion that I was the front of Professor de Meyer's offending in striking at the roots of his system.—C. W. C.

hold appliances as one might reasonably demand. You have probably seen that the Liernur system admits the use of a quantity of water sufficient to insure a perfectly clean condition, not only of the closets, but of the privy, soil-pipes, and drains.

"You are also positively wrong in your judgment that some of the details of that system include engineering fallacies, as, for example, the one illustrated on page 43 of my pamphlet. I suppose that you have not rightly considered the signification of the hypothenuse of the triangles, with regard to the total amount of forces in relation to the resistances. In my exposition (page 113) the hypothenuse xy, xy, xy are represented as the expression of the force resulting from the sum of the different moving forces through the pipe in its total length—that is to say, 'to the extreme outlet.' I am fully prepared to prove that the device of Captain Liernur for increasing the flow of horizontal sewers by the stand-pipes, which I have described and explained, is NOT an 'engineering absurdity of which any hydraulic engineer would at once see the fallacy.' But I cannot here enter into the discussion of these points; such a discussion would involve the necessity of writing another pamphlet.

"Your pamphlet, 'The Sewerage of Paris,' a copy of which you have courteously sent me, is based on the same *sanitary* errors which are advocated by the so-called 'Commission Technique,' of Paris.— Allow me to say, frankly, that I cannot conceive— *First*, how sanitarians venture to say that in (well-flushed) sewers, '*running only* ONE-HALF *full*,' containing fecal matter, and connected with atmospheric air, there is not a good condition for the growth of germs of disease; and, *second*, how 'sanitary' engineers can overlook the fact, that your system leaves entirely unsolved the important question: 'What to do with the sewage without involving danger to health?' Every main sewer not *completely* and *constantly* filled is dangerous to health; and all sewage containing fecal matter is a danger to health wilfully created. Fecal matter should never be mixed with other wastes in the centre of population!

"You are positively wrong in saying that the discharge of all waste directly into the sewers 'receives the approval of the *best* authorities on the subject.' I maintain that 'sanitary engineers' (*exceptis excipiendis*) are no authority at all on this subject. Excuse my candor in expressing the opinion that, so long as the care of 'urban sanitation' is in the hands of men—'health officers,' 'sanitary engineers," or officials, however called —animated, it may be by excellent intentions, but not thoroughly schooled in the science of hygiene, and having, of course, no clear idea of the sanitary conditions which must be urged, errors like those which I have combated will constantly arise.

"Finally, dear sir, I must unbosom myself completely in reply to your observation that, 'being already old in the consideration of the Liernur system, I am very sorry to see you showing such an infatuation as you do for this system." I am now nearly fifty-three years of age, and, of course, I, too, am 'already old' in a knowledge of the Liernur system, having, moreover, had the opportunity in my former capacity as Deputy Sanitary Inspector, in 1867, now sixteen years ago, to hear M. Liernur, in the Department of the Interior, at the Hague, explain, himself, the principles of his system. Since that date I have studied the matter very carefully, and it is, therefore, with a full knowledge, that I, from a sanitary point of view, call your system decidedly A BAD ONE, and Liernur's system eminently A GOOD ONE.

"Excuse my frankness, and believe me,
"Very truly yours,
(Signed) "V. O. DE MEYER."

Twelve years ago the German Government organized an Agricultural Bureau or *council* charged with the important and responsible duty of looking after the agricultural interests of the Empire. This "Council" is composed of the leading agriculturists of the country, the members being either farmers of large estates and experience, Professors of the State Agricultural schools or Directors of State institutions for agricultural experiments. This Council meets annually to discuss and vote upon whatever questions relating to agriculture the Government may submit for its consideration, or which in the opinion of the Council, may seem paramount in the interests of the Empire.

In 1881, the Council appointed a subsidiary commission to investigate the entire question of sewerage in all of its details, but especially with reference to the utilization of fecal matter. This commission called to their aid experts and other persons likely to prove useful in obtaining an exhaustive and conclusive report on the subject. This report was completed and submitted to the Council in Frebruary, 1884, and was by that body unanimously adopted for the guidance of the Empire. It is entitled "Maxims of Experience" in the sanitation of towns, and is, probably, the most valuable and reliable authority extant upon the subjects of which it treats.

To be brief, I shall give only a few leading paragraphs translated from the report, as published by the Council:

"SEC. 9. Impure liquids should be excluded from streams, lakes, bays or other public waters, *also from the soil* for the purpose of letting them ooze away as effluents. The degree of danger connected therewith depends upon the quantity and quality of the liquid and upon the local circumstances, but as a rule it must be held that impurities in a state of solution are less dangerous than putrefying solid matters, all matters in solution being subject to the process of self-purification.

"SEC. 10. The attempts to solve the problem of purifying, by means of precipitation, clarification or irrigation, the enormous masses of sewage produced in large and populous cities, and augmented by water-carriage, have not thus far met the demands of sanitation and economy, and have nowhere succeeded.

"SEC. 11. All attempts to get rid of water-carried sewage have resulted in intervention on the part of the Government, both on account of the nuisance created and the increase of taxation incurred. The expectations of the water-carriage system, therefore, have neither been realized by towns nor by agriculture.

"SEC. 12. Sewerage by water-carriage and irrigation are to be classed with works subject to Government control, so as to allow the exercise of a rigorous authority. Professionally schooled officers should be appointed to guard against the pollution of the subsoil and water-courses; both as it respects towns and irrigation fields.

"SEC. 22. The only practical way of returning to the soil the manurial elements taken from it, in supplying provisions for large communities, is by reducing the fecal matter and other filth possessing manurial value to a dry powder, that can be stored or transported at will, for which ready sale at good prices is at all times certain.

"SEC. 23. The manufacture of such a poudrette or manure powder has been successfully accomplished in two different ways:

    (*a*) By means of separating the water from the fecal matter in vacuo—method of Liernur.

    (*b*) By means of compression and distillation—method of Buhl and Keller.

"SEC. 24. The financial result of these methods depends chiefly upon the cost of delivering the fecal matter at the factory.

"SEC. 26. The cheapest delivery is effected by the pneumatic tubular arrangement of Liernur.

"SEC. 28. The differentiating sewerage system of Liernur (one set of tubes for fecal matter and another for house and rain-water) solves more completely the problem of sewering large cities, from a sanitary and economical point of view, than either the water-carriage system or the separate (small pipe) system, and with an equal degree of comfort and convenience in the houses and on the streets.

"SEC. 29. The Government of Prussia has declared—April 24, 1883—that 'there is no objection to the Liernur system in a *State sanitary sense*,' and has also advised its 'rapid introduction into the towns and cities of the kingdom.'

"SEC. 30. The Director of the Joint Stock Engine-Building Company of Berlin, Privy-Counsellor L. Schwartshorff, has, in a writing addressed to the Imperial Council for Germany, dated February 25, 1884, declared himself prepared to build and work the Liernur sewerage system on his own account and at his own cost and risk, in the same manner that gas and water-works are built and worked by private enterprise."

The above report is dated February 28, 1884, and was unanimously adopted by the "Council" the same day. I have quoted the above paragraphs to show that Colonel Waring is mistaken in believing that the Liernur system is no longer a "live issue in sanitary improvement."

Before proceeding to notice specifically the objections to Colonel Waring's system, known also as the "Memphis System," the "small-pipe system," the "separate system," etc., it may be well to state briefly upon what the claims of Colonel Waring to an original system of sewerage are founded.

Colonel Waring has taken out patents for a *combination* of certain features relating to sewerage, and collects a royalty of ten cents per running foot of sewer for the whole system. This "combination" happens never to have been made before—singly, however, the features have been used, partly as long as forty years.*

The royalty on this system, if it should be introduced into the city of Baltimore, would amount to upward of $100,000, and it is therefore natural that Col. Waring should try all possible means to have people believe

---

* See Opinion of Mr. Rudolph Hering in Sanitary Engineer, April, 1883, p. 483.

that his system is far superior to any other. As a business matter no fault can be found with Colonel Waring for this; but, why should the people of Baltimore pay so large a royalty for *practically nothing?* If in the place of the Field flush tanks, the roof water from one house at the head of every sewer were allowed to enter the same, the system would then be nothing more than the English separate system, *on which there is no royalty.*

It is a pertinent question to ask, why has Colonel Waring secured agents and endeavored to introduce his patent into Germany, France, and elsewhere, but never in England? The answer is plain. Because he knows that in England he could not collect a penny of royalty, and that English engineers would laugh at his pretensions. In Germany he has failed to find adherents among municipal engineers, because they are well acquainted with English practice. In Paris he has secured, no doubt, the services of some excellent engineers, who are said, however, to have more railroad than sewerage experience. They have only laid an insignificant length of the sewers, stretching a few blocks, but it has been so extensively advertised that the impression seems to prevail, in this country at least, that quite a lot of work has been done.

It is not difficult to find intelligent and experienced engineers, in this country as well as in England, who maintain that the admission of roof-water, clean as it is, secures an admirable flushing, better for several reasons than automatic flush-tanks alone, which are placed at the highest ends of the sewers. Indeed, "the absolute exclusion of roof-water is simply to throw away a great natural and economical aid in rendering sewers clean;" but without discarding this advantage Colonel Waring could not have secured a patent.

The "separate system" with roof-water flushing exists in many of the English towns, and has been recommended by Mr. Rudolph Hering and other engineers in this country, more or less extensively, in not less than twenty places; but Colonel Waring, in spite of his able writing and extensive advertising, has not succeeded, I believe, in more than six or seven places in convincing the people that his is the only rational system, and in a less number that he is entitled to a royalty for it.

Speaking of the Memphis system, Mr. Edward S. Philbrick, C. E., says: "There are matters of detail in the Memphis system which I would question—among others, the absence of man-holes. Now, in constructing a separate system for sewage alone, *the cost of manholes would be a very large item, the pipes being small, and their absence in Memphis is, therefore, a very considerable item when compared with the cost of the sewers alone. It seems to be questionable whether any permanent success can be had by building a large number of sewers in such a condition.*"

The correctness of Mr. Philbrick's judgment, expressed in 1880, the year in which the Memphis sewers were constructed, has been fully verified by experience, as will appear from the following extracts, taken from a letter of Mr. A. Ross, engineer in charge of the Memphis works, dated November 3, 1884. In response to inquiries made by myself, Mr. Ross says:

"Our main lines (East, twelve-inch diameter; West, from twenty, fifteen, twelve, ten, to eight-inch) have been supplied with man-holes; two lateral lines, six-inch diameter, have also been supplied, *on account of frequent stoppages.*

"Our four-inch house connections answer their purpose; if people throw things in them not allowed by ordinance, they are liable to stop up first, before the articles reach the main sewer, thus acting as a safeguard to prevent stoppages in the latter. The house-owner will have to clean them out pretty soon. *They will learn to do better.*"

In speaking of the liability of the pipes to become foul, Mr. Ross says:

"The only place where the pipes get foul is at the junction of the house connection with the main, where the grease gets chilled, and, in the course of time, will accumulate and form a barrier.

"The flush-tanks," he says, "work well." But he adds: "The only trouble we have is with the half-inch supply-pipes. These get stopped by mud, and it takes one man to inspect them every few days, and, by opening the supply-cocks, wash them out occasionally.— Some pipes have been stopped up solid, and we had to replace them with larger pipes.

"Our main sewers, particulary the East main (twelve-inch diameter), are too small, and should be larger, as, during the winter, the waste of water is twice that in the summer. We obviate this for the present by having five escapes or overflows, two for the West main, and three for the East main. If the flow of sewer-water reaches a certain height, it overflows into Bayou Gayoso."*

---

* This, of course, must convert the bayou into an open sewer, or elongated cesspool, and, though the trouble may only occur in the winter season, as Mr. Ross states, it is nevertheless, to say the least of it, *not very nice.*—C. W. C.

Mr. Ross naively remarks: "In general we cannot complain *much;* whenever we find a man-hole necessary, we build one *instanter*." And he might have added:— Whenever we find a sewer runs too full, we let it overflow into Bayou Gayoso.

"Another source of complaint," says Mr. Ross, "is that *some* of our sewers are not deep enough to take the drainage of cellars and basements. Sewers should be laid deep enough at the outset to drain these places."

I need make no comment upon the above account of Colonel Waring's system as it has been found to work in Memphis. Every one can draw his own conclusions as to whether it has proved a success or not. Certainly, as Mr. Robert Moore, C. E., and Sewer Commissioner for St. Louis, says, "The work done in Memphis does not commend itself as a precedent," and, "The mode adopted of ventilating the (Memphis) sewers, through the house drains, is one which, after trial, has been condemned by Dr. Buchanan (chief medical officer of the Local Government Board of England), and sanitary engineers generally, as dangerous to health."

In regard to the boasted advantages of the small-pipe or separate water-carriage sewers, there exists a very great difference of opinion; some able engineers and experienced sanitarians maintaining that without certain precautions, such as open grated man-holes, and disconnecting traps in the house-drains, small sewers are as dangerous as large ones; and some believe that the air from small sewers is *more dangerous than from large ones.*

In 1875 there occurred in Croydon, England, which is drained by a system of small-pipe water-carriage sewers, an epidemic of typhoid fever in which, in a population of 81,000, there were nearly one thousand two hundred cases.*

Dr. Buchanan, of the Local Government Board of England, made an examination into the cause of this outbreak, and his conclusion, as given in a printed report, was that the sewers of Croydon had been the chief agency in propagating the fever. After mentioning other causes of the same kind, "in Rugby, in Carlisle, in Chelmsford, in Penzance, in Worthing, all sewered with small-pipe water-carriage sewers, and in the last two of which epidemics had broken out, severe and sudden, without there being any question of other distribution than through the sewers," Dr. Buchanan adds,

---

*Croydon is one of the cities cited by Colonel Waring as an example of "wonderful success" in sewage irrigation.

"Towns with large sewers have not appeared to have the same suddenness of outbreak. . . . In them the evil influence of sewer infection is more gradually manifested, as might be expected from the different physical circumstances of the two kinds of sewers. It is plain that means of ventilation are wanted more numerously in proportion as the displacement of air may be local and sudden; for any want of freedom of current, and lack of proper exit-means for displaced air, tells far more than in larger sewers."

Dr. Buchanan also refers to the great danger, as shown by the experience of Croydon, of connecting houses with the sewers without the invention of a trap, which is the Memphis plan, and by which the air of the sewer is brought directly into the houses. He strongly recommends a disconnecting trap in all cases.

In speaking of the report of Dr. Buchanan on the Croydon epidemic, above referred to, Mr. Moore, C. E., of St. Louis, says: "From this testimony, then, which is of the very highest order, it appears that the separate system (water-carriage), and particularly Colonel Waring's form of it, is not 'universally admitted to be healthy and safe,' but is tainted with grave suspicions, that in point of fact, *it involves greater dangers and requires greater care than does the combined system.*"

Part II.

"IRRIGATION AS A PROCESS FOR PURIFYING SEWAGE."

In a paper read by me before the Medical and Chirurgical Faculty of Maryland, in April, 1883, the following paragraphs occur:

"The chief trouble of the water-carriage sewage is the question of the ultimate disposal of the noxious matter after it is out of the city.

"In England, where this system had its origin, they tried to remedy the evil (of river pollution) resulting from it, by using the sewage for irrigating lands, and those who originated the scheme promised not only exemption from sanitary evils, but also the most wonderful agricultural results. Experiments on a small scale at first seemed to corroborate this theory; but very soon it was demonstrated that, easy as it was to find land enough to receive the sewage of small towns, it was next to impossible to do so for large cities, and the larger the city the greater the difficulty; hence, in every instance of the kind the land used has been gradually overdosed with sewage matter, and become a noxious swamp instead of a productive farm. The Berlin irrigation fields are notable instances of the kind."

The sum and substance of the above is that sewage irrigation may, under certain circumstances, do for small towns, but it cannot be relied upon for large cities.

Col. Waring differs with me on this point; he contending that sewage irrigation is applicable even to such large cities as Berlin and Paris, and he produces a letter from Mr. James Hobrecht, the engineer who devised and built the Berlin works, to prove that my statements in regard to these words "lack the truth." If we are to accept the *ipse dixit* of an interested party as to the value and excellency of his own work, then we would be constrained to believe, from the attestations of Col. Waring, that the Memphis system of sewage is a success, notwithstanding the evidence already given to the contrary.

Mr. Hobrecht seems to think, with an Eastern prince, that "where a throne is the stake, any stroke is fair play," and, therefore, he does not hesitate to deny statements which are based upon absolute *facts*, as I shall hereafter show by official documents from his own compatriots and fellow-townsmen. In order, however, to give some color of respectability to his denial, he produces a letter of courtesy from two American engineers, Messrs. Gray and Swan, who had been accorded the rare privilege of inspecting the Berlin field. These gentlemen, it appears, wrote to Mr. Hobrecht, as any well-bred American would have done, expressing their acknowledgment and thanks for attentions received, and concluded by saying: "Any one at all familiar with the difficulty involved in the disposal of the sewage of a great city, cannot fail to be impressed with the high degree of success which has been attained at Berlin." It would be interesting to know in what this "success" consists. Messrs. Gray and Swan do not tell us. *Aliud corde premunt, aliud ore promunt.*

But before allowing ourselves to be greatly disturbed by this rather vague testimony of Messrs. Gray and Swan, it will be well to inquire whether they thought well enough of the success of the system to recommend its adoption by the city of Providence, R. I., in behalf of which they were acting, and of which Mr. Gray is the City Engineer.

I have now before me a letter from one of the most eminent civil and sanitary engineers in this country, dated November 2, 1884, in which the writer incidentally mentions Mr. Gray's visit to the various sewerage works in Europe, and adds: "He (Mr. Gray) went and returned, and is just about issuing an excellent and full report. PRECIPITATION IS RECOMMENDED." The writer adds: "It is found to be less expensive in that particular case than irrigation, and the works will cause no nuisance, while sewage farms would be quite objectionable amidst the summer resorts of Narragansett Bay."

Without doubting the capability of Messrs. Gray and Swan to form a correct judgment, and not questioning in the least their frankness in stating the impressions made upon them by the Berlin Works, it is nevertheless to be regretted, that they did not give a detailed statement of their investigation, or at least specify what particular part of the system impressed them with the idea of a "high degree of success." Few things, I fancy, are more deceptive than the "pastures ever green" of a sewage farm. The beautiful exterior that these fields sometimes present does not always indicate their real sanitary condition; it simply indicates that vegetation will grow luxuriantly with an ample supply of liquid manure. But as this fact has been known for centuries, no one need refer to a sewage farm to prove it. To ascertain the more important facts, however, involves the necessity of a laborious inquiry.

In order to determine whether the system works well it is necessary to ascertain:

1. The total quantity of sewage produced, and collected at each pumping station, as compared with the total quantity actually applied to the irrigation fields, in order to be certain that the whole of the sewage is actually applied to the purposes of irrigation, and no part of it allowed to flow away uncleansed into the nearest water-course, as is often the case.

2. The quality of the effluent water, in a chemical and microscopical point of view, must be ascertained so as to determine to what extent it has ceased to be a *pabulum* for the nourishment of dangerous organisms, as well as a carrier of them.

3. The quantity of marketable produce actually grown, as compared with the quantity of manurial mat-

ter actually applied, so as to determine the value of the method of cultivation, as compared with ordinary tillage.

4. The total amount of expenses, as compared with the total receipts, so as to determine accurately how much the process really costs.

To ascertain all this in regard to the sewerage works, especially works as extensive and peculiar as those of Berlin (there are, I believe, eight large sized farms), would require simultaneous measurements and observations at a number of sewage lifts, discharging places, feeding ditches, and effluent outlets; and a dozen men having the requisite local knowledge, with free access to the plant and books belonging to the works, and also proper scientific training for such special investigations could not accomplish the work in less than one month of ordinary professional labor. Messrs. Gray and Swan, evidently possess the requisite scientific training, but unless they ascertained all the facts above mentioned, I respectfully submit that they could not, as I think they had not intended to, testify to the success of the Berlin *system*.

But Col. Waring has further attempted to establish the merits of the irrigation process by instancing an abstract generality, viz., that sewage can be purified by filtering it through a stratum of earth. This fact has never been denied by me nor by any one else that I am aware of. The nearest approach to a denial of the proposition has come from Col. Waring himself, when he said, in his paper read before the Sanitary Council of Maryland, November, 1883, that: "He (Dr. Chancellor) is wrong in supposing that the putrescible matters of household waters can be removed by straining, and that diluted urine is unobjectionable."

"However well we may strain household wastes," says Col. Waring, "and however much we may dilute urine, they will both become active sources of offence when putrefying in the waters of a harbor."

Irrigation and filtration are quite different processes. That a liquid, however impure, will if properly filtered, present all the physical characteristics of pure water, and yet not be chemically pure, is something any one may convince himself of by the simple experiment of pouring a quantity of urine in a proper funnel filled with a mixture of clean sand and clay, moistened with clean water to saturation. A quantity of fluid equal in amount to the volume of urine poured on will run off, and this effluent will have all the *physical* qualities of pure water. Upon the relative proportion of earth and urine, however, depends the success of the experiment; and the amount of earth required in proportion to the quantity of liquid to be purified is so great that even the filtration process is applicable only on a limited scale. The land, too, must be of a certain quality, as to porosity and composition; it must be located at a reasonable distance from the city; it must have a free water outlet at a drainage depth of not less than six feet, and finally the cost must not be excessive. If lacking in any one of these requirements the land will not answer the purpose; and the difficulty of finding such land increases with the extent of the area required. He who thinks that a small area will suffice for a great quantity of sewage will find that he is egregiously mistaken.

According to some authorities, one acre of land for every twenty persons is the least quantity that can be got along with for *irrigation purposes*, and it is safer to reckon one acre for every ten persons, inasmuch as the fecal matter from this number contains double the amount of manurial ingredients which an annual harvest of breadstuffs grown upon one acre of land requires. The posssibility, therefore, of securing a sufficient quantity of land for disposing by irrigation of the sewage of a large city presents a difficult problem. It means that for every 1,200 persons a square mile, or 640 acres of land, of the requisite quality and in a suitable locality, must be found; but to each 640 acres an additional 40 acres is to be added for loss of surface on account of ditches, roads, etc., which is the smallest quantity estimated for this purpose by practical sewage farmers. The amount of land, then, required for every 1,200 persons will be 680 acres. However easy it may be to find one or two square miles of land of a certain price, quality, and locality, it is quite a different matter when we come to provide say 30 square miles, or about 20,000 acres, for the sewage of a place the size of Baltimore. With a less quantity the fields would be liable to become super-saturated, and the public streams receiving the effluent insufferably polluted.

But this is not all. The proportion of one acre for every twenty persons is based on the cultivation chiefly of rye grass, which is the only growth capable of assimilating the enormous quantity of nitrogen contained in the sewage. This grass is so watery as to be almost worthless. It must be used when in the green state, and this limits the market to the wants of the farmers in the immediate neighborhood. There is consequently but little demand for it, and where, as in Berlin, there is a large quantity, it has to be given away. This may in a measure account for the large annual deficit, which we shall hereafter see, results from operating the Berlin fields.

In speaking of the difficulties attending sewage irrigation, Mr. R. Scott Burn, the eminent sanitary engineer of Glasgow, says: "Land cannot be obtained of sufficient extent in the neighborhood of towns in which the sewage is produced; and this may safely be accepted as the rule, when we consider that one acre is required for every twenty to twenty-five individuals of the population. The land, moreover, must be, to give the best results, of a certain quality and locality."

"Every point," he adds, "connected with the utilization of town sewage by the irrigation of land, is so surrounded with difficulties, that corporations find it practically impossible to come to any right decision on any one of them. The Birmingham Corporation, for example, found, after the most extensive and searching inquiry into what had been done in sewage irrigation, that all the questions 'are practically unsolved.'" *

Again, The Birmingham Sewerage Committee, in pushing their inquiries on the subject, found that the average of seven towns which have had their sewage utilized by irrigation, gave 5,768 tons of sewage as the yearly quantity applied per acre; and applying this to the case of their own town they found that 4,800 acres would be required. "Now," as the Committee remarked, "it would be manifestly absurd that an area of this extent (nearly 5,000 acres) could be devoted to such a system of farming."

Continuing, they say: "If there is now a difficulty in disposing of the rye-grass grown upon the small experimental sewage farms at Saltly, how could there be any reasonable expectation of disposing of the enormous quantity grown upon 5,000 acres? Apart from the difficulty of getting this quantity of land in the neighborhood of large towns, the mere cost of preparing the land—averaging this at £25 ($125) per acre—for irrigation with sewage, would be so enormous, that this difficulty alone would act as a strong deterrent in such cases."

In considering the management of such monstrous farms, the Committee asks: "Are corporations to add to

---
* Burn's work on Sanitary Science, page 132.

their own duties those arising from farming on such a gigantic scale? And, moreover, where are the tenants to come from? Very few farmers would undertake farming if they were compelled to use all the sewage sent them, at the risk of being indicted for creating a nuisance."

But to return to the Berlin works; for I have not done with Mr. Hobrecht's letter, which Colonel Waring read with exultation before the late Sanitary Council of Maryland, as a crushing denial of statements made by me, that "I was not permitted to visit the 'fields' myself, the interdiction, so far as strangers are concerned, being peremptory, on account, it is said, of their insanitary condition." And again, that the fields are, "as I was credibly informed, already over-saturated," and that a "pestilence was feared unless speedy relief was afforded, either by *increasing the area of irrigable surface*, or adopting another system of sewerage."

Mr. Hobrecht says these statements "lack the truth." Let us bring the witnesses into court, and then decide who has told the truth, Mr. Hobrecht or myself.

FIRST. I have in my possession a letter from a distinguished resident of Berlin, in which the following statement is made: "At one time all roads leading to and through the estate were provided with sign-boards, forbidding entrance *upon pain of being arrested*, and admittance to strangers was only possible by means of tickets procured from the administration of the sewage farm in the city. Three years ago a Commission was appointed by the Imperial Council of Agriculture to report upon the question of sewerage, and the utilization of fecal matter. In their inquiry into the various methods for the removal of filth and sewage, of course the water-carriage and irrigation works of Berlin claimed a large share of attention. The Commission accordingly applied to the administration of the irrigation works for permission to visit them, which permission was not granted. At least, Dr. V. Langsdorff, Secretary General of the State Board of Agriculture of the Kingdom of Saxony, who acted as spokesman for the Commission, reported to the Council that *admission was refused;* and the Commission was compelled to rely for information about the irrigation fields partly upon the official statements of the managers themselves, and partly upon such facts as could be ascertained by visiting the fields *incog.*"

SECOND. Below will be found a statement from one of the most distinguished engineers in Europe, who is entirely familiar with the working of every part of the Berlin system. After enumerating several causes for the failure of the system, he adds: "Another cause of this lies in the circumstance that they began with far too small an amount of land. According to Chief Engineer Hobrecht's estimate, one hectare was sufficient for 735 persons (one acre for about 300 people), and his brother, at that time Mayor of Berlin, pronounced the rules upon which this calculation was based to be 'so undoubtedly true, that within ten years one would have to hunt with a lantern for persons willing to acknowledge that they had opposed the process.' The repeated warnings of scientific men were not listened to, and the plan was carried out. How well founded these warnings were, soon came to light. Although large parts of the land were dyked in, so as to form sewage ponds, and all other parts had received as much as they could bear, still there remained large quantities of sewage which nobody knew what to do with, and this either inundated the adjoining farms or polluted the water-courses. The complaint about this caused the government to appoint a permanent commission to guard against such occurrences, and this, in connection with the ever-increasing super-saturation, occasioned *a demand for more land*, which cry was repeated until it could no longer be resisted, and consequently *Berlin has been compelled to purchase additional land* at enormous prices, in order to reduce the 735 persons per hectare to about 100 persons per hectare, or 40 persons per acre.

"Leaving the rest to the future, enough has been said to show that it is altogether a mis-statement of facts to call the Berlin irrigation works a triumph or even a success. The only triumph which can be pointed to is that due to a forced acknowledgement of nature's immutable laws over a stubborn maintenance of manifest errors."

THIRD. With regard to the sanitary condition of the Berlin fields, it is stated on page 11 of the Annual Report of the Mayor and Aldermen of Berlin, for the year ending March 31, 1883:

(a) "The drain-water flowing from the sewage meadows and planting beds contains, in the form of ammonia and nitric acid about 2.5 grains of nitrogen in 100 litres of water, thus showing that about two-thirds to three-fourths of the nitrogen has been converted into vegetable albumen, and that the remainder flows off with the effluent water."

And on page 127 of the weekly journal, *Das Grund*

Eigenthum, the official organ of the Property Holders' Club of Germany, for the 1883, it is stated:

(*b*) "The Imperial Board of Health of Germany reports the following results of a microscopic examination of effluent water from the Berlin irrigation fields by Dr. Koch. . . . 'In *one cubic centimetre* were found in February, 1883 (winter), 403,000 bacilli colonies and 6,500 bacteria; in August and October, 1882 (summer), 830,000 bacilli colonies.'"

If Col. Waring calls such water *clean*, or *sanitarily safe*, there is between his standard and mine considerable difference.

FOURTH. In referring to the cost of the Berlin water-carriage and irrigation system, Dr. Schultz, Chairman of the Commission appointed in 1880 for advising upon the proposals of the mayor and aldermen of Berlin for the sewerage of the suburban districts, says:

"Taking the Third Radial District of Berlin, with its 106,000 inhabitants, for the comparison, we arrive at the following summary of cost for the year 1879:

Interest on capital for construction of sewers, pumping station, and forwarding pipe, five per cent. on $1,742,572	$87,128
Interest on capital for purchase of irrigation fields and cost of grading, etc., five per cent. on $540,023	27,001
Renewal fund and repairs, two per cent. on $2,282,592	45,652
Cost of lifting sewage and of sewer-cleaning service	23,125
Cost of working the irrigation farm	24,386
Total annual expenditure, third district	$207,292
Deduct receipts from sale of irrigation farm produce	34,285
Annual deficit, third district	$173,007

(or about $1.64 per head of population.)

"According to this the *annual deficit* will amount, when the entire city is sewered (population 1,250,000), to about $2,000,000."

So much for the real facts in connection with the irrigation fields at Berlin, of which Mr. Chief Engineer Hobrecht boasts so loudly, and which Col. Waring would have the public believe I have misrepresented. Let the unprejudiced judge as between the correctness of my statements and the truth of Mr. Hobrecht's denial.

But Berlin is not the only city where sewage irrigation has proved a failure. If Col. Waring had been as well up in the literature of irrigation as he pretends, he would scarcely have referred, as he did in a former paper, to Dantzic as one of the instances of " wonderful success " in sewage irrigation. Of this place it need only be said, in refutation of any such claim, that the lessee of the farm, an English gentleman and skilfull engineer, has, like William Hope, of England, fallen a victim to his faith in irrigation. *He failed more than a year ago.*

Col. Waring also claims that the Croydon works are a "wonderful success," and I am free to admit that the process is regarded with favor, in a sanitary point of view, by the Local Board of Health. But let us examine into the conditions under which this "success" is attained.

1. There is no irrigation by *crude* sewage; but all the sewage is first passed through a patent extractor, and only the liquid portion is sent to the farm. The extractor delivers the solid matter into a trough at its side, whence it is removed by hand. This, of course, involves delay and expense, and must necessarily, to a greater or less extent, create a nuisance.*

2. According to Mr. Baldwin Latham's gaugings of the sewage from Croydon, passing through *one* outfall (Brimstone Barn), the volume of sewage in twenty-four hours varies from a minimum of 2,860,821 gallons, on November 7, 1878, to a maximum of 12,166,173 gallons, on January 2, 1879, the increase being occasioned by "thaw and rain;" so that provision has to be made for 10,305,352 gallons of liquid, in excess of the minimum sewage, flow through this single outfall. In speaking of this excess of water to be provided for in the sewerage system, the Croydon Local Board of Health say: "The average flow of sewage at the Norbury extractor is about 750,000 gallons. *In wet weather this is increased to two or three million gallons.*" The sewage, therefore, cannot be discharged day by day upon the land in a known and fairly equable quantity.

3. In a book called "Sewage Disposal," p. 29, the government inspectors of England say: "Italian rye-grass is probably in all respects the most advantageous crop to be grown, as it absorbs the largest volume of sewage

---

* See Report Local Board of Health, 1879, page 3.

and occupies the soil so as to choke down weeds;" but, says the Local Board of Health of Croydon, "The difficulty is to find a sufficient market for this produce. In a dry season, when grass is scarce, this difficulty *may* not arise; but in a *moderately* wet season, when ordinary grass is plentiful, the rye-grass cuttings are not so much in demand."

Then, again, "The rye grass cuttings will not keep, or bear long carriage, nor can the rye grass be made into hay with advantage, owing to the great quantity of moisture it contains and the damp state of the ground on which it is grown. *These causes involve greater labor and cost in making the grass into hay, and the produce is not worth so much as ordinary hay.*"

In referring to other crops, the Board says, "corn crops do not thrive on sewage, in a great measure, because they cannot do with the moisture incident to its use. * * * An ordinary farmer can manure the land when he pleases, but a sewage farmer must deal with the sewage day by day whether he wants it or not;" and, "will often be obliged to turn sewage on to land, that, so far as the crop is concerned, would be better without it." This is especially the case with melons; turnips, potatoes and other farinaceous tubers. The conclusion, therefore, is that rye grass is the only crop that can be grown upon sewage farms, and this is quite valueless.

4. The cost of the Croydon works seems to have been enormous. The Beddington farm consists of 465 acres and the Carshalton estate of 74 acres, making a total of 539 acres, of which 500 acres are under irrigation. I have not been able to ascertain the total cost of this land, including sewers and other work, but it may be approximated. The Croydon Rural Sanitary Authority is carrying out (with the sanction of the Local Government Board) a scheme for purifying the sewage of their district for which they purchased 30 acres of irrigable land. In noticing this scheme the *Croydon Guardian* says: "The land has been purchased at a cost of £11,300, and the engineering and superintendence will bring the total outlay (including sewers and other works), up to £90,000 or $450,000."

Estimating the Croydon works (500 acres of land) upon the same basis, it is fair to assume that they cost not less than $7,000,000—a pretty considerable sum for a city of 81,000 inhabitants.

With the foregoing exhibits, taken from the official report of the Croydon Local Board of Health, it would be interesting to know, specifically, upon what ground

Col. Waring bases the assertion that the Croydon works are a "wonderful success." The Croydon authorities seem well pleased with the works, but they are not so enthusiastic over them as Col. Waring. In a letter received from the Hon. John Cooper, Jr., Mayor of Croydon, dated Nov. 13, 1884, he says:

"The irrigation works of our borough have proved entirely satisfactory as a means of sewage disposal. The irrigated lands are utilized for agricultural purposes with varied success. * * * There were at times statements made that the irrigation fields emitted an obnoxious smell, but for years past no such complaint has been received."

This is a very straightforward statement from Mayor Cooper; but in comparison with Col. Waring's enthusiasm, it really seems to "damn with faint praise."

In referring to the cost of sewage disposal by irrigation, Mr. Robert Rawlinson, C. E., says: "There are undoubtedly manurial elements of value in crude sewage;" but he fails to see any advantage in utilizing it by irrigation, "if it must cost 30 shillings to earn 20 shillings." In speaking of the sewage of the metropolis, 160 millions of gallons per day, Mr. Rawlinson says: "For broad irrigation there should be some 40,000 acres of land available, which at $500 per acre would cost $20,000,000, and might cost $20,000,000 more to drain, form roads and irrigation conduits; but no such area of land could be purchased for so low a price. It has been found that when land for sewage irrigation purposes has been taken compulsorily, the price has, in some cases, mounted up to six and is never less than three or four times the ordinary selling or letting value for ordinary agricultural uses." *

According to the above estimate, the maximum cost for irrigation fields to dispose of the sewage of London, exclusive of the sewerage works proper, would be as follows:

For 40,000 acres of land.............. $120,000,000
For preparation of same.............. 20,000,000

Total...................... $140,000,000

At this rate it would cost to dispose of the sewage of Baltimore by irrigation, exclusive of the cost of building the sewers the sum of $14,000,000; or, in round numbers, including the construction of sewers by the Waring plan, about $18,000,000.

---
* See Inaugural Address delivered before the Sanitary Institute at Dublin, by Sir Robert Rawlinson, C. B., President of the Congress.

Col. Waring satirically alludes to my translation of M. Aubry-Vitet's article in the *Revue des deux Mondes*, for October, 1880, in which the author strongly condemns the irrigation process as practised at Paris, and declares that M. Aubry's article was "written in special advocacy of a particular method of chemical purification." To this I have no reply, as I am indifferent to Col. Waring's satire and have no means of knowing what M. Aubry-Vitet's object was in writing the article.

To cite Paris and Breslau as examples of success in irrigation proves nothing. In neither of these cities has any attempt been made to utilize *all* the sewage produced, only such a quantity as can be conveniently used, the remainder being discharged into the rivers. The whole sewage of Paris amounts to about 60,000,000 gallons per day, and of this, according to Col. Waring's own statement, only about four and a half million gallons is used per day in irrigation. The statement of Col. Waring, that the effluent from the irrigation fields at Gennevilliers is as pure as the best drinking-water of Paris, can only be explained by the fact that the water, escaping from the under drains at Gennevilliers, is only to a very small extent sewage effluent; it is the groundwater from a large territory, and therefore supplied greatly by rain-water filtering into the soil. The people on the farms at Gennevilliers use, comparatively speaking, very little sewage; and, *cæteris paribus*, it would have a better chance to get purified than at Berlin, where the fields are flooded to their maximum capacity.

But the most important question is, "Does the irrigation process answer fully the demand of public health?" Dr. Koch has shown that the comma bacillus multiplies to a terrible extent in water-carriage sewers, and that the spread of cholera keeps pace with this increase. Accepting this theory, we must also believe that the particular bacillus of cholera nostra or Asiatica, of diphtheria, of typhoid fever and of yellow fever, will, when present in the excreta of some sufferer from the disease, increase and multiply in the sewers of the water-carriage system; and so long as there is no proof, nor even claim that these germs of mortal disease are not destroyed by the process of irrigation or filtration, we must look upon irrigation fields with great suspicion, if not dread.

This theory was accepted and promulgated by the Paris Sewerage Commission of 1881, at the head of which stood the celebrated *savants*, St. Claire Deville,

Pasteur and Brouarkel. This Commission maintained that as there was no reason to believe that the particular microbes of the various miasmatic diseases were destroyed on irrigation fields, all human excreta should be excluded from the Paris sewers, and be removed preferably by some pneumatic process. This exhaustive report culminates in the maxim, *"les matieres excrementite elles doivent etre exclues des egouts de Paris,"* and to this it adds the advice to treat the remaining sewage, not by irrigation, but by "intermittent downward filtration," which is entirely different from the process of irrigation.

The investigations of Dr. Frankland show that even after the most careful filtration, sewage-water cannot be considered as safe. He says, " Water once contaminated with sewage matter, even if purified subsequently by filtration in the most perfect way attainable, if not positively dangerous, is still unsafe to be used. However pure water may appear to the eye, and however agreeable to the palate, it may yet contain animal organisms of a dangerous type."

In speaking of the bored wells on Manhattan Island, numbering about 60 or 70, and varying in depth from 26 to 2,000 feet, 18 being more than five hundred feet deep, Dr. C. F. Chandler states that the water from such wells can never be free from danger if drank before being boiled. The geological formation renders it impossible, he says, for water to come in from beyond the limits of the island, except possibly in one locality for a short distance south of Harlem River. It is only filtered surface water, he says, and *however clear it may be, it is always in danger of containing disease germs which cannot be filtered out by the soil.**

The experiments by Professor Thiersch and Dr. Saunderson also show that "water poisoned by sewage is capable of propagating cholera, even though the water be boiled and drank in the form of tea." Clearly, then, the utmost care ought to be taken to exclude impure fluids and other offensive matter, not only from watercourses, but from the soil as well.

Mr. Henry Robinson, Member of the Institute of Civil Engineers of London, one of the most recent authorities upon sewage disposal; says: "It is well recognized by physicians that the poison of several diseases is received

---

* See "Sanitary Engineer." March 22, 1883, p. 366. The reader is also referred to a paper by Professor Chandler, on "The Sanitary Chemistry of Water," published in the Reports of the American Public Health Association, in which the author says: "Many diseases of the most fatal character are now traced to the use of water poisoned with the soakage from soils charged with sewage and excremental matters."

through the lungs in a worse form than through the stomach; and there must be times when the sewage carriers, or films of solid sewage over a large surface, are capable of evolving gases or germs which are likely to pollute the air."

Referring to the effect of sewage irrigation upon the public health, Dr. Allen Sturge, in his paper read before the Institution of Surveyors, says: "Great complaints have been made at Gennevilliers that the health of the inhabitants is not so good as before its introduction (irrigation by sewage) in consequence of a rise in the level of the subterranean water, which now invades the cellars of the houses." This statement is corroborated by M. Lefevre, President of the Societe des Geometres de France, who has to make valuation surveys of this district for the Civil Courts of Paris. He says: "Gennevilliers is a large agricultural village, and at one time had fine prospects of extension. The value of building land had increased to a very large degree, but as soon as the neighborhood between Gennevilliers and Asnieres was seen to be invaded by the muddy and infected waters of Paris, this land lost a great part of its value." He adds: "My personal opinion is, that the dispersion of the sewage outside the great towns must be considered as a public misfortune for the localities infected."

In the Health Department of the recent Social Science Congress at Birmingham, the question, "What is the best method of dealing with town sewage?" was answered in a paper by Mr. E. Pritchard.

Mr. Pritchard said: "Had this question been asked me some fifteen or twenty years ago, I, like many others, would have suggested irrigation; but experience of the last few years has caused a modification of my views, and the answer now would be to the effect that local circumstances must of necessity govern the particular method of treatment."

He continues: "With suitable land and proper management good results are obtainable without the creation of a nuisance; but, as the true value appears now to be more generally known, sewage treated by broad irrigation, unless under exceptional circumstances, does not at the present time find much favor. It is estimated that one acre will purify the sewage from fifty to one hundred persons; *this is on the assumption that such land is not continuously treated.*" In speaking of the Earl of Warwick's farm at Leamington, Mr. Pritchard says: "The first consideration would generally appear to be 'how to make it pay,' leaving the purification of the sewage as the lesser factor."

Another authority on this subject is Professor Virchow, of Berlin. At the tenth meeting of the German Health Society, this great physician and scientist submitted, among other propositions, the following: "The agricultural employment of fæcal matters must be subject to strict sanitary supervision." He showed that "excrementitious matters when applied to land, if washed into streams and rivers, *even as effluents*, may give rise to heavy, wholesale pollution."

Once more. In a paper read before the Section for Clinical Medicine, Pathology, and Hygiene of the Suffolk District Medical Society, Mass., April 30, 1884, Dr. Henry I. Barnes, in noticing the drainage of the Woman's Prison in Sherborne, Mass., says: "Epuration of sewage is attempted by what is known as Col. Waring's method. Five acres of land are employed, the sewage is distributed over the land by open-joint tile drains, and the effluent drainage is led off by tiles laid five feet under the ground." The water coming from the ground is represented to be as clear as spring-water, but an analysis obtained in the office of the State Board of Health, says Dr. Barnes, "is proof beyond dispute that the system amounts to nothing by way of purifying the sewage, and that it (the irrigation field) is practically a mammoth cess-pool, the contents of which the citizens of Boston drink."*

I have now done with this discussion, so far, at least, as further controversy with Col. Waring is concerned. As to the criticisms which I have been led to make upon his system, they have been inspired by no ungenerous feelings, but have grown naturally out of the discussion. As far as the excellencies of his system are founded on sound principles they cannot suffer from such an examination; if the system possesses defects, there is no reason why they should not be pointed out, still less reason why it should not, at least, be submitted to that criticism to which all inventions are exposed.

While this is a philosophical age, which is little inclined to take anything for granted without investigation, I must say that I have observed with regret that my efforts to bring to the attention of the public the merits of the Differentiating Pneumatic System of Liernur have been met by certain sanitarians and journals with irritation and clamor, rather than with that coolness and rationality of inquiry and argument which alone form the road to truth.

---

* See THE SANITARIAN, September, 1884.

REPORTS FROM COUNTY BOARDS OF HEALTH.

The only report received from any county in the State is from Olney District, Montgomery county, which is hereto appended:

"SANDY SPRING, MD., *Dec.* 31, 1885.

"To DR. C. W. CHANCELLOR,

"*Secretary Maryland State Board of Health:*

"In pursuance of one of the rules adopted at the first meeting of the 'Board of Health for Olney District,' in Montgomery county, (created by Act of Assembly, approved April 8th, 1884,) we beg leave to submit the following report:

"The Board of Health for Olney District has held meetings regularly on the stated days during the year, and with generally good attendance.

"All nuisances coming to the knowledge of the Board have been promptly remedied on notification from the Board, or the President, without call for the exercise of authority, and without unkindly feeling.

"On several occasions the President delivered lectures on 'Sanitary Science and Rules of Health,' to large and interested audiences.

"Printed addresses to the public have been issued whenever caution or information was necessary.

"Public attention to the rules of health has largely increased, and the improvement in the sanitary condition of the district is very marked.

"The people seem to be in kindly sympathy with the Board, as shown by their ready compliance with official and and personal requests, and by applications to members of the Board for advice regarding the surroundings and arrangements of their houses.

" At the December meeting of the Board, delegates were appointed to the convention (held in Washington, D. C.) of 'The American Public Health Association.'

"HENRY C. HALLOWELL,
"President.

"B. D. PALMER, *Secretary.*"

APPENDIX.

THE DRAINAGE OF THE MARSH LANDS OF MARYLAND,

*And its Influence Upon the Agriculture, Population and Health of the State.**

BY C. W. CHANCELLOR, M. D.,
Secretary State Board of Health of Md.

If the enclosure and tillage of land which naturally yields little profit deserves commendation, how much more credit is due to the skill and labor of those who have recovered and rendered valuable vast areas which were before abandoned to the use of the waters.

The Egyptians, whom both necessity and profit induced to exercise their wits for the improvement of their country, may be reckoned as the pioneers in the art of land drainage. We learn from Heroditus that their first works, consisting of embankments to protect their cities and lands against the overflow of the river Nile, were built by Sesostris and subsequently heightened by Sabacon the Ethiopian, who employed for this purpose all criminals and persons condemned to death. In the execution of this work 120,000 Egyptians are said to have perished from the pestiferous nature of the country; but after its completion the improvement experienced was such that the cities and towns of note increased from 18,000 to upwards of 30,000, or 60 per cent. in population.

Sir Walter Raleigh informs us that the Assyrians spent much time and treasure in draining the overflowed marshes of Babylon, an improvement which added

---
*Read before the Agricultural Convention of Maryland, February 25th, 1885, and republished by request.

greatly to the agricultural and commercial prosperity of the country, as well as to the general health of the people.

Among the Greeks, drainage was practiced with great success. Thessalia, at one time a sea, was reclaimed by a remarkable work of drainage, and became so productive, that as an emblem of plenty it was called "The Cornucopia."

The extensive drainage accomplished by the Romans is familiar to every one who has given any thought to the subject. The most noted work of the kind was the drainage of the Pontine Marshes, a pestilential stretch of the Campana di Roma, eight miles in breadth and thirty miles in length. From having been uninhabitable, these marshes were made good ground, and the country people, allured by the richness of the soil, settled there in great numbers. It was through these marshes that Claudius Cæcus carried his famous Appian way, but subsequently the State, distracted by civil wars, neglected the drainage works, and those rich pastures and fertile fields were again abandoned to the wild luxurience of nature. It is indeed melancholy to reason and humanity to behold an immense tract of fertile land, in the immediate vicinity of one of the greatest cities in the world, pestilent with disease and death, and to know that like a devouring grave, it annually engulfs all of human kind that toil upon its surface.

In the magnitude of the enterprise, the drainage of the Fucine Lake by the Romans was scarcely less than that of the Pontine Marshes. It is stated that the Emperor Claudius employed 30,000 men for the period of eleven years, without intermission, on this work.

The ancient provinces of Gallia, comprising what is now Belgium, part of Holland and the northeast part of France, was at one time so full of bogs and marshes that the victorious Cæsar was unable to conquer it after ten years of war; but modern ingenuity and enterprise have succeeded in converting these once pestilential marshes into the richest and most populous districts in the world, the population averaging at this time about one individual to every acre of land.

The reclaimed lands of Holland deserve particular notice, especially the districts of Purmeer, Beenister and Haarlam, all three of which are drained lakes. Purmeer is about five miles long and more than two miles broad. The Beenister lake embraced an area of 7,000 acres of water, which, after four years of labor, was made dry land, and is now so planted with gardens, orchards and rows of trees that it presents one of the most delightful summer landscapes in the country. Haarlam lake, with an area of nearly 50,000 acres and an average depth of 10 or 15 feet of water, has been converted into fertile meadows, thickly dotted here and there with the neat homes of the tidy peasantry. The drainage of this lake was a work of such magnitude, that during its progress incredulity was excited as to the ultimate possibilities of the project, but it proved to be an entire success, and the thrifty and enterprising Hollanders are now considering the practicability of shutting in by an embankment and draining a large area of the Zuyder Zee, greater in extent and volume of water than Chesapeake bay.

We may regard these industries and thriving Dutch communities as the parent and pattern of marsh engineering. In the magnitude of their works, in the strength of their dykes, barring out a boisterous ocean; in their many thousand wind-mills, raising the drain-water from millions of acres of land, they have surpassed every other people.

We come now to speak of the Fen lands of England, which have been successfully drained, and form the most productive and healthy sections of the country. The lands are located in the maritime districts, and lie considerably below the level of the sea at high tide, the drainage being discharged by cuts and sluices into the rivers. The central basin of Somerset, more than 200 miles in extent, exists under the protection of sea walls. In the southeast corner of Kent and Sussex the "Romney Marsh" and other low grounds are protected against the battling waves of the channel by massive walls and embankments. Embanked marshes border the river Thames and flank the Essex coast, and in East Norfolk there are extensive low-lands maintaining a perpetual struggle with the moving sand of the seashore. But the most extensive district of all is called "The Great Level of the Fens," which occupies a large part of Lincolnshire and Cambridgeshire, and extends into four other counties, having a length of about seventy miles, with a breadth varying from five to forty miles, and embracing an area of several hundred thousand acres of land. This whole country lies several feet below the level of the ocean at high water; all its farms, towns, and population depend for safety upon the ability of the various embankments, which stretch along the shore and ramify over the entire plain.

These are certainly interesting memoranda, for we have here presented an example of Saxons in rural life—not the statesmen, capitalists, merchants or mechanics, but the husbandmen—assembling to concoct measures of relief, and ultimately falling to work to dyke out the sea, embank the rivers, and drain the lands for mutual safety and advantage.

It is an interesting inquiry how a rough, semi-barbarous population could have first combined together in an enterprise of such great and general utility, but in the recorded instances we seem to have a clue to the motives and purposes actuating these early agriculturists to labors of unusual magnitude. Co-operation for mutual benefit was soon upheld and enforced as a *custom*, and then usage and precedent became authoritative as *law*.

It is stated as a fact that the least watery portions of the Fens of England have been brought into cultivation with greater facility and less expense than the woodlands on the hills could be cleared into farms, and that these fens have attained to a higher order of farm management than any other parts of the kingdom.

The young power of steam, applied to the the drainage of marshes, has quite supplanted wind-mills in all parts of England, and is also extensively used in Holland. The usual arrangement is a vertical scoop-wheel which dashes the water up an ascending curve with great power. In what is called the "Great Level," where there were formerly 700 wind-mills, there are now only a few, but the number of steam pumps employed is about seventy, varying from ten to eighty horse-power, and raising the drainage water of at least 250,000 acres. The centrifugal pump surpasses even the wheel in the percentage of duty it performs in proportion to the power employed. One of these pumps has been found to drain effectually a marsh of upwards of 3,000 acres. The disk, four feet and a half in diameter, worked by a twenty-five horse-power engine, throws up 75 tons of water per minute, five feet high, or 100 tons per minute between two and three feet high. Exaggerated conceptions are frequently formed of the cost of raising water with pumps worked by steam power. It appears from the best evidence collected on this subject that the cost is really an insignificant item.

There, is, however, a more recent and less expensive means than either the wind-mill or steam-engine. It consists simply of a siphon, which passes over the bank impounding the water. At Warwick, in England, a contrivance similar to this has been adopted, whereby a very great saving in cost is effected. It has been in operation a number of years, and works very satisfactorily.

Siphons working automatically involve but little outlay in maintenance, and they would undoubtedly be used much more frequently than they are at present if their special nature and advantages were more fully understood. Thus far, they have been used for the drainage of land with great advantage. In Scotland the Earl of Stair drained by this means a wet marsh near Culhorn House which had rendered the entire neighborhood unhealthy. The siphon pipe, seven inches in diameter, was half a mile long, and it reduced the water nine feet. There is every reason to believe that most of the marshes in Maryland could be drained in this way, and with comparatively small expense.

The drainage of the marsh lands of Maryland is certainly a work of the highest importance, when we consider the advantages which would follow, both in an agricultural and sanitary point of view. Malarial diseases which deter emigration and drive out population, are principally associated with these lands. Their drainage, therefore, would not only enhance the value of surrounding lands, by improving the public health, but would thereby remove the chief obstacle to the ingress of population, and add greatly to the agricultural resources and material wealth of the State.

A great error prevails in this State in reference to the utilization of marsh lands. It is generally thought that they are devoid of agricultural interest, but the experience of England and Holland should correct this false judgment and cheer those who are willing to look at home for resources, where, after all, industry will be better rewarded than at a distance. Industry meets with just reward everywhere; and the assertion may be safely ventured, that the same amount of enterprise *at home* would secure more comfort and happiness than can be expected under any circumstances in a newly-settled country, where all that is obtained is at the cost of solid enjoyments. The adventurous merchant or speculator may find a wide field in the "Far West" to satiate, if possible, his thirst for wealth; but the industrious farmer of Maryland needs no better patrimony than that which he already possesses.

A soil easily cultivated, and susceptible of being largely increased and improved; the necessaries and even luxuries of life in great abundance; a temperate climate which can be made exceptionally healthy; free and constant intercourse with the chief commercial centers of the country, by means of both water and railroads reaching to the very door of the granary; surrounded by a peaceful, orderly, intelligent and refined population, such are some of the advantages of which our farmers can boast, as a set-off to those of any new country. "Let the waters be gathered together, and let the dry land appear," then the earth will "bring forth grass, and herb yielding seed, and the fruit tree yielding fruit after his kind."

Of course, no accurate estimate as to the cost of draining the marshes of Maryland can be made without proper surveys and levels, but judging from the results in other countries, we may at least approximate an estimate. The embanking and draining of the vast lakes, fens and marshes of England and Holland averaged a cost of about $11 per acre—a very moderate sum for the benefits derived.

The drainage of the Maryland marshes, as compared with the drainage of the lakes of Holland or the fens of England would be a mere bagatelle, especially with the improved apparatus now in existence for executing such works. Taking the most extensive of our marshes embracing from five thousand to fifty thousand acres, we may safely estimate that the average cost for embanking and draining will not exceed $10 per acre. Some of the lands probably would not bear so large a tax even as $10, but others would bear a much larger sum, and considering the question of improved health and consequent increase of population, the benefits to be derived would more than counterbalance the expenditure, even if it were increased by one hundred per cent. above the estimate.

To ascertain the quantity of marsh-land in the State, susceptible of being brought into successful cultivation, would also require accurate surveys, but from the data at hand we may roughly estimate the combined area at not less than 500,000 acres.

In consequence of the water-logged condition of most of the marsh-lands in Maryland, especially on the Eastern Shore and in Southern Maryland, they are almost entirely valueless, or would only bring a price when sold in connection with other lands, and for this purpose they are not worth an average of more than fifty cents per acre. Insalubrious in themselves, they are also the cause of unhealthfulness to the surrounding country, and, therefore, their drainage, apart from any agricultural consideration, is imperatively demanded as a sanitary measure.

That these lands can be successfully drained may be inferred from the experiences of other countries where such works have been accomplished under much more adverse circumstances, with the result of improved health and largely increased productions. The State has expended, in principal and interest, about $30,000,000 in developing, by canal and railroads, the resources of Western Maryland, and has doubtless been repaid by the outlay. Not more than one-tenth this amount would be required to drain the principal marshes on the Eastern Shore and in Southern Maryland, and the result would be improved salubrity, augmented population, and a largely increased basis of taxation.

A brief reference to the physical geography of the counties on the Eastern Shore and in Southern Maryland, derived principally from Martinet's map of Maryland, the maps of the coast survey, and Ducatel's Geological Reports, will serve to indicate the large areas of water-logged land in the State, a great part of which could be brought under cultivation by embanking and draining.

Dorchester county lies between the Choptank and Nanticoke rivers. It contains very large areas of marsh land at present valueless, but which could be readily drained and brought under successful cultivation. The neck of land between the big and little Choptank is a low, flat country that suffers generally from want of proper drainage. In this neck alone there are several thousand acres of land which could be reclaimed, and from being malarious and worthless would become one of the most healthy and productive portions of the State.

Meekins' neck, on the bay shore, is also a waste of marsh land, and this is the case with nearly one-half of Hooper's Island, the extent of which is nearly fourteen miles in length, and from one to two miles in breadth—fully 10,000 acres of land. At the head of Honga river and bay, there are also extensive marshes, which if brought under cultivation would yield large crops. Bishop's-Head neck presents the same physical aspect. At the heads of big and little Blackwater rivers there are also extensive marshes. In Drawbridge District the country is low and marshy, and, judging from the neigboring lands, would, if reclaimed, yield abundant and lucrative crops. Hurley's neck, south of Vienna, terminates in extensive marshes that could be made productive.

In Wicomico county, that portion of the neck of land lying between the Nanticoke and Wicomico rivers, forming the third district of the county, terminates in extensive marshes, and generally speaking, the necks of land extending along the creeks and rivers in the south and south-east extremities of the county are a waste of marsh lands.

In Somerset county, between Wicomico river and Monie creek, and Monakin creek, there is a considerable expanse of marshy lands. The soil of the land that terminates Monakin neck, called "Deal's Island," is very productive and the adjoining marshes, if reclaimed, would be especially valuable for the cultivation of corn and sweet potatoes. The extensive swamps known as "Jerico Marshes" in Potato neck, from the extreme end of the borders of this county, in the midst of which are some few inhabited spots. These salt marshes rise by gradual deposits of decayed vegetable matter above the surface of tidewater, and are not healthy; but if they were properly embanked and drained there is no reason why they should not become as healthy as any part of the State.

From the head of Annimessex river reaching to the southern limits of the State, there is a broad expanse of salt marshes, which, judging from the healthy appearance of the hardy population who inhabit the country immediately about them, may not be considered as the seat of malarious diseases, but their influence at a distance is believed to be prejudicial to health. A northerly direction from Princess Anne to Salisbury leads through a swampy district which is said to be more unhealthy.

The clearing of the Pocomoke river, in Worcester county, would add greatly to the agricultural resources and improve the salubrity of the county. This river rises in an extensive stretch of marsh land, called "Cypress Swamp," which is located in St. Martin's district, and extends into the State of Delaware. The bed of the river is obstructed at various points by trees and deposits of various kinds, which, if removed, so as to confine the waters of the river in their natural channel, would facilitate if not completely effect the drainage of a very large area of land, now an almost impenetrable swamp, covering a rich and fertile bottom. East of the Pocomoke river the country is more marshy than on the western side, the creeks that feed the river being principally on the eastern side. Extensive marshes are also to be found on Sinepuxent neck, stretching a considerable distance along Sinepuxent bay.

The marshes belonging to Caroline, Queen Anne and Talbot counties are extensive, and similar to those in the counties already mentioned. To ascertain the location of these marshes and their extent, is a matter which would involve some expense and considerable time. Without pretending therefore, to give anything like an accurate account of them, it may suffice to say that they are principally found:—

1. In Caroline county along the east side of Choptank river and its tributaries, and between this river and Tuckahoe creek, above their junction. There is also a very extensive swamp in the upper part of the county, known as the "Long Marsh."

2. In Talbot county, as may be expected, there is a great deal of marsh-land in "Bay-Hundred," also on the Choptank, Miles and Wye rivers, and the creeks that feed them.

3. In Queen Anne's county the principal marshes are in Kent Island district, and along the courses of Chester and Wye rivers.

In considering the marshes of the Eastern Shore, mention might be made of a great deal of waste land in Kent and Cecil counties, but as the area is not so extensive as in the counties above mentioned, it is only necessary to call attention to the fact that a vast amount of land of this character does exist, without specifying the localities or extent. It is sufficient to say that there are rich alluvial bottoms at the heads of most of the creeks in both Kent and Cecil counties, now covered by water, which could be drained without great difficulty or cost, and if drained, would greatly improve the health of the respective localities, and furnish sites for meadows equal in productiveness to the valuable meadow lands of Holland.

From what has been said, it is obvious that the best and most improvable lands on the Eastern Shore are to be found in the marshes, which if brought under cultivation would make that section, literally, the "garden spot" of Maryland. The great desideratum is population, and this cannot be secured under existing circumstances, for not withstanding the claim of the inhabitants, that the average health of the Eastern Shore is equal that of Western Maryland, the experience of more than a century has shown that the marshy sections of the State are more liable to malarial fevers than the upland counties.

There is, perhaps, no section of the State the agricultural resources of which are so little known as Southern Maryland, and certainly no section that has suffered more from the effects of malarial fevers, induced by the existence of extensive marshes which could be reclaimed without great expense or trouble.

Mr. J. H. Alexander, in his "Report on the new map of Maryland," 1835, calls attention to the importance of constructing a canal or canals to drain the extensive marsh lands at the head of Wicomico river, in Charles county, known as "Zekia Swamp" or "Allens' Fresh," embracing an area of more than 5,000 acres.

The physical outline of this swamp is that of a long basin hollowed out between adjacent highlands, with an average width of nearly a mile, to a distance of twelve miles from tidewater. The bottom of the basin, formed of the soil of the hills, and decayed vegetable matter, is for the most part covered with water. In speaking of the survey made of this swamp, Mr. Alexander says: "The foot in passing over it finds nothing but a succession of miry knolls, whose unpleasant monotony is varied, from time to time, by plunging into water three or four feet deep. Nevertheless," continues Mr. Alexander, "amid all these apparently unfavorable circumstances, there is good ground for believing in the possibility of the ultimate and not disproportionately costly or difficult redemption of the swamp."

The other swamps in Charles county are Piscatawa, Mattawoman, Port Tobacco, Pomonky, Maryland Point, Nanjimoy, Piscawaxen and Cobb's Neck.

It is needless to call attention in detail to the extensive marshes in Calvert, St. Mary's, Prince George's, Anne Arundel, Baltimore and Harford counties, or to expatiate upon the benefits which would result from their being properly embanked and drained. An examination of their actual condition would undoubtedly show that these marshes can all be drained and made firm and safe pasturage, if not permanently arable land.

There is no *physical* difficulty in the way in draining any or all of the marsh lands of Maryland. Engineers can furnish plans and execute the work, if the financial means are provided. But when we come to consider the actual performance of the work, there will be a host of conflicting interests; and even many whose lands and health would be benefited will persist in declaring their satisfaction with the present state of things, miserable as it is, and their disbelief in the practicability of any scheme of improvement or the ultimate profit to be derived therefrom.

I have stated that there are not less than 500,000 acres of marsh lands in Maryland which could be reclaimed. Now, if for more accurate and closer calculation, we should deduct one-fifth, we will then have 400,000 acres remaining, which when drained and prepared for cultivation will readily produce 40 bushels of corn, or 1½ tons of hay per acre, and will command from $30 to $50 per acre, or in round numbers an average of $40 per acre. Upon this basis, which is believed to be reasonably accurate, we formulate, as the practical result of good drainage and cultivation, the following:

ESTIMATE.

400,000 acres of unreclaimed land at $1 per acre	$ 400,000
Expenses of draining and improving 400,000 acres at $10 per acre	4,000,000
Total cost	$4,400,000

CREDIT.

Reclaimed lands, 400,000 acres at $40 per acre	$16,000,000
Deduct cost of drainage, &c	4,400,000
Net profit	$11,600,000

In their present condition these marsh lands are worth nothing, and yield nothing but an unlimited supply of malarial fevers. When drained and cultivated in a proper manner they will produce forty bushels of corn, or 1½ tons of hay per acre. Two hundred thousand acres then will give 16,000,000 bushels of corn, which at 50 cents per bushel will be $8,000,000 gross product. It will require about ten million bushels of corn in addition to the wheat and other crops to supply man and beast in the counties where these marsh lands exist, which when deducted from the gross product will still leave 6,000,000 at 50 cents per bushel—equal to $3,000,000 saved annually to the farmers of this section. If the above estimate is within just and correct limits, there cannot or should not be any reason in the minds of practical, thinking men, in or out of the Legislature, to cause them to look upon this important work with fear and trembling, or want of faith in the possibility of executing the same.

But let us state the proposition in another way. It is estimated that one good laborer will reclaim an average of 37 acres of the marsh lands of Maryland annually; therefore 1,000 laborers will reclaim 37,000 acres annually. The cost of labor may be reckoned at $30 per month per man, or $360 per annum per man. At this rate the total cost of 1,000 laborers will be $360,000 per annum, or an aggregate of $3,960,000 for eleven years, which would be required to drain the entire 400,000 acres, with 1,000 laborers, or 5½ years with 2,000 laborers.

Now, according to this statement, the estimate of expenses in draining 400,000 acres of marsh lands in this State, and the actual profits from the same, would stand thus:

Present value of 400,000 acres of marsh lands at $1 per acre............................ $400,000
1,000 laborers for 11 years at $360 each per annum............................ 3,960,000

Gross expenditure..................... $4,360,000

CREDIT.

By 400,000 acres of reclaimed land at $40 per acre $16,000,000
Deduct expenses........................... 4,360,000

Net profit $11,640,000

In comparing the two foregoing estimates, it will be found that there is a difference of only $40,000 in the general results, and that the average cost of drainage by either calculation is about $10 per acre or $1 less per acre than the average cost of draining the marsh lands of England and Holland.

Thus far we have only estimated the pecuniary advantages in an agricultural point of view which would result from the drainage of the Maryland marshes; we come now to consider the importance of such a measure from a sanitary standpoint, and to show the pecuniary advantage the State would reap on this score.

It is well known that marshy districts are peculiarly unhealthy. From tables prepared by M. Maret, of several parishes of Switzerland, in which comparison is made between well-drained and marshy countries, it appears that one-half of all born in a well-drained district live to the age of 47; whereas, the same proportion in a marshy parish live only to the age of twenty-five. In the hills, one in twenty of all born live to eighty; in marshy districts, only one in fifty-two live to this age.

The evil consequences resulting from malaria, prior to a country being drained and improved, is ably depicted in "The Statistical Accounts of Scotland." In some districts of that country malarial distempers were so frequent that it was with difficulty the farmers could carry on their work, especially in the fall of the year. Hence, in some parishes liable to the disease, when a farmer wanted four laborers for any piece of work, he generally hired six, knowing the probability that some of them would be rendered unfit for labor by an attack of the ague before the work could be finished. It now appears from unquestionable authority that wherever the land has been thoroughly drained, intermittent and remittent or bilious fevers have disappeared.

There are no less than thirty parishes in Scotland to which this observation is applicable, but it will be sufficient to give only one---the parish of Fife—in illustration of what has been said. Before the land in this parish was drained, the families who lived near the marshes were subject both in the spring and autumn to intermittent fevers. Whole families were to be seen in such distress that none of them could assist the others, and were dependent upon the aid of persons at a distance for the necessaries of life; but since the marshes have been drained and cultivated, those disseases to which the inhabitants were formerly so liable, and the sad train of complaints connected with them have been unknown.

The experience of England and Holland has also proved in the most conclusive manner that by drainage and the introduction of agricultural improvements the greatest changes may be effected in the health of a district; and that it is quite possible to have luxuriant crops produced on the same soil where formerly noxious vapors abounded and impregnated the inhabitants with disease and death.

Before the marshy districts in England were drained, strangers hardly ever ventured to visit them from the certainty of being subjected to an attack of ague; but since the improvements, which have been effected by drainage, they have become as healthy as any other part of England.

Every case of sickness, and the loss of every life from preventable disease is a tax upon the material wealth of the State, besides being a great loss to the families in which such cases occur. It has been estimated that the industrial interests of Maryland are damaged every year to the extent of more than one million of dollars by malaria alone, and this loss falls more heavily on the Eastern Shore and Southern Maryland counties than any other section of the State.

We have seen that in other countries districts once rife in pestilential fevers and dreaded "swamp ague" have become perfectly healthy under proper drainage and cultivation. The same happy results would ensue in this State if the marsh lands were drained and the amount of surface evaporation reduced by means of drying and warming the soil.

In France the evil was first measured by a careful survey of all malarious districts, to ascertain their dimensions and to calculate the area subjected to the malign influence of this poison. The same thing should be practiced in our State. Such a work would require much time and a considerable sum of money, but the expense involved would be a mere trifle when contrasted with the beneficial results which would inevitably follow.

It is our familiarity with malarial diseases which makes us endure them as we do. If some new disease should develope in this country of the same frequency and violence as the usual malarial fevers, a panic would be produced; but if a remedy were suggested for the new disease, as simple and reasonable as the one which experience and observation has taught us will give immunity from malarial diseases, how quickly and how thoroughly would it be carried into execution!

Attention to this interesting subject ought not to be restricted to any one district or section, but should embrace every part of the State until all the water-logged lands, wherever they may exist, are drained and brought into productive cultivation.

For accomplishing so important an object, the following suggestion is submitted for the consideration of this convention, viz: That a committee be appointed to urge upon the next Legislature the desirability of creating a commission invested with power and provided with sufficient means to make a careful survey of all the marsh lands in the State; to consider their present influence upon agriculture, population, and health; and so ascertain the means by which said lands can be most effectually drained and brought into cultivation.

THE SQUALID DWELLINGS OF THE POOR—A SOCIAL AND SANITARY REPROACH.*

By C. W. CHANCELLOR, M. D.,

SECRETARY OF THE STATE BOARD OF HEALTH OF MARYLAND.

Careless manipulation in the prosecution of an analysis may adulterate a long and laborious investigation, but the disappointment occasioned by such a failure can only be measured when we know the practical consequences of the genuine result. In studying the laws of dead matter, an ungrounded conclusion will seldom endanger life or induce sickness; in ascertaining the weights and distances of the heavenly bodies the discrepancy of a few grains or inches can never be a fatal error.

Mind may be analyzed according to the taste of the metaphysician, and dissected into five or fifty rudimental principles; stars may be weighed by avoirdupois or apothecaries' weight, as it may best suit the fancy of the astronomer; and the world may stand forever marshaled into two or more conflicting sects on any abstract question of theoretic science, without involving in their difference the welfare of a single interest, or the safety of a solitary individual. But in a science having for its objects the prevention of disease and the preservation of health—of all desired objects the most desirable—the simplest theory cannot be indulged in without involving a thousand lives. A random step upon such sacred ground must lead to danger, may lead to death. The lives of our fellow-creatures are the material we experiment upon; their happiness or misery is the issue to which every experiment must tend. A faithless rule or fanciful theory may occasion a wide-spread and woeful pestilence. Reasoning, therefore, in such a science should be conducted on the most rigid principles, and the chaste prose of sober truth should never be adulterated with the meretricious poetry of drunken fancy.

A careful consideration of the dwellings of the poor in crowded cities has led to this admonitory preface. It is an important ques-

---
*Read before the American Public Health Association, at its annual meeting held at St. Louis, Mo., October, 1884.

tion, involving the very essence of urban sanitation, and as the points about to occupy attention relate immediately to this question and its bearing upon the public health, we are anxious the public should look with their own eyes into the consequences of the evil, in order that they may see the exceeding hazard which its continuance must occasion.

Were the extent of disputed territory limited to a few inches or a few feet, the value of conquest might be of little importance; but it is a wide and spacious interval which is the subject of contention. The grand point at issue is not a verbal difference, or a conventional technicality; it is an important practical question. It is whether we shall continue to maintain in our cities and villages the most fruitful source of zymotic fever; a disease which spares no age, nor sex, nor condition; which comes into our families unseen and unprovided for; which creeps from house to house with noiseless progress, and covers entire districts with death and desolation—it is whether such a monster can be more effectually killed by being starved, or by being fed.

If an investigation should be carried on, and a report made upon the insanitary condition of the dwellings of the poor in our large cities, it would reveal a frightful picture of misery and vice, fitted to excite and shock humanity. Public inquiry would show these dwellings to be an infamy to civilization—places where no care can protect their occupants against disease; where sobriety and decency are physical impossibilities; and where men, women and children are smothered in filth and vice. A writer in an English paper, calling attention to these habitations a short time ago, says that in them, "disorder is perpetual, and disease never absent. At times whole streets are blockaded, as it were, against the police, and then a pandemonium of violence proceeds unchecked. Every Saturday and Sunday the inhabitants of these rookeries give themselves up to a drunken orgie, and scarcely a week passes without some shocking crime is perpetrated, thus demonstrating the connection between filth and immorality."

If we turn our eyes to the condition of these dwellings in our own country, and the forlorn condition of those who occupy them, we are at once impressed with a melancholy conviction of how little has yet been done to improve the lot of the great mass of the human race. Modern ages have witnessed the growth of many sciences to maturity, of some to perfection. Mathematics and chemistry, the most complete and extensive as well as the most valuable instuments by which the dominion of man has been extended over the powers of nature, have long attained a degree of certainty, beyond which their advancement may seem rather an object of curiosity than of use. Every branch of physical knowledge has been explored with a success that has seldom failed to reward the toil of the inquirer; the art and science of logic and the philosophy of mind have long assumed their places in the rank of exact sciences. The effect of this advancement of knowledge has been for ages apparent, and is daily more obvious in the increase of wealth, the multiplication of securities against evil, and the production of fresh means of enjoyment; but in the distribution of these good things, a very small class of the community lays claim to a lion's share, and the poor "are sent away empty." It is plain, therefore, that none of these are the sciences by which the misery that has always marked the lot of the lower classes can be removed. It is equally plain that, to the discovery of the means of removing it, the resources of the human mind should be intensely applied. To such discoveries we look forward with confident hope, but this hope is founded solely on the expectation of the diffusion of sound principles of hygiene.

The principal sources of happiness are the social affections; but the man whose thoughts are perpetually harassed by the torment of immediate, or the dread of future want, loses the power of benevolent sympathy. Another result of suffering is, that it produces an extraordinary greediness for immediate gratification; a violent propensity to seek compensation from any sensual indulgence which is within the reach. As a consequence, the poorest individuals in civilized society are generally the most intemperate; the least capable of denying themselves any pleasure, however hurtful, which they can command. Hence their passion for intoxicating liquors.

There is really no *a priori* cause why the poor more than others should be addicted to intemperance, unless it be a sense of their own misery, superinducing a condition—a disease it may be called—which craves for stimulants. It might be well if our social reformers would regard the prevailing intemperance of the laboring class from this point of view, for it is quite certain that it is an incredibly fruitful, if not the chief, source of it. Our great industrial class is entitled to be cared for and protected, both as to their health and the pursuit of their avocations. They are the backbone and sinews of the nation's strength.

We cannot consider here the loss, in an economical point of view, from intemperance. It would amount to many millions of dollars. But what of the useless waste of life and its attendant sickness? of the consequent impoverishment, pauperism, and demoralization, and the increasing legacy of hereditary disease? There are two primary and fundamental considerations upon which national stability and permanency rest. The first regards the health of the people, the other their education. Any system of government without full provision being made for these will be incomplete, and in regard to the former, the best guaranty of a nation's security will be wanted. Therefore, above all things, let no government, in its administrative capacity, be without a health department, presided over by wise and energetic health officers, whose supreme duty it shall be to vigilantly administer laws, the aim of which shall be to protect the health of every citizen, and especially to surround that of the dependent, industrial population with every possible safeguard.

A nation such as ours, of fifty-five millions, with a vast manufacturing industry, a busy and flourishing commerce, and a large agricultural and mining interest to attract the most vigorous and enterprising of our people, cannot afford to waste the lives of its citizens. Are not labor and capital the two pillars upon which a free country rests? Disease paralyzes labor and wastes capital. It ought then to be the primary object of an enlightened government to prevent disease, preserve health, and prolong life; to maintain the whole people in a condition of the highest efficiency, alike for the labors of peace and the struggles of war.

Though "social reform is in the air," never before was the misery of the very poor more intense, or the condition of their daily life more hopeless or more degraded, than at the present time. There is a boundless field for the labors of the philanthropist; and it does seem strange, that, while the sufferings of the heathen in distant lands should unfailingly touch a chord of enthusiastic generosity in the hearts of all religious sects, the mission at home should awaken the coldest response. The courts and alleys of our crowded cities too often furnish a spectacle of squalor and misery which is a disgrace to our civilization, and should arouse public misgiving and inquiry. It is here that persons must come who wish to see for themselves what destitution and degradation is. It is here that the fever dens are to be found which figure so largely in perfunctory official reports. Here resides a population which is a people in itself, ceaselessly ravaged by fever; plagued by the blankest, most appalling poverty; cut off from every grace and comfort of life: born, living, and dying among squalid surroundings, of which those who have not seen them can form no adequate conception. The atmosphere in these courts and alleys is in almost every case foul in the extreme; and in the houses, unless one has a very strong stomach, it is difficult to remain for a minute, so intolerable is the stench.

These houses are filled with women, and diminutive urchins "engaged in the pleasing occupation of stirring around the filth in a sewer with their fingers." They evidently know what they are born to experience, and deem it advisable to accustom themselves to dirt and bad smells at as early an age as possible. They will declare "there is no sickness in the house," when you know certainly to the contrary. A further inspection reveals the fact that in an upper room, on a bundle of filthy rags in one corner, the eldest son perchance is "down with the fever," and in another, on a still sparser supply of rags, a little girl—it may be she is fast dying of diphtheria. Mark Twain once declared that he had been up a mountain so high that he could not tell the truth on the top of it. You will readily perceive that the people who occupy these dwellings are so poor, so dirty, so degraded, and so low in the scale of Christian civilization, that they cannot tell the truth; and if you should stay long enough amongst them, you would soon begin to entertain doubts of your own veracity.

The vast wealth created by modern progress has run into the "pockets" of the fortunate few; but the great majority of the "toilers and spinners" have derived no proportionate advantage from the prosperity which they have helped to create. It is true that many members of the working class, who have the moral and intellectual qualities essential to material success, have had their full share in the prosperity of recent times. Numbers of them have risen, and others will rise, into the rank of capitalists; but there is good reason to believe that the lowest dregs of the population in large cities are constantly exposed to the direst extremities of want and suffering—a circumstance which affects injuriously their life, their health, and their prosperity. There must, moreover, always be a residuum in any community—recruited frequently from higher classes as the inevitable penalty of individual vice, recklessness, or calamity—which no amount of general prosperity, no ingenuity or drastic severity of legislation, can wholly extirpate; but much is to be gained by grappling, in a proper way, with the evils which actually exist. The wretched dwellings of the poor, together with poverty, ignorance, and crime, are a chief incident in the general condition of this class. These various factors are interdependent, and any one may be the determining cause of the others. The remedies, therefore, must be as manifold as the disease.

With regard to the direct and immediate means of dealing with the evils of over-crowding in the dwellings of the poor, Mr. Chamberlain, of England, goes to the root of the matter, and speaks out with uncompromising plainness.

In the first place, he would have the authorities proceed on the assumption that the houses which are unfit for habitation are public nuisances, and that the community in such cases should justly compel the owner to put them in proper condition, or require them to be closed or demolished.

It is certain that much more is capable of being done than has yet been undertaken, to require the owners of these shameful dens of vice and disease to keep their property in good sanitary condition. If over-crowding were strictly prohibited under the penalty of a heavy fine, it would seem that all these nests of crime and misery might be at once closed out; and their re-establishment in other localities be prevented by the due enforcement of proper regulations.

For this purpose municipal authorities must have the hearty and consistent support of public opinion. When property takes alarm, the outcry which it makes is deafening. Personal interests can generally take good care of themselves; it is the public good which is so often powerless and voiceless in presence of the audacity of private wrong. A municipal government, charged with the protection of these undisciplined and disorganized natural rights, has no chance against the eager, persistent, and vociferous clamor of the vested interests with which it has to contend; and the experience of health officers, in their endeavors to enforce the most moderate precautions for the preservation of health and the safety of life, has not been encouraging.

Whenever, for the purposes of sanitary improvements, or where property has been declared unfit for human habitation, it has been necessary for the authorities to interfere, the owner generally obtains from the public, under the guise of compensation, amounts altogether and demonstrably in excess of the market value of the property, even on the most favorable compensation. Surely the sound principle in such cases should be, the real value of the land and buildings, used under legitimate conditions, and not the exorbitant value arising from criminal practices. For example: There is a certain class of property found in unhealthy, crowded areas, and used for immoral purposes actually prohibited by the laws; but the illegal occupation is the justification of the exorbitant rents demanded from the wretched occupants by the persons who trade in their vices. A house which for honest occupation is worth $200 a year, will bring in double or treble that amount to an owner who winks at the traffic which it is permitted to shelter.

When this house is required by the municipal authority, the demand for compensation is based, and often allowed, on an income which represents, not a fair return for an investment, but the profit on complicity with vice. The same result obtains where tenements, which could properly accomodate a single family, are made to do duty for three or four times as many persons as can be decently housed in them. The income derived is proportionally increased, and compensation follows as a premium on evil practices. In this way a premium is offered for neglect and wilful indifference to sanitary provisions. It is a question simply between the rights of property and the rights of the community, and until this fact is faced, no reform is possible; and it may be laid down as the principle of future effective action that to make certain localities in cities habitable for the toilers who live in them, the expense must be thrown upon the property-owners.

When these owners, not satisfied with reasonable rents and the increment which the general prosperity of the city has created, obtain exorbitant returns from their investments by permitting arrangements which make their property a public nuisance and a public danger, the state is entitled to step in and protect the citizen, paying only such compensation or damages as will fairly represent the worth of the property legitimately used. It is very well worth the while of the public to face this question and solve it. It would be of great benefit to all, and especially to the working population. It is not only a waste of life, but a waste of money, to educate the growing population, and send them to live in such miserable dens as they are often obliged to live in. The welfare of society demands that this matter of the housing of the poor shall be trifled with no longer. Public opinion is beginning to assert itself, and the prospect of action draws nearer daily.

The following project of a law is presented with the hope that, if applied, it may effect some good in promoting sound and trustworthy ideas upon this vitally important question, and bring within closer range the possibility of thoughtful and effective action. It possesses not only a large element of intrinsic justice, but, if enacted, would have the effect of placing upon the owners of unsanitary property a responsibility which undoubtedly belongs to them, and would be incalculably more effective in rectifying the evils of overcrowded tenements than all the "peddling" legislation of municipalties, or an army of sanitary inspectors.

1. The law should make it an offence punishable by heavy fine to own and rent property for habitation which is unfit for the purpose.

2. Local authorities should have power, subject only to appeal to the courts of proper jurisdiction, to close such property, or to make, at the expense of the owner, such alterations or repairs as may be ordered by the sanitary officer; the property to be closed during litigation.

3 When necessary to acquire any property or destroy any building, for the purpose of preserving or protecting the public health, or for any sanitary purposes whatever, the local authorities should be empowered to acquire the said property or destroy the building, without the city having to pay more than a fair market value for the same, to be settled by proper arbitration, but in no instance should the value assessed be greater than the seller could obtain in the open market from a private purchaser, with no allowance for prospective value or compulsory sale. Provision should also be made to prevent owners from exacting extortionate prices for their tumble down-houses, often bought for speculating upon the necessities of the city or community.

4. The owner should be required to prove before the arbitrators, not what the nominal rent is, but what the actual rent received during a given period has been, and the amount of purchase-money may be estimated on that basis, unless the house has been used for improper purposes, or by too large a number of tenants.

5. The valuation should be made in every case, where an agreement cannot be arrived at between the parties, by official arbitration, and no appeal should be allowed from the decision.

6. The scheme of improvement should include any surrounding property which will be benefited by the reconstruction of the unhealthy area, and the confirming order should authorize a rate to be levied on the owners of such adjacent property, fairly representing the appreciation of their holdings by the proposed improvement.

7. The cost of any scheme for the reconstruction of an unhealthy area should be levied on all owners of property, including long leaseholders within a certain district to be determined by the arbitrators; but if the improvement is essentially local in its character, and the nuisance is created solely by the condition of one or more houses, the cost may be thrown entirely on the owners of such house or houses.

The effect of these or similar provisions would be simply that improvements on a large scale, and in every large town, could be undertaken by the authorities without fear of excessive cost. This is the age of municipal reform and enterprise; and there is not the slightest doubt that local authorities would, under these conditions, joyfully embrace the opportunity afforded to them, and that they would quickly put an end to the scandals and disgrace which have at last forced themselves on public attention, and alarmed and shocked the public conscience. It remains to be seen whether practical effect can be given to the only measure which affords hope of permanent relief. Political power is the means to the end of solving some of those social questions which intimately concern the welfare of the masses of the people, and in the settlement of which they have a just right to make their voices heard.

www.ingramcontent.com/pod-product-compliance
Lightning Source LLC
Chambersburg PA
CBHW020804230426
43666CB00007B/840